FEMINISM, GENDER AND UNIVERSITIES

For a feminist-friendly future in a globalizing world

Feminism, Gender and Universities

Politics, Passion and Pedagogies

MIRIAM E. DAVID

University of London, UK

ASHGATE

Published by
Ashgate Publishing Limited
Wey Court East
Union Road
Farnham
Surrey, GU9 7PT
England

Ashgate Publishing Company
110 Cherry Street
Suite 3–1
Burlington, VT 05401–3818
USA

www.ashgate.com

British Library Cataloguing in Publication Data
A catalogue record for this book is available from the British Library

The Library of Congress has cataloged the printed edition as follows:
David, Miriam E.
 Feminism, gender and universities : politics, passion and pedagogies / by Miriam E. David.
  pages cm
 Includes bibliographical references and index.
 ISBN 978–1–4724–3711–2 (hardback : alk. paper) – ISBN 978–1–4724–3712–9 (ebook) – ISBN 978–1–4724–3713–6 (epub)
 1. Feminism. 2. Women's rights. 3. Women college teachers. 4. Women in higher education.
 I. Title.
 HQ1155.D38 2014
 378.0082–dc23   2013049435

ISBN 9781472437112 (hbk)
ISBN 9781472437129 (ebk – PDF)
ISBN 9781472437136 (ebk – ePUB)

Printed in the United Kingdom by Henry Ling Limited, at the Dorset Press, Dorchester, DT1 1HD

Contents

List of Tables and Figures

Tables

Figures

Preface and Acknowledgements

This book is about how the political project of feminism became a worldwide social movement in the twentieth century, and how it is now embedded in academia and in the wider society in untold ways. To tell the story of how feminism became not only a political project but also an educational one, and to remain true to feminist principles of collective and collaborative action, I have relied on many dear friends and colleagues: what we call sisterhood. *Sisterhood and After* is the name of the British Library's most recent archival collection of oral histories of the Women's Liberation Movement (WLM) collected together by the University of Sussex also in association with the Women's Library and funded by the Leverhulme Trust, and launched at a celebratory event on international women's day (8 March 2013). This major project is to ensure a collective record of the twentieth-century women's movement in the UK and that the lives of women would not be lost to history. Over sixty interviews are now available on the *Sisterhood and After* learning website www.bl.uk/sisterhood and on the *Sisterhood and After* project page http://www.sussex.ac.uk/clhlwr/research/sisterhoodafter.

Some women involved in the oral histories are also participants in my study, which is also to ensure that women are not erased from the histories of the transformations in global higher education in the twentieth century. My participants are not only British feminists but also from as many countries as I could reach out to and include feminists from Australia, Canada, France, Germany, India, Ireland, Israel, New Zealand, South Africa, and the United States of America (USA). I have tried to be expansive but it remains a study largely of the 'global north'. I too have used interviews, conversations and written testimony, to develop a life history and collective biography of academic feminism. My material covers a wider canvass but is also sketchier, relying as it does on the stories of well over a hundred international feminists. I have provided a list of the names of the women on whom I have relied for my cohort analyses to develop the collective biography in Appendix 2. I am very grateful to all the women who gave their time and energy including: Judith Abrahami, Sandra Acker, Nafsika Alexiadou, Pam Alldred, the late Jean Anyon, Madeleine Arnot, Alison Assiter, Barbara Bagilhole, Jackie Barron, Tehmina Basit, Liz Bird, Jill Blackmore, Lucy Bland, Avtar Brah, Penny-Jane Burke, Pam Calder, Claire Callender, Kelly Coate, Amanda Coffey, Barbara Cole, Davina Cooper, Fin Cullen, Vaneeta D'Andrea, Bronwyn Davies, Sara Delamont, Kari Dehli, Carol Dyhouse, Ros Edwards, Margrit Eichler, Debbie Epstein, Mary Evans, Joelle Fanghanel, Sally Findlow, Michelle Fine, Harriet Freidenreich, Jane Gaskell, Jay Ginn, Alison Griffith, Gabriele Griffin, Dulcie Groves, Helen Haste, Val Hey, Yvonne Hillier, Sue Himmelweit, Chris

Hockings, Christina Hughes, Maggie Humm, Gabrielle Ivinson, Carolyn Jackson, Heather Joshi, Jane Kenway, Hilary Land, Annette Lawson, Carole Leathwood, Ruth Levitas, Wendy Luttrell, Meg Luxton, Ruth Madigan, Meg Maguire, Frinde Maher, Pat Mahony, Janice Malcolm, Ellen Malos, Catherine Marshall, Jane Martin, Heather Mendick, Sue Middleton, Heidi Mirza, Merilyn Moos, Louise Morley, Gemma Moss, Audrey Mullender, Rajani Naidoo, Mica Nava, Caroline New, Anna Paczuska, Carrie Paechter, Ann Phoenix, Marilyn Porter, Nirupama Prakash, Jocey Quinn, Judy Glazer Raymo, Diane Reay, Terri Rees, Sheila Riddell, Jessica Ringrose, Delia Langa Rosado, Maxine Seller, Jenny Shaw, Chris Skelton, Suzie Skevington, Maria Slowey, Carol Smart, Corinne Squire, Mary Stiasny, Helen Taylor, Penny Tinkler, Clare Ungerson, Elaine Unterhalter, Linda Ward, Kathleen Weiler, Gaby Weiner, Lois Weis, Jackie West, Fiona Williams, Elizabeth Wilson, Gail Wilson, Lyn Yates, Nira Yuval-Davis.

Along the way I also spoke and shared ideas with my group that I coordinate for the North London University of the Third Age (U3A) initially on *Women's Learning Lives* and more recently on *Women and Wisdom*. I am most grateful to them all for their ideas and wisdom. They include: Dorothy Barnes, Daphne Berkovi, Barbara Cantor, Jenny Clark, Annie Scott Faulkner, Katja Goldberg, Maureen Hanscomb, Norma Hines, Annie Hopewell, Diana Impey, Patricia Isaacs, Barbara Kushner, Anne Vaughan, Josephine Zara. As part of the process of thinking through my material, I discussed these matters in depth with the original group of nine women. It became a pilot study about women and their education in a changing British context, because, as it turned out, none of them are or were academics. I later narrowed the focus to only feminist scholars and activists in academe. Over the course of the summer term 2011, we gathered together autobiographical stories about how important education had been and continued to be in their lives. These women's lives reflect the changing contexts in the UK at least, with only half of them having attended university at the conventional age of 18 (at least for young men who were the traditional beneficiaries of university education). These ranged from three women who were my contemporaries and in their mid-60s, only one of whom had also gone straight from school to university, in her case as a working class woman to study classics, and going from there through research to becoming a secondary school mistress. One of the others went as a mature student and became totally enamoured with HE and its potential for women, leading her to remain a very active supporter of women's causes. The third woman was a talented linguist and became a bi-lingual secretary and involved in informal educational activities, joining her first university as U3A. Two of the women were around the age of 70 from relatively middle class families, and one had gone straight to university from school, becoming a professional psychologist as an eventual career. The other, again, became a mature woman returner, training to be a primary school teacher, alongside her daughter attending university, a rather typical career path for many of my participants of that same generation. Yet two more of the women were in their late 70s, from upper middle class backgrounds, both of whom had gone to elite universities, one to study history and the other French. They both had active and fascinating lives in struggling with traditional family expectations and wishes. The two eldest were both born in the 1920s and fascinatingly, both in a city in the north of England near my birthplace and from relatively modest (working) class backgrounds. Both had gone to university and onto educational activities, although not in universities. One, married to a university professor of education, had involvement with changing forms of educational opportunities as both a schoolmistress and educator, and the other has, over her life-course, become a very feisty feminist. Indeed, she has become involved in a range of feminist activities and causes and continues, at the age of 90 to teach about memoirs and women's writing for the U3A in a most engaging fashion. To celebrate her birthday we put together and self-published a birthday booklet, entitled *Josephine @ 90.* We all wrote stories, poems and/or tributes to her life as an inspirational feminist and educator, teaching as she continues to do for theU3A, and other organizations, both here and abroad. These stories illustrated for me the vibrancy of women's learning and the importance of education in their lives. They helped me to think about the wider ramifications of university and lifelong learning but they also made my task of trying to synthesize social and educational changes and transformations more difficult.

Some of my other networks of friends and former colleagues – from Queen Mary, University of London, Dame Colette Bowe (also a former chair of council), and Lady Elizabeth Vallance (former chair of council of the London University Institute of Education) were always extremely encouraging. Both introduced me to Sir Adrian Smith (former principal of QMUL), who at the time was Director General of the UK Government Department of Business Innovation and Science (BIS) and to whom I am grateful for the interview and time he gave me. I am also grateful to Mabel Encinas for giving me lots of technical help and advice on how to transcribe the interviews.

Other long-standing supportive colleagues and feminist friends including from my co-counselling and new Facebook networks are: Andrea Abbas, Peter Archard, Melissa Benn, Mimi Bloch, Jude Bloomfield, the late Kevin Brehony, John Brennan, Liz Charlesworth, Gail Chester from Feminist Library, Sylvia Cohen, Gill Crozier, Luke Daniels (insistent that I write as he was revising and rewriting his book about male violence), Viv Davies, Phillip Davies of the British Library, the late Celia and Mary Davis, Rosemary Deem, Rayah Feldman, Irena Fink, Becky Francis, Mary Fuller, Naomi Fulop, Eva Gamarnikov, Clare Gartland, Rosalyn George, Anne Gold, Maggie Gravelle, Helen Green (of U3A), Jane Green, Jalna Hanmer, Annette Hayton, Mary James, Jean French Jones, Ken Jones, Tessa Joseph, Adah Kay, Mary Kennedy, Terri Kim, Richard Kuper, Ruth Lister, Melanie Mauthner, Marg Mayo, Mavis Mclean, Monica Mclean, Julie Mcleod, Dorothea Morris, Ruth Schmidt Neven, Ruth Pearson, Andrew Pollard (formerly director of TLRP), Jane Rarieya, Barbara Read, Hilary Rose, David Ruebain, Andrew Samuels, the late Sheila Saunders, Pam Schickler, Monika Schwartz (chief executive of the Women's Therapy Centre of which I am chair of the trustees), Bev Skeggs, Farzana Shain, Chloe Stallibrass, Judith Suissa, Anne Summers (chair of the Friends of the Women's Library), Pat Thomson, Nancy

Kirton Trawford, Valerie Walkerdine, Eileen Marchant Wearmouth, Marlene Hanson Wertheim, Anne West, Olivia Vincenti, Gill Yudkin. My current PhD students – Alison Palmer Chaney, Sayaka Nakagomi, Janice Tripney – have been incredibly helpful in keeping my ideas current as have colleagues from the current Gender and Education Association (GEA) executive – Kimberley Allen, Claire Maxwell, Rosamund MacNeill, Kate Reynolds McKenzie.

And finally I want to thank my real and true sisters – Judy Berle and Anne Sultoon – for also keeping my feet on the ground, and my children – Toby Reiner and Charlotte Reiner Hershman – for both being truly inspirational as teachers of life and in school; and Jeff Duckett, for being there and for listening … Hopefully my study reaches beyond the 'global north' and has implications for, and impact upon, the 'global south' especially for educational futures and to make the world more 'feminist friendly', thereby reducing gender-related violence in its myriad forms.

List of Abbreviations, Acronyms and Names: A Glossary

ACU	Association of Commonwealth Universities
AERA	American Educational Association
AIDS	Auto-Immune Deficiency Syndrome
AHRC	Arts and Humanities Research Council
AJR	Association of Jewish Refugees
AKU	Aga Khan University
ASA	American Sociological Association
ASHE	American Society for Study of HE
BA/BSc	Bachelor of Arts/Bachelor of Science degree
B.Ed	Bachelor of Education
BERA	British Educational Research Association
BIS	Business, Innovation & Science, UK Government Department of
BJSE	British Journal of Sociology of Education
BME	Black and Minority Ethnic groups
B.Phil	Bachelor of Philosophy
BSA	British Sociological Association
BWSG	Bristol Women's Studies Group
CBE	Commander of the British Empire; UK Government honour
C of E	Church of England
CHEER	Centre for Higher Education and Equity Research, University of Sussex
CNAA	Council for National Academic Awards (UK)
CND	Campaign for Nuclear Disarmament
CR	Consciousness-raising groups
CREG	Centre for Research on Education and Gender
CROW	Center for Research on Women
DPhil	Doctor of Philosophy (especially awarded by the University of Oxford)
CV	Curriculum Vitae
EC	European Commission
ECU	Equality Challenge Unit, independent body concerned with UK HE
EO	Equal Opportunities
ERA	European Research Area

ESF	European Science Foundation
ESRC	Economic and Social Research Council
EU	European Union
FAAB	Feminists Against Academic Bollocks
FDR	Franklin Delano Roosevelt, US President from 1933 to 1945
FE	Further Education
FWSA	Feminist & Women's Studies Association
GEA	Gender and Education Association
GER	Gross Enrolment Ratio
GEXcel	Gender and Equality Centre of Excellence
GPI	Gender Parity Index
HE	Higher Education
HESA	Higher Education Statistical Agency
HIV	Human immunodeficiency virus
IBM	International Business Management
ILEA	Inner London Education Authority
IMF	International Monetary Fund
IOE	Institute of Education, University of London
IS	International Socialists
IWD	International Women's Day celebrated on March 8th for over 100 years
JCR	Junior Common Room
LGBTQ	Lesbian, Gay, Bisexual, Transgender and Queer
LSE	London School of Economics and Political Science
MA/MSc	postgraduate Masters degree
MEd	postgraduate Masters in Education
MBE	Member of the British Empire: a UK government honour
M.C.	Middle Class
MDG	Millennium Development Goals
MLitt	Masters in Literature
MOD	Ministry of Defence UK
MPhil	Masters in Philosophy
MRC	Medical Research Council
MS	The early US feminist magazine
NAC	National Abortion Campaign
NAWO	National Association of Women's Organisations
NCCL	National Council of Civil Liberties
NIACE	National Institute for Adult and Continuing Education
NGO	Non-Governmental Organisation
NLU3A	North London University of the Third Age
NOW	National Organisation of Women
OBE	Order of the British Empire: a UK government honour
OECD	Organisation for Economic Cooperation and Development
OFN	Older Feminist Network

OISE	Ontario Institute for Studies in Education, University of Toronto, Canada
OU	Open University
PG	postgraduate students
PhD	Doctor of philosophy
PGCE	Postgraduate Certificate of Education
Poly	Polytechnic, became a new university in the UK in 1992 Education Act
SCR	Senior Common Room
SCUM	Society for Cutting Up Men manifesto
SET	Science, Engineering and Technology subjects
SPA	Social Policy Association UK
SRHE	Society for Research in HE
STEM	Science, Technology, Engineering & Maths &/or Medicine subjects
SWP	Socialist Workers Party
SWS	Sociologists for Women in Society
TU	Trade Union
UC	Upper Class
UCU	Universities and Colleges Union
UG	undergraduate students
UK	United Kingdom of Great Britain and Northern Ireland
UN	United Nations
UNESCO	United Nations Educational, Scientific and Cultural Organisation
USA	United States of America
U3A	University of the Third Age
UUK	Universities UK, the organization of UK leaders of HE
VSO	Voluntary Service Overseas
WACC	Women's Abortion and Contraception Campaign
WC	Working Class
WEA	Workers' Educational Association
WHEM	Women in HE Management
WL	Women's Liberation/Lib
WLM/WM	Women's Liberation Movement or Women's Movement
WNC	Women's National Commission
WS	Women's Studies courses
WSWW	Women's Studies Without Walls

Chapter 1

Feminism as an Education Project to Transform Women's Lives

Introduction

This book is about the feminist project to transform women's lives towards gender and social equality over the last 50 years. This is fundamentally an educational and pedagogical project: to understand how the current gender, sexual and social structures have come about and to develop knowledge and wisdom to further that understanding and transform such relations in the direction of what has become known, in the twenty-first century, as gender and social justice. It has been a project increasingly in universities, as higher education (HE) has expanded, with changing socio-economic and political systems globally.

The origins of this feminist project lie with the social and political movements for change in the post-Second World War period: movements for civil and human rights across the now so-called 'global north', in North America, Europe and parts of Australasia. Many of the early participants in the women's liberation movement (WLM), which is what has become known as 'second-wave feminism', had been or were students in these expanding systems. Book titles such as *The Second Sex* (Beauvoir, 1949, 1953 in English); *The Feminine Mystique* (Friedan, 1963); *Women: The Longest Revolution* (Mitchell, 1966); *Patriarchal Attitudes* (Figes, 1970); *The Dialectic of Sex* (Firestone, 1970); *The Female Eunuch* (Greer, 1970); *Sexual Politics* (Millett, 1970); *Women, Resistance and Revolution* (Rowbotham, 1973) *Of Woman Born: Motherhood as Experience and Institution* (Rich, 1976) are key examples of the books that 'inaugurated' the women's movement, between 50 and 60 years ago. They were variously written by Simone de Beauvoir, the French intellectual and existentialist; Betty Friedan, the American Jewish feminist writer, socialist campaigner and founder of the National Organization of Women (NOW); Juliet Mitchell, the New Zealand-born socialist-feminist academic, later psychoanalyst; Eva Figes, the German Jewish refugee to England becoming a novelist; Shulamith Firestone, the Canadian orthodox Jewess who sought refuge in New York; Germaine Greer, the Australian émigré academic to England; Kate Millett, the American artist who wrote this as part of her doctorate; Sheila Rowbotham, the English feminist historian, and Adrienne Rich, the American lesbian feminist poet and essayist. These writers were all passionate about changing women's lives: in the family as daughters, sisters, wives and mothers, as sexual beings, and in education, paid and unpaid work or employment. How could women's lives be transformed and made more equal with men's lives in both public and private? How could patriarchy and sexual oppression be overcome?

Just how successful has this project been? What has been accomplished over the last 50 years, in terms of feminist knowledge and wisdom and what remains to be done? What changes have been made that need to be undone in the changing global contexts towards neo-liberalism? How successful has the feminist project been in educating women and girls across the globe about their rights in both their public and private lives? How has the education system itself been transformed? Just what do feminist academic activists, like me, think of the changes that we have achieved over the last 50 years? To what extent have our own transformed lives led to wider and global educational and political transformations? What are the educational and political obstacles still to be overcome, especially in an era of near global neo-liberalism? What precisely is the legacy for future generations within and outside of global universities?

Whilst there have been innumerable studies of feminism and the women's movement, changing politics and policies, there is relatively less about how feminism has become a part of academe, developing feminist knowledge, contributing to critiques of the traditional academic subjects, and as a subject in its own right, as, for instance, women's studies. Many of the women who wrote the initial books and pamphlets of 'second-wave feminism' were, indeed, women who had been college students, as the American women in Friedan's (1963) study of housewives and mothers and their dissatisfaction with 'the problem that has no name' had been, but just how did feminism continue to impact upon HE itself (Stambach and David, 2005)? How did feminist knowledge emerge, and become a vital part of the transformations of HE? What did the feminists who, perhaps surprisingly at first, became academics think and feel about this project, and just how did they engage with it? Looking back how do they now feel, and what are their views of the prospects for the future?

Clearly socio-economic and socio-political transformations over the last 50 years are such that education, and HE, is now a key part of the global economy. We now refer to this as the knowledge economy or 'academic capitalism', a term coined by the American feminist Sheila Slaughter, with her colleagues Larry Leslie and Gary Rhoades (1997; 2004). Whilst there are many ways to describe and theorize these manifold and global transformations, a key part has been played by changing forms of education, especially in relation to information and computer technologies (ICT), and these are often now known to comprise the knowledge industries as important forms of networking.

Questions of gender and sexual relations, and violence against women or sexual harassment and child sexual abuse, are now more overtly in the public eye (David, 2013). For instance, it was a young woman paramedical *student* whose murder through a brutal gang rape in India dominated the global news headlines over the New Year period (2012–2013). Similarly, the Taliban's general political violence in that region of the Indian sub-continent, Afghanistan and Pakistan, has been perpetrated on young women fighting for *girls' education*, such as Malala

Yousafzai – who was shot in the face by a Taliban gunman for campaigning for girls' education in Pakistan in October 2012. Miraculously she survived the gun attack and was brought to the UK for treatment. Given her recovery in the Birmingham hospital she is now being educated in the UK, was nominated for the Nobel peace prize, and celebrated her 16th birthday giving a pleading speech at the UN on 12 July 2013 about education for all and universal girls' education. She has also written her story (Yousafzai with Lamb, 2013). In South Africa, Reeva Steenkamp, the girlfriend of Oscar Pistorius, the Paralympic gold medallist, whom he shot, was described *as a law graduate* and model who was about to deliver a Valentine's day talk to schoolgirls on sexual abuse. These are some stark examples of the violence and sexual harassment of women and girls that also occur closer to home.

In the UK there has been a recent furore over a BBC celebrity, Jimmy Savile, whose sexual harassment and rape of young women, over a 50 year period only came to light publicly recently and after his death two years ago. It is only now that questions of sexual abuse and gender-related violence are being discussed in public arenas. Such violence against women is not confined to the developing regions of the world, although it is clear that it remains a serious problem for the implementation of education for all. Even in the developed regions of the world such as the UK and the USA gender-related violence remains rife. But the roots of such gender-related violence are not adequately tackled and remain sidelined in political discourse. We must continue to argue for a more appropriate form of education for all that tackles issues of gender, gender-based sexual abuse as part of child sexual abuse, and all violence against women as integral to a proper education for all.

Why are these questions of gender and sexual relations now so visible when they were not on public agendas 50 years ago? Is the way in which they are publicly debated a result of feminist activism or is the question more complex than simply that? Is it more to do with transformations in culture, social media and communications, contributing to new forms of capitalism and commercialization of gender and sexuality as new forms of sexualization? Has this become a toxic mix of globalization and changing gender and social relations? What has really changed to make these questions of such intense media debate and will the resolution of some of the issues bode well for a more women- and feminist-friendly future? Or is it the case that the 'cycle of domination of top roles by men' [in universities], as Louise Morley (2012) argued in the *Times Higher Education*, will continue to hold sway? What needs to be done to break out of that vicious cycle to make education, higher education especially, and society more broadly, more feminist-friendly and less misogynistic? And, can education be used to try to transform wider social and sexual relations and reduce, if not eliminate, male violence against women?

Looking back on my own life as a feminist academic, I remember that Savile was launching his career as a DJ on the public stage when I was becoming an undergraduate student of sociology at the University of Leeds. Among my friends and acquaintances in Leeds were young women who did encounter him – and around the same time other women friends were beginning groups as part of the early stirrings of the women's liberation movement (WLM) that was later to become known as feminism. It was in these consciousness-raising (CR) groups that women began to talk personally about intimate sexual relations, but in the relative safety of the privacy of groups of like-minded women, reaching out towards some understanding of sexual power relations, and how they were not only individual but also political. Yet they were certainly hidden from the public gaze.

The phrase 'the personal is political' was then coined, leading into discussions about the sexual division of labour, women's rights and women's work, and, more importantly, the rise of intellectual curiosity about how these structured gender relations had come about (David, 2003). Through the women's movement, based, as it tended to be, around young women as students or new graduates, feminists began to develop new 'knowledge' and new approaches, including feminist pedagogies grounded in personal experience. At the same time, HE was expanding and opportunities for women not only as students but also as researchers and academics were opening up: women, including feminists, quickly were afforded opportunities to enter academia. In the UK, for example, the policy to expand HE was initiated through the Robbins Report, published in autumn 1963 (Robbins Report, Cmnd 2154, 1963). At that time, very few of the age cohort went to university, and of that tiny proportion, only a fifth were women. Over the last 50 years, this pace of change has speeded up such that women now comprise over 50 per cent of the undergraduate students in HE across most countries, especially the 'global north', although these percentages do not translate into academe and nor do they transform gender relations (UNESCO, 2012). The differences here are stark as I shall show.

Women's Learning Lives as a Background

This book began life as a project reflecting on the global transformations in HE as they impacted upon women's lives and education across the life course. Tentatively called *Women's Learning Lives* I particularly wanted to capture the vitality of the changes for women through education, school and universities. As a feminist social scientist, I had always been passionately interested in the relations between social and political changes, family, work and education and had written extensively about these issues in an academic activist vein, including an intellectual biography (David, 2003). I now wanted to devote my time and attention to providing an overview of the changes for women through universities and the question of changing forms of pedagogy, especially feminist pedagogy, for the practices of HE. Although I had touched upon these questions in my more recent studies on social diversity and widening access to and participation within HE in the twenty-first century I had not had the liberty to concentrate solely on these, given the changing nature of universities moving towards a performative, managerialist culture (David, 2009a). In an inaugural professorial lecture at the University of London's Institute of Education, which was also a valedictory, entitled *Transforming*

Global Higher Education: a feminist perspective I began to address some of my passionate interests, questioning how feminist perspectives had been incorporated into the global academy without their critical and radical edge (David, 2009b).

My aim remains focused on my own feminist passions and politics as a woman educator and intellectual: different from what has become, in an era of neo-liberal accountability and 'metrics', academic research assessable and accountable only to university peers. As Morley (2011) has argued so passionately the moves towards creating new 'metrics' and 'the numbers game' in assessing gender equity or parity amongst students in HE is a form of 'misogyny posing as measurement'. She also suggests that it is important for feminist academics today to consider how to change 'the rules of the [patriarchal] game' (Morley, 2013) so as to have a more gender-friendly future for universities. What precisely should this entail, given our experiences as feminist academics in neo-liberal universities?

The term pedagogy may appear abstruse but it has come to have meaning amongst educators as a perspective on knowledge and ways of learning through committed and critical forms of teaching about ideas: an intellectual approach (McLean, 2006). It is also about a commitment to social and gender justice. Yet, as HE has expanded, and more women have participated, it has become increasingly difficult to attend to questions of women or even gender alone, with social and political commentators arguing that gender equality has been accomplished with the advent of mass HE globally (e.g. Bekhradnia, 2009; Altbach, 2010; Willetts, 2010). This is what has been called the 'feminisation crisis debate' (Morley, 2011; Leathwood and Read, 2008). I have also become fascinated by the contested nature of these global changes and how gender equality in education has become emasculated, or certainly not feminized, by its incorporation into neo-liberal global universities.

This idea of gender equality or the more lukewarm notion of gender equity has been one of the key international policy changes in the last 25 years, and certainly in the first decade of the twenty-first century in an era of near global neo-liberalism. Starting as an academic sociological concept to distinguish different forms of sexual relations or sexual divisions and the social relations surrounding sex, it had entered the political lexicon by the end of the twentieth century. Most countries of the 'global north' have developed policies for gender equity in the public sphere and education especially; and many countries of the 'global south' also have developed frameworks for gender equity in public life (Morley, 2011). In 2010 in the UK, for example, the 'gender equality duty' was renamed and strengthened in law as part of the 'public sector equality duty' and yet three years later the Coalition government has decided to review it with a view to repeal (Government Equalities Office, 2013a and b).

Such is the extensive usage of the term, it now has also become a major vehicle for social research, particularly and interestingly in the Nordic countries for instance, with research centres of excellence on the topic, funded by government in Sweden and Norway, and with devoted research funds for gender and women's studies in Finland. There remains a huge disparity in what is meant by gender equity, and even more so by gender equality, under different political regimes, despite all the recent moves towards austerity cultures. Perhaps the most notable exposition is that expressed at the world congress on *Education For All* in the 1990s, and through UNESCO's (March 2012) publication of the *World Atlas on Gender Equality in Education* that I will elaborate in Chapter 2.

Using feminist methodologies of biographies, life histories and narratives, I construct a collective memoir to reflect on what has been accomplished over the last 50 years, and what the problems are with gender equity in HE today. I had originally intended to survey women's education and learning through the transformations in the economy, linked to socio-cultural and political systems, but this proved to be too vast to be able to illustrate all the nuanced transformations. I have therefore opted for an account as seen through the eyes and in the words of the participants in these changing processes. By concentrating on how a select group of academic women's lives have been transformed through HE I am able to demonstrate how important education has been in these changing contexts, and what further changes are necessary. I have woven a tapestry of their values and voices to create a collective life history and biography.

Women's learning lives as a double entendre had escaped me, but when my U3A group in north London pointed it out to me approvingly as I discussed it with them in the spring of 2011, it seemed most apposite. Women's learning does live on in both formal and informal universities. The vast majority of students and participants in U3A, as in universities, are women: here usually over the formal or 'official' age of retirement. Of course, women also outnumber men in their life expectancy in older age, although there are class and cultural differences, but what was particularly important was how these women seemed particularly thirsty for discussions, talks and learning more broadly; less hidebound by the old strictures of age than their male counterparts. This is indeed a testimony to how alive women are to continual learning and development across their lives. It may also be because women were traditionally denied opportunities for learning and work at younger ages and stages. This passionate and spirited engagement in lifelong learning has indeed developed apace as higher and adult education has grown and the notion of lifelong learning has been given credence and become a policy mantra. As I have argued 'a particular transformation, I would contend, that is often occluded in the dominant strands of the literature is that of women's learning and involvement in aspects of HE' (David 2012).

Initially seen as being 'the university of life', adult, continuing, extra-mural or extension education from universities in the UK also developed alongside workers' education, especially through the Workers' Educational Association (WEA), including the independent Ruskin College in Oxford, founded as a working men's college at the turn of the twentieth century. Ruskin was home to the first-ever British women's liberation movement (WLM) conference in 1970 and we shall hear about how influential it was in the stories of some British feminists. The extra-mural departments of universities and community education were often the beginnings of women's studies, and seen as safer places and spaces than the more overtly political consciousness-raising (CR) groups and where feminist work could blossom before it was allowed formal entry into university curricula. These were the courses that we, in the Bristol Women's Studies Group (BWSG), comprised of budding academic scholars and activists, for example, set up outside of universities in the early 1970s (BWSG 1979). There has recently been an attempt in London, at the Feminist Library, to recreate what is called Women's Studies Without Walls (WSWW) (20–21 January 2013). For those adults in later life it grew into what, in the UK, became the U3A 30 years ago.

Nevertheless, despite women's activism in courses and teaching for adults in community education, U3A was said to be founded by three *male* university professors – all distinguished social scientists and historians – who were also interested in what today might be called 'outreach' or university extension: 'Thirty years ago, in 1982, three men began the UK version of the University of the Third Age. They were [Professors] Peter Laslett, Michael Young and Eric Midwinter. Eric Midwinter MA, DPhil, OBE ... talk[ed] about the early days, the principles and the future. Dr Midwinter is a distinguished social historian, former Professor of Education at Exeter University, former Director of the Centre for Policy on Ageing and currently its Chairman ... ' (Richard Callanan, NLU3A, 6 June 2012, email communication). Women as relatively formal learners have been the mainstay of these developments but the gender dimension has remained occluded even in recent official reports for example, the UK's National Institute for Adult and Continuing Education (NIACE) by Shuller and Watson (2010): another aspect of the paradoxes of gender equality, perhaps, or of the continuing sexism and patriarchal relations in British society. This is limited assessment of how the processes of educational change occurred is what I hope to rectify.

Feminist Scholarship and Reflections in Academe Today

The question of gender equality in universities, and the contribution of feminist or women's studies is a highly contentious topic, arousing very strong emotions amongst both protagonists and detractors. The claim that gender equality has been achieved usually refers to the question of the balance of male and female students, whether of undergraduate or graduate degrees and courses (HEPI, 2009). It is rarely about the numbers or proportions of women as academics, teachers or researchers, where it clearly has not happened but feminist knowledge, pedagogies and wisdom have developed apace. As is argued in the USA's *The Chronicle of Higher Education* (November 2012) special issue on 'Diversity in Academe' devoted to the academic profession in the USA: 'Gender issues have fascinated and confounded people for ages. That certainly holds true for academe these days ... Not long ago, women were the focus of most gender discussions in academe. But now it's more complicated, with each sex drawing attention for different reasons ... Educators are still trying to figure out what attracts men to certain fields, like computer science and philosophy, and women to others, like biology and teaching ...' (2012, B3).

Quite clearly there is a lot of evidence now about the continuing richness and vitality of feminist work in and across the global academy, in the arts, humanities and social sciences. As I write this, in the last 18 months, there have been a series of events that illustrate how both feminist and gender work have become embedded in the global academy. The UK's Gender and Education Association (GEA) has grown into an international organization over its 12-year lifespan and its biennial international conference was held in Gothenburg in Sweden in late April 2012. Entitled *Gender and Democracy: Gender research in times of change* this conference provided rich evidence of the work of European feminists: all part of international networks of academic feminists. For example, Professor Lisa Huusu, a Finnish feminist and the inaugural director of the centre of gender excellence (GEXcel), a joint centre of excellence of Örebro University and Linköping University in Sweden – with its research theme on how gender paradoxes in changing academic and scientific organizations is changing and being changed – asked how gender equality is promoted via diverse interventions for change, and how these initiatives are evaluated, implemented, resisted and disrupted. The symposium was organized jointly with Louise Morley of the Centre for Higher Education and Equity Research (CHEER) at the University of Sussex, whose recent innovative studies of gender equity in two African countries (Ghana and Tanzania) have been a theoretical breakthrough; it addressed a key question about how gender is undone and redone in HE via policies, practices and micro-political relays of power. Drawing on empirical data from Austria, Germany, Sweden, the UK and the European Union, Ghana and Tanzania the symposium showcased work on how gender equality will fare in different national and international contexts, including austerity, privatization and post-neo-liberal cultures (Morley, 2011).

There have also been more directly celebratory events to mark the work of a broad and global network of academic feminists, ranging from a UK *Feminist Review* party to celebrate the 100th issue publication alongside a celebration of the work of the feminist scholar especially of the notion of intersectionality, Professor Avtar Brah. This was quickly followed by a workshop seminar at Goldsmiths College, University of London, on *Feminist Genealogies* directed at Masters students that proved to be so popular it became a closed event. It reviewed feminist ideas from the 1970s on debates about the demise of the welfare state in the UK today. The presentations by Professors Sara Ahmed, Avtar Brah, and Bev Skeggs were helpful in focusing upon generations of feminist thinking as not simply chronological but linked to socio-economic and political shifts. The renowned sociologist and feminist Professor Angela McRobbie emphasized the importance of the transformations in HE, for women, and the pleasures or freedoms entailed in being able to think autonomously.

More globally, The Aga Khan University (AKU)'s Institute for Educational Development East Africa based in Dar es Salaam, Tanzania organised its annual research institute on '*Inclusion and Equity in Education: Focus on Gender current issues for research and practice*'. This conference took place in November 2012 drawing participants from across not only Africa but also parts of Asia, and developing an exciting agenda for international research on HE leadership and management, as well as in schools. Organized by Dr Jane Rarieya, together with Professor Anjum Halai, originally from the AKU, based in Karachi, Pakistan particularly important questions raised ranged over girls' education in Muslim societies, ICT in African schools, gender and social justice, and how to teach about gender-based violence in African society, given the obstacles to change and traditional attitudes to family. The debate was passionate and strong, with colleagues participating from major NGOs creatively to meld together policies and good practices across the 'global north' and the 'global south'.

My aim is to capture the feelings of excitement, pleasures and challenge in the heyday of feminists' entry into academe, as budding feminist scholars and activists and to re-evaluate them in the light of the fact that feminist scholarship is clearly now embedded within the global academy, as these examples illustrate. It is, indeed, 60 years since the publication of Beauvoir's *The Second Sex* in English and 50 years since the publication of Friedan's *The Feminine Mystique* in the USA. Given this time span I decided to develop a 'collective biography' of international feminists, in keeping with feminist life histories, ranging over their passions and reflections on involvement in feminist scholarship, knowledge and activism.

Initially I focused on the generation of women formed through involvement in university education from the late 1960s who became known as 'second-wave' feminists, by contrast with the 'first-wave' feminists of the turn of the twentieth century who had campaigned for political changes such as women's suffrage. Whilst this wave analogy is problematic, I use it to analyse my stories of women across three generations of academic feminism borrowing from the late British feminist sociologist of education, Professor Olive Banks (1986) who developed a collective biography of 'first-wave' British feminists (as we shall see in Chapter 3). Her feminists were public and political, and 'best-known' differing from mine in the sense that education was not a key to their involvements. Indeed, only a small minority of her feminists had any higher education, an indication of the massive changes that have occurred over the 100 or more years since the origins of 'first-wave' feminism. I am concentrating solely upon feminists involved in academe, none of whom are 'best-known' in the public sense but who have produced an amazing body of scholarship, knowledge and wisdom to further the cause of women's liberation.

As Mary Evans (2004) had pointed out the women's movement was one of the major social movements of the twentieth century. Given the global economic recession and changing political complexions of government, there are also urgent questions about the changing role of HE and its part in global economies as well as the changing contributions of women, especially university-educated women. As feminism began to develop in the global academy almost 50 years ago, many feminists of this generation are now either retiring or already deceased[1] and yet

---

1 British, American and Australian women such as Professors Sheila Allen, Jean Anyon, Irene Bruegel, Rosemary Crompton, Jill Forbes, Alison Kelly, Gail Kelly, Diana Leonard, Sue Lees, Alison Lee and Mary Macintosh have already passed away.

such contributions are now critical for new gender agendas for HE. There is a lack of collective memory about the challenges and struggles of these women in academic life, as the pace of change in universities and the knowledge economy quickens. I want to capture the particular contribution of feminist academics in the arts and social sciences, as their collective ideas and insights of generations of feminists to the global academy may be lost to future generations.[2, 3]

Have the political and social changes that we campaigned for, from the 1960s, in what was then the women's movement been achieved, as many were beginning to argue at the turn of the twenty-first century or are feminist politics, drawing on generations of feminists, still important for transforming women's lives in the direction of equality? What part especially did feminists in the global academy play in developing the theories and evidence to assess the claims about the achievements of gender equality and feminist pedagogies and practices for the now contested neo-liberal universities of the future? How sustainable are feminist strategies for academic and educational developments in universities of the future?

Changing Approaches to the Study of Feminism in Academe

Originally, the idea for the book was linked to an unsuccessful research grant proposal for funds to complete projects as an emeritus professor. Given that the research proposal required me to say how I would disseminate my work, I planned to produce a book. My disappointment with the rejection of the research bid was mitigated by my plans to write up the work as a book, although the implications were that I would have *no resources* for undertaking the research, except for library and office facilities at the Institute of Education, University of London (IOE) and supportive colleagues at both IOE and at the University of Sussex's Centre for Higher Education and Equity Research (CHEER) where I am a visiting professor.

The lack of the grant initially felt bitter-sweet but it has enabled me to widen the scope of the study to involve more participants from across the generations. I have benefitted from many supportive national and international networks of feminist scholars, through national networks such as the British Educational Research Association (BERA), British Sociological Association (BSA), Gender and Education Association (GEA), Feminist and Women's Studies Association (FWSA), Social Policy Association (SPA) and Society for Research in Higher

---

2   For example, the late Professors Diana Leonard and Sheila Allen together organized the first British Sociological Association (BSA) annual conference in March 1974 on sexual divisions and society, processes and changes, from a feminist perspective (Barker and Allen 1975a and b).

3   In January 2014, the Feminist Library in London organised a reunion of 1960s and 1970s Sisters who were eager to meet together again to capture the old spirit of the time, and continue in supportive groups to deal with growing old together. A large email list has also now been created.

Education (SRHE), amongst others. In the 1970s, as an academic and member of the Bristol Women's Studies Group (BWSG), we developed pedagogical materials for both the University of Bristol and beyond in what were then extra-mural courses (David, 2003). As I moved universities, this continued with colleagues in the UK at other universities such as London's South Bank, Keele and IOE and more recently through national professional member organizations, building networks of international collegial and collaborative relations.

Since the 1990s I have also been involved with an international 'education feminist' network of the American Education Research Association (AERA) itself a major international professional organization of educators. GEA and the FWSA have also been committed to promoting educational change, feminist education research and gender equality in public policies. I had begun the process of thinking through the questions of the role of feminist activism linked to scholarship with three journal special issues:

1. *Discourse: Studies in the Cultural Politics of Education* (2008) with the American Professor Kathleen Weiler drawing on an international symposium that we jointly organized at American Educational Research Association (AERA) annual meetings in 2006 entitled *Second Wave Feminism and educational research.* Whilst recognizing the Anglophone, classed and raced limitations, in both the symposium and special issue we tried to account for the national and global contributions of the generation of second-wave education feminism with papers from, *inter alia*, Australia (Lyn Yates), Canada (Jane Gaskell), USA (Catherine Marshall, Kathleen Weiler) and myself (UK).

2. *Higher Education Policy* (2009) with Professor Louise Morley *Celebrations and Challenges: Gender in Higher Education,* drawing on a symposium at the SRHE annual conference 2007.

3. *Contemporary Social Science* (2011) the journal of the Academy of Social Sciences entitled *Challenge, Change or Crisis in Global Higher Education* with Professors Val Hey and Louise Morley (again), based on their Economic and Social Research Council (ESRC) seminar series on 'imagining the university of the future'. I argued that 'a major theme of contemporary research has been whether educational expansion has reduced or reinforced educational, economic and social inequalities. Most of this international research evidence points to how educational and economic inequalities in global and local labour markets are reinforced, internationally and nationally, although gender inequalities are either occluded or ignored' (David, 2011, p. 147). Hey and Morley argued that their rationale was 'our desire to imagine the future cohabitation of equity and universities, in the light of the present continuing and compounding of persistent inequalities' (Hey and Morley, 2011, p. 165).

As I began to gather my evidence for the book, talking to other feminists, both in the global academy and outside, I began to see how awesome the task was of trying to capture all the changes. The expansion of universities has indeed been huge, even if it is the case, as Delia Langa-Rosado and I argued (Langa-Rosado and David, 2006), that now we have 'massive universities, and not universities for the masses', not only in the UK but also in Spain for example. Inequalities in educational opportunities and provisions remain, despite the changes. I wanted to look at the debates and how they had impacted upon women's lives, as well as what the transformations had been in terms of the 'the numbers game' (Morley, 2011). Given that I did not get the research grant that I had applied for, I needed to rethink my approach and methods. How could I write about feminism, gender and universities without resources? And was my concern with women's learning *per se* or more about the changing perspectives of women as feminist educators and researchers in the academy? How could I weave in my politics and passions if I were surveying the transformations in global HE? And how could I confine my work to just what was happening in universities, even though they were playing a bigger part in national economies and international than in the twentieth century? Just what part did growing inequalities, and poverty or social disadvantage especially for women have in this story? My feminism had always included activism as part of the picture: campaigning as well as theorizing and reflecting. Aiming to change the world in the direction of greater equalities, and transforming it for women inevitably, in my book, means for social class, ethnicity and race too.

I decided to talk to feminist activists and others mainly in universities, and as public policy analysts – professors and researchers. I asked them a series of questions designed to target certain key issues that I see as the criteria to zero in on what feminism is and how it plays out in their and others' lives. I asked them to assess and reflect on how successful feminism has been in educational arenas, in politics and public life, and how important it remains to them today. I wanted to capture their initial feelings of excitement about being a part of the women's movement and campaigning for political and social changes. I also wanted to see whether they felt that they had achieved their personal and political goals, and how far these had changed over time. Had the goals of the women's liberation movement been achieved as some were beginning to argue at the turn of the twenty-first century?

In addition, I wanted to assess what the obstacles as well as opportunities to social change had been. Just how far had we been successful in transforming academic, educational and political lives? What had not been achieved and could the transformations that were desired yet be accomplished? Were some of the social and political changes during our lives inimical to feminist aims and was it possible to continue to campaign to change these? I also wanted to capture the range of emotions that the women had and have: the passions for being a feminist and also the desires for and disappointments of being in academia, and the pernicious effects of the business and managerial systems in global education today. I wanted to show how contested the current managerial or business approach to university and education systems is and how odiously different in approach to that of feminism.

I developed a series of questions, as a way of collecting my data (see Appendix 1 for the questions sent out). Given the developing technology of email and Skype, I invited responses to my questions from my international networks by email, Skype, as well as face-to-face interviews. The questions could be used as either interview or conversations based loosely on a set of prompts, or ones that could be used as an online quasi-questionnaire, with written answers via email, with occasional follow-up telephone, Skype or face-to-face conversations.

Starting with the feminists that I had come to know well through my UK networks and through the AERA, I specifically drew upon the special issue of *Discourse* and its loosely framed network which extends to Australia, Canada, New Zealand, USA and UK.[4] Inevitably this also involved snowballing techniques as my contacts suggested other people who might reply. My emphasis quickly became, however, 'education feminists' in the UK through my own involvement in the sociology of education, through my work with the *British Journal of the Sociology of Education* (BJSE). This initial set of contacts was primarily of 'second-wave' feminists but I subsequently extended the range to include younger generations of feminist scholars. Here these drew on my knowledge and acquaintance with education sociologists through the GEA, and especially its current executive and the BJSE executive editors. I also contacted members of the executive council of SRHE most of whom had initially been involved in educational development rather than discipline specific studies.

My second core network drew upon my initial involvement in 'second wave' feminism at the University of Bristol, the BSA and the SPA. I had remained in contact with the women who made up the BWSG (1979)[5] as we had met to celebrate anniversaries, most recently the belated 30th anniversary of its publication in October 2010 and a contribution to the FWSA annual conference in July 2011 at Brunel University on the *Futures of Feminism*. The loose feminist network in Bristol had become international with some now resident in North America and many crossed the Atlantic frequently: I thus had a huge array of feminist academics to email for responses in writing or by Skype, and by their visits to the UK.

Who Are the Women and Feminist Academics as Participants in My Study?

I aimed for international feminist 'voices', but all in English. I did not anticipate a large number of respondents but hoped for a spread amongst Anglophone metropolitan countries, and some countries of Africa and Asia where I knew of feminist academics. As I proceeded I found that some of my respondents preferred to be interviewed whilst others were happier to write to me by email. I have had an

---

4   A photograph provides a glimpse of some of the network dining during the AERA annual meetings in New Orleans, April 1994.

5   A photograph provides a glimpse of our reunion for the thirtieth anniversary of publication at Helen Taylor's home in Bristol, October 2010.

amazing and extensive array of responses, far more than I had initially expected, and finally ended up with well over 100 participants, who have provided interview materials, conversations and transcripts or written replies to my questions. I am immensely grateful to all of these wonderful women for giving their time to me so generously and warmly. I hope to do justice to their wisdom in creating this collective biography of their lives. Many of the participants have also sent me copies of scholarly publications, papers, CVs and other evidence of their writing and research: a testimony to the breadth and richness of feminist scholarship and writing today.

I have also obtained a spread of feminists across the arts, humanities and social sciences, as well as across the ages and generations, although, perhaps inevitably, most of my participants' replies were from women either already or partially retired, or in that age bracket of women about to retire. Especially important, here were the reflections on feminist work in the academy put together by a group of Canadian feminist scholars, entitled *Minds of Our Own: Inventing Feminist Scholarship and Women's Studies in Canada and Quebec, 1966–1976* (Robbins et al., 2008). Two of the editors, namely Professors Margrit Eichler and Meg Luxton, have participated in my study, showing the importance of preserving the memories of the heydays of feminist involvement in creating new knowledge and wisdom for global education.

Whilst I have a fascinating array of participants, my study is inevitably *partial*. It is partial because it celebrates the feminist scholarship and knowledge that has grown in academe, although there are debates about what exactly this now constitutes and I have only captured feminists in the social sciences, with a tiny number from the arts. It is also partial because of the limitations of my networks (and my resources) but also because several people I approached many times, either did not reply or refused to participate. I found it very difficult to mount an argument with some of those who ignored my requests (and I had no effective leverage), whilst others I knew to be far too busy to be willing either to be interviewed or respond in writing to my questions, and I did not feel like putting further pressure on such pressurized academics, as this might be seen as a further instance of the intensification of academic work today, rather than the pleasure and passionate engagement with feminist scholarship.

Contextual Material

As I was penning this introduction, a former colleague of mine – Alison Wolf – published a book that covered some of the same ground called the *XX Factor: How Working Women are creating a New Society* (2013). It is an engagingly written and well documented review of the societal changes that have been occurring for women, and well-educated women especially, over the last several decades. And she uses a similar method to mine: she interviews women from across the generations – some of hers and my generation, and many younger women who are now rising up in education and professional jobs – her book is about elite university-educated professional women. But there the similarities end and we part company. Wolf argues that the expansion of universities for elites has meant that such women are now in the ascendance in the professions and business and are able to live lives of privilege and non-traditional women, dependent though they may be on other less privileged women for forms of care and support. She applauds this system of individual class-based educational and professional success as heralding a new society. She does not think to question its downsides.

Sylvia Walby, another colleague of more feminist inclination, reviewed the book and argued that: 'Fascinated by the emergence of highly educated, fully educated women Alison Wolf here takes us on a scenic tour of their brave new world to marvel at this exotic species ... Greater attention to variations in the lives of women between countries, in the forms of gender regimes that structure choices differently in different places, would have enabled a more nuanced account of the pattern of contemporary gender relations ... other work shows that other worlds are possible and already exist' (*Times Higher Education*, 27 June 2013, p. 48).

Sylvia Walby herself had already published several books that demonstrate other worlds that exist. Her 2011 book entitled *The Future of Feminism?* appeared to promise a reflection on the future as seen from an educational perspective. However, Walby's current version of feminist politics, as articulated here, is not at all about the processes within universities, although she is an extremely distinguished professor of sociology, also holding the title of the UNESCO chair in gender research at the University of Lancaster. Rather she is interested in exploring the impact on European politics and issues of gender equality or equity within the polity, and she does this with considerable flair.

As Marilyn Porter, a Canadian feminist sociologist, argues in her review (2012) too: 'It is neither about the future, except in a rather brief final chapter, nor is it about feminism except in her rather narrow definition and range. It is an analysis of women's activities generally directed at increasing women's equality with men in the UK, in Europe, to a much lesser extent in the USA and to an even smaller extent "globally" by which she means in UN domains. Indeed, early in the book, she both broadens and narrows the definition of "feminism" almost out of existence by defining it as "people or projects that pursue the goal of reducing gender inequality (Walby 2011, p. 3)". She does this because she avers that "feminism" has become stigmatized, and that the most effective response is to abandon the word but retain what Walby sees as the heart of the enterprise ... Feminism ... has simply changed its manner of working and become less visible and more effective because it is institutionalized and integrated into mainstream activities including government' (Porter, 2012, p. 50).

Both books and arguments stands in marked contrast to my interests in the contradictions between different political perspectives within current economic structures and beyond an analysis of 'mainstreamed' equality seeking feminisms and their work within current structures of power, especially in the UK and Europe. I am interested in both a more traditional and radical notion of feminist politics as they relate to the personal, and within an institutional arena, of education: about both activism and understanding the roots of women's oppression with the family, work and the polity.

Illustrating quite how important reassessments of the contemporary state of affairs are, another exciting book is that by Janet Newman (2012) *Working the Spaces of Power: Activism, Neoliberalism and Gendered Labour*. Like Walby, she is interested in traditional politics – through the local as well as the national state, as well as lobbying and pressure groups or social movements. Like Wolf, she too uses a similar method to mine: here of interviewing women across generations, mainly but not only academics: some academics manquée. She is interested in talking to her feminist participants about involvements in activism – in local or national politics, and in pressure groups for social change and social welfare. Interestingly, although we are the same age, she creates four rather than three generations or cohorts of participants. Four of her 50 (British) participants are also participants in my study – Avtar Brah, Davina Cooper, Sue Himmelweit and Hilary Land. We have complementary interests: in the transformations achieved by feminists and in the blockages to change wrought by more conservative and constraining contemporary governments. Janet Newman does not focus on education or changing politics specifically in academe, leaving yet another space for feminist assessments of the past and thoughts about possible future scenarios. This is where my book is different from hers.

In an altogether different vein from Walby and Newman, Kathy Davis and Mary Evans (2011) as editors of the *European Journal of Women's Studies*, were interested in the trajectories of feminist theories amongst generations of scholars in the global academy. Davis and Evans, as sociologists and both from a generation of 'second-wave' feminism, invited their contributors to consider whether there now is a 'feminist canon', drawing upon the US by contrast with European and/or UK ideas. The contributors to their edited book entitled *Transatlantic Conversations: Feminism as Travelling Theory* all produced autobiographical reflective essays. Davis and Evans grouped the contributions around three overlapping themes, which were also used as a way to structure the sections of the book namely (i) becoming a feminist in a transatlantic context (ii) activism inside and outside the academy and (iii) theoretical engagements.

Interestingly this thematic approach to feminist perspectives turned out, quite serendipitously, to be similar to how I had framed my questions. But I did not confine mine to the transatlantic context, given my focus on obtaining contributors from Australia, New Zealand and Canada. Whilst also 'Anglophone', my approach addresses a slightly wider canvass, and does not engage with the dominance of American English or indeed American feminist theories. Davis and Evans invited their 16 contributors to make specific considerations about the European/US relations of domination, and, as an aside, the imperialism of American English in the forming of these ideas. Interestingly, another four of my participants (Mary Evans, Kelly Coate, Gabriele Griffin and Ann Phoenix) were also contributors to the Davis' and Evans' (2011) edited volume, although perhaps it is equally odd that my networks did not overlap more with those involved with this edited volume given that it was based upon feminists directly involved with women's studies and feminism in the current climate.

The vast majority of my participants turned out to be *professors* in the US sense of being 'full' professors (although in the UK not necessarily tenured). There are 82 professors out of 110 participants or almost three-quarters of my participants are professors (or emeritus and retired). The other 28 participants are in relatively senior positions as academics or researchers, with a small number having left academe for more activist and policy pursuits. The majority of my participants are also doctors, either with PhDs, professional doctorates, or doctorates by publication. Ninety-nine of the 110 were doctors. The 11 who were not were all living in the British Isles, mostly senior participants, in terms both of age and professional status. The reasons for these women not having doctorates was because it had not been a necessary pre-requisite of becoming an academic when they entered the profession, and they had risen through doing research and scholarly work without its need. Some decided later in their careers to obtain a doctorate by publication as 'a swansong' as Jackie West put it. There were a small number of older academic feminists that were neither doctors nor professors: all of them resident in the UK.

Given this increasingly intensive nature of academic work in universities today and the constrained and constraining individualized academe, I was not surprised that the responses from the older and retired women also tended to be more full: those who had been fired by feminist passions for political activism and who had eventually become, as I had too, jaundiced by the constant struggles within academia to maintain an emancipatory place and space. Yet all my participants feel passionately about how important the feminist project has been to their own learning, involvement in the academy and to their own lives.

My study is therefore made up of a diversity of women academics, across the generations and ages, and also extremely varied in terms of their social and geographic locations: illustrative of the mobile, transnational academics who are characteristic of the overall academic profession in the twenty-first century, as Terri Kim and Rachel Brooks (2013), among others (Brooks and Waters, 2011), have argued so cogently. They have recently shown that: 'The proportion of foreign and migrant academic staff in UK universities has increased significantly in recent years: 27 per cent of full-time academic staff appointed in 2007/2008 came from outside the UK (Kim and Locke 2009), but in some of the major research universities, the proportion is much higher: e.g. in the University of Oxford, over 60 per cent of academic appointments in 2011 went to non-UK nationals (unpublished interview data, April 2011). The proportion seems also higher at the professoriate level: according to the unpublished survey data provided by INCHER-Kassel (Teichler, 2010), 41 per cent of UK university professors have foreign citizenship. Within the UK, the highest numbers of new appointments from the EU are: Germany 4200, Ireland 2895, Italy 2695, France 2340, Greece 1905, and Spain 1570. From outside the EU, the highest numbers of appointees are US 2950 (2380 academic staff + 570 researchers), China 3730 (2280 academic staff + 1450 researchers), and India 1900 (1330 + 570)'.

Similarly, Rajani Naidoo (2012) has shown how diverse and transnational the global academy now is. While most of the women participants are now resident in the UK, many were not born here but come from former British colonies such as Australia, Canada, the Caribbean, India, Pakistan, South Africa and the US and other parts of Europe – France, Greece, Spain. Equally, my participants from Canada, for example, are originally from other countries such as Germany, Norway, the UK and the US: few were born in Canada. By contrast, the participants still resident in Australia were born there although there is one Australian feminist now resident in England.

Table 1.1 **Mobile academics: origins and current countries of residence of participants, 2012**

Countries	Countries of Current Residence	Countries of Origin/Birth
Australia	4	5
Canada	7	3
British Isles:		
UK:	83	75
England	76	69
Scotland	2	3
Wales	5	3
Ireland (Eire)	2	1
Caribbean		1
France		1
Germany		2
Greece		1
India	1	2
Israel/Palestine	1	1
New Zealand	1	1
Norway		1
Pakistan		1
South Africa		2
Spain	1	1
USA	10	14
TOTALS	110	110

Importantly, the stories of how these diverse women entered the academy and became feminists – through university or not – and specifically types of subject – women's studies, sociology, psychology – is immensely varied. The theories and/or books or writers who contributed to and impacted upon their learning is, interestingly much less varied, and it is much clearer about the developments of feminist practices and influences of generations of writers and theories, including Eureka moments, and feminist contributions through their own work such as doing PhDs and teaching courses etc. We also have a range of accounts of the contributions through feminist activism in the academy, changing positions and changing lives, influences through obstacles and opportunities and the impact of gender in the twenty-first century.

The Ethical Dilemmas of Feminist Research: Anonymity Versus Giving Voice

In pulling together these stories and presenting this collective biography there were inevitably ethical questions to be addressed, particularly in honing in on the travails of life in the academy today. This was not an issue that Alison Wolf (2013) raised and she has presented her stories, naming all her women quite openly. Janet Newman (2012) though had a similar problem of balancing giving voice and recognition to the creativity of feminist activists as opposed to maintaining confidentiality and anonymity. How could I maintain confidentiality and yet provide evidence of the creativity of feminist activities in the academy? There is some ambiguity about whether social science research ethics imply that anonymity will be maintained at all times or whether participants be named to ensure that it is their own voices that are heard rather than their words being plagiarized or at least rendered bland, dispassionate and impassive. There is also a fundamental question to be raised about detailed biographical material giving too much exposure to personal and intimate matters at the expense of broader political and professional issues. There is again the complicated question of the difference between anonymity and confidentiality, given global and technological transformations. Belonging to communities such as feminists in academe means that people can be identified even if one does not name them explicitly and so the question of attribution is never straightforward. Furthermore, given that we 'belong' to social groups and the feminist movement is nothing but an intrinsically social group our ideas and views are never solely our own, our work is itself the product of belonging to a community of scholars, thinkers and activists. So our individual ideas come to have more social meanings and this is what I have striven for in writing these individualized accounts.

As already mentioned, in the 1970s, these emerging ideas of the women's movement became known as the debate about the 'personal as political' and it has continued to be a thread in feminist research, mirrored by sociological research around what C. Wright Mills (1959) saw as 'personal troubles becoming public issues' and linking biography with social structure and history to form a narrative account. Of course, times are different now, and the democratic optimism of sociologists in framing questions at that time can no longer be sustained.

Given the so-called 'biographic turn' in the social sciences and the now accepted methods of auto/biography in feminist work (Stanley and Wise, 1979; Stanley, 1990) the majority of my participants were not precious about revealing personal, political or social issues in their professional and family lives. Indeed, they were happy to talk and have their words and conversations transcribed for use here and have given their permission freely. They have spoken in open and accessible ways, illustrative of feminist values about publication. Some, though, felt unsafe in the context of their ongoing lives in academe and I have tried my best to be faithful to their wishes, whilst also not claiming more for myself than is appropriate, namely naming individuals where possible to ensure that feminist integrity is maintained but also striving to ensure that their lives will not be harmed by my revelations: no psychic damage. This is something of an acrobatic feat in the current context of neo-liberal global universities where secrecy is difficult but 'open access' a misnomer if ever there was one.

Finally, I am struck by how these networks of feminists have become more than just professional and collegial but also friendships based upon shared values and knowledge, and the desire to maintain that development and creation and recreation of feminist knowledge through our daily and pedagogical practices. By this I mean developing and maintaining feminist critiques, through collective actions. So whilst it may be the case that feminist activism from and through the global academy may have been muted during the first decade of the twenty-first century, increasingly, as the socio-political climate in a global era of austerity tightens, resistance to the changes and limitations for women, particularly as feminists has increased and become more dramatic.

In the following chapters, I aim to provide a collective biography through narrative accounts and assemblage based upon feminist genealogies, and including reflecting on the past to build feminist pedagogies for a feminist-friendly global university of the future.

In Chapter 2, a contextual and conceptual chapter, I set the scene by reviewing the changing evidence about gender equality in global universities today, considering the changing 'numbers game' and debates about changing forms of gender equality versus feminist activism. I also briefly consider the expansion of the modern university, and its current European and global situation, especially in terms of the gender balance across students and academics: to what extent are the figures a mask for misogyny? There is clearly now gender equity amongst all kinds of students across the Europe, UK, USA but there are huge disparities amongst all levels of academe with male predominance continuing as, for example, *She Figures* so clearly demonstrates for all EC countries. I conclude with some feminist critiques of management and leadership in global academe, and the necessity to change the rules of the [patriarchal] numbers game for a feminist-friendly future.

In Chapter 3 I consider the methodology of developing a life history of academic feminism, starting from so-called 'second wave' feminism as the WLM. I also present how I approached a collective biography based upon Banks' (1986) method of developing a cohort analysis. My three cohorts of feminists born between 1935 and 1970 are presented and then I review the debates about 'second wave' feminism, and how this wave analogy plays out with my participants across the three cohorts or generations. I conclude with my participants' views of their feminist values and commitments.

In Chapter 4, I discuss my participants' current professional and academic status, and their educational and social origins. I focus on the social class backgrounds of the women in the three cohorts, as compared with whether they are 'first-in-the-family' (a UK concept) or first generation (a US concept) to go to university. What is clear from this is analysis is that the vast majority of my participants from across the generations are 'first-in-the-family' illustrating one of the major achievements of educational expansion – the university education of women. Overall, there are twice as many participants who are 'first-in-the-family' compared to those who have working class family backgrounds, although those who come from working-class or lower middle-class families increase across the younger generations or cohorts, illustrating how gendered social mobility has worked, maintaining a clear gender gap across class and culture.

The stories of the (66) feminist academics of cohort 1 are told in Chapter 5, to review how second-wave feminism first broke onto the shores of academe borrowing the lovely title from Lorna Marsden's (2008) essay. What are the different and diverse trajectories of becoming a feminist in academe from the women's political engagements? What kinds of feminist writing such as the popular texts and tracts, and political activism, were important? Who influenced whom to remain an active feminist in academe?

In Chapter 6, I focus on the early ripple effects of feminism through the stories of cohort 2 (some 32 women): the trajectories of becoming a feminist as feminism establishes itself in academe. To what extent does being of a different age cohort affect becoming a feminist scholar? What kinds of literature and texts are important in this journey and how is it changing as the academy changes? What role does academic feminism play in the creation of this generation's feminist knowledge?

In Chapter 7, the youngest generation of feminists in academe (the twelve women of cohort 3) is the centre of our attention, becoming academics and feminists in the heyday of the expansion of the neo-liberal university. What kinds of feminist knowledge and pedagogies have influenced their stories of academic engagement, given the contradictory transformations in gendered academic life today? Are they on the crest of the wave of feminism in academe? Additionally, I then ask about the pressures and constraints on being an academic in an era of the neo-liberal global university. How is this generation experiencing life in academe – as pleasure or pain or both – and how are they developing feminist pedagogies and practices for the future?

In Chapter 8, I move to my concluding comments about feminism and feminist knowledge or activism in the increasingly business and managerially oriented university and education systems. How constraining has this malign managerial approach been and will it continue to be? I conclude that collaborative feminist values have held the women together although the three cohorts of feminists entered academe in entirely different contexts and despite the range of social, cross-cultural and familial backgrounds from which my participants came. Indeed the vast majority of the women were 'first-in-the-family', 'first girl' or first generation to go to university whether from middle or working class families. What of new feminist pedagogies for the future of the university, and how are they to be challenged including the obstacles and opportunities for feminist pedagogies in the future? What kinds of critique of the increasingly sexualized culture for young people might constitute a feminist project and equally what are the necessary tools for feminist leadership for the future of higher education? Having revealed the fundamentally educational nature of feminism, can misogyny and the gender-based violence culture be overcome through education?

Figure 1.1   Photograph of Bristol Women's Studies Group (BWSG) taken in 2010

**Figure 1.2   Photograph of embryonic American Educational Research
Association feminist network taken in 1994**

Chapter 2

Gender Equality in Global Higher Education: The Misogynistic Numbers Game?

Introduction: Feminist Activism or Gender Equality?

Given the overall growth in global HE participation, student life and life after university has become a fundamental part of popular culture in the global north with films, novels and series on television. *Fifty Shades of Grey*, the best-selling (salacious) novel of all times, published in 2012, opens with two young female Canadian students about to graduate. Nevertheless, the author reverts to a nineteenth century habit of not revealing her forenames, acknowledging perhaps the ongoing sexist and misogynistic nature of public life. Many feminists have argued that this book contributes by being either 'mommy porn' or sado-masochistic gender violence but whichever, Lisa Appignanesi, together with Rachel Holmes and Susie Orbach, have edited a book entitled *Fifty Shades of Feminism*, acknowledging that 'fifty million women readers can't be altogether wrong ... [but] our times are still embroiled in misogyny ... so it is fifty women exploring what feminism means to them today' (*The Observer*, 17 March 2013, *The New Review*, p. 38). Clearly the culture is shifting towards contradictory forms of gender equality, and at very least the commercialization of feminist publications in an era of neo-liberalism by contrast with the previous era of social democracy.

What is the contemporary situation as regards the 'real' numbers of women and men participating in HE? This is heavily contested, at least in the UK, as gender equity of students is assumed and the question of gender equity amongst academe is not seen as an issue. 'The feminisation crisis' in the UK is currently rather dramatic with the UK Conservative Minister for HE, David Willetts, reasserting the argument in his 2010 book, *The Pinch*, that working-class men should be favoured over middle-class women in accessing HE, given his fear that 'feminism had trumped egalitarianism'. A more measured approach has been expressed in the USA, by *The Chronicle of Higher Education*, the magazine for academe, in a special issue on 'Diversity in Academe: The Gender Issue' (2 November 2012). As the editor notes: 'Gender issues have fascinated and confounded people for ages. It certainly holds true in academe these days'. John Kerry, the new Secretary of State in the US, replacing Hillary Clinton in January 2013, in his first article for a British newspaper (*Evening Standard*, 8 March 2013, p. 14) entitled *Malala's Vital Lesson for US Foreign Policy* stated that 'the US believes gender equality is critical to our shared goals of prosperity, and peace, and why investing in women and girls worldwide is critical to advancing US foreign policy'. Let us start with a map of the global situation with respect to gender equity in education, and HE especially.

Serendipity would have it that the UNESCO *World Atlas of Gender Equality in Education* was published (March 2012) as I wanted to present a global picture. UNESCO is the United Nations Educational, Scientific and Cultural Organization and as such gathers together statistics from across the world, namely all the countries that sign up to the United Nations. Most interestingly it is now committed to global gender equality across and including all levels of education, but different from feminism. It has produced the first world atlas on gender equality in education covering students across forms of schooling, up to and including researchers, but it includes very little on the academic labour market or forms of employment, whether academic or not! And it shows that gender equity is nowhere near being achieved in academe today anywhere in the world.

This atlas provides the most challenging information about gender equality across the life course but including also what is called, in this publication, tertiary education: this covers all post-school or post-compulsory education, namely HE and universities. It is signals how gender equality in education is on the global public agenda in ways in which it was not at the beginning of the twenty-first century, and certainly not as an international issue during the twentieth century. Have these questions been put on public policy agendas because of women's and feminist activism, through women's involvement in universities or are the discourses of gender equality different from feminism? The production of this 'evidence' is an important indicator of public policy debates about gender equality, including both the economic and social interests of the global powers, as Kerry's (2013) argument illustrates.

First, I review this evidence and second, critique the various statistics about gender equalities in universities across the globe, using feminist work to illustrate paradoxes about the future of HE. This sets the scene for how global academic feminists developed their expertise and knowledge. As the Director-General of UNESCO, Irina Bokova, argues in her foreword: 'Good policy is sharp policy. It is policy that targets specific problems and bottlenecks. For this, we need a clear picture of what is happening and good data. This first *World Atlas of Gender Equality in Education* responds to this need on one of the most important questions for human rights and sustainable development today.

Girls and women remain deprived of full and equal opportunities for education. There has been progress towards parity at the primary level, but this tapers off at the secondary level in developing regions. The global economic crisis is deepening inequalities, made worse by cuts in education budgets and stagnating development support. Gender equality is one of the six goals of the global Education for All campaign that UNESCO leads. This was launched in 2000, when all the countries of the world agreed to "eliminate gender disparities in primary and secondary education by 2005, and achieve gender equality in education by 2015, with a focus on ensuring girls' full and equal access to and achievement in basic education of good quality" … this allows for a clearer picture to emerge on gender progress and gaps. This Atlas is a map of the world; *it is also a call to action, to concentrate ever more on promoting gender equality in education as a human right and development multiplier'* (UNESCO, 2012, p. 1).

Gender equality in education has been accepted as a global human right, but how is this interpreted? Does it include sex and sexuality as well as social relationships between men and women, or boys and girls? This issue is clearly still a pressing socio-political question in 2013–2014, when issues of violence against women, and sexual abuse, bullying and harassment, are on the global political agenda. UNESCO used statistics from the Organization for Economic Cooperation and Development (OECD) and European organizations such as the European Union through Eurostat, supported by the World Bank.

Bringing together the countries of the world through the UN was an incredible achievement and getting a public policy commitment to the more modest goal of 'gender parity' was a major victory for campaigners. This process had been started over 70 years ago through the then US President, Franklin Delano Roosevelt's wife, Eleanor Roosevelt – the first lady of the US – arguing for human rights. After FDR's death, she pressed the US to join the United Nations (UN) and championed the new UN post-war legislation. Indeed, she became the first chair of the UN Commission on Human Rights and oversaw the drafting of the Universal Declaration of Human Rights in the late 1940s. [In the 1960s, she chaired the Kennedy administration's Presidential Commission on the Status of Women.] Setting revised goals for human rights and sustainable development through national governments was a means of trying to provide hope for the new millennium. It was also partly achieved through cooperative organizations other than the UN, although the UN has been at the forefront.

The European Union (EU) and the European Commission (EC) through its various organizations has also developed statistics about gender equality, especially through Eurostat, also through the European Research Area, and the European Science Foundation (ESF). This was inspired by political activism and international networks of women's rights campaigners as well as being seen as important as part of global economic competition and development. Moves towards markets in public policies may also contribute to the rise in gender equality policies in a contradictory way including UNESCO by its appointing professors of gender research, including one in the UK, Professor Sylvia Walby (mentioned in Chapter 1).

The European Commission (EC) has produced specific statistics on gender equality in 'science', where science is the umbrella term for research across all subjects and disciplines in universities. Their nicely named *She Figures – Statistics and Indicators on Gender Equality in Science* (EUR 23856 EN) have provided evidence and indicators on gender equality in universities every three years during the first decade of the twenty-first century. It is argued that: 'The *She Figures* data collection is undertaken every three years as a joint venture of the Scientific Culture and Gender Issues Unit of the Directorate-General for Research of the European Commission (EC) and the group of Statistical Correspondents of the Helsinki Group' (From the Clement C. Maxwell Library, 5 January 2010).

In the USA,[1] there are also numerous debates about gender equity in HE, with *The Chronicle of Higher Education*, publishing its special issue (2 November 2012, part B). As the editor notes: 'It's well known, for example, that female undergraduates outnumber their male counterparts ... the undergraduate gender gap is especially striking among black students ... women are advancing in the professoriate as well' (Carolyn Mooney, senior editor, special sections, B3, 2012).

In the UK the aim of providing evidence for policies on gender equality seems to have been more of a political struggle than these supra-national and global organizations indicate. There is, in fact, no one organization that provides such comprehensive figures and statistics in the UK as those of the EU, EC or UNESCO. Although the UK Government departments collect statistics about schooling and HE these figures are published separately and do not provide a comprehensive public account of gender or other equalities in and across education.

As regards universities, however, the organization of university leaders or vice-chancellors, now the Universities UK (UUK), set up a unit to gather together gender statistics, initially named as its Equalities Unit, in the early twenty-first century. This unit built upon and paralleled a women's equality unit, set up under the New Labour Government, in the Cabinet Office in the late twentieth century. The Government's equality unit was moved between departments and administrative units over a ten-year period and was eventually abolished by the incoming Coalition Government, despite its excellent work in providing a forum for women to develop a strong network of researchers and campaigners.

Similarly, the UUK's unit has been transformed and changed over the last decade in line with neo-liberal tendencies. Although continuing to be financed by public funds, the unit is no longer under the umbrella of the UUK, but has become an independent and autonomous organization, renamed the Equalities Challenge Unit (ECU). However, in its current guise it provides detailed evidence about *Equality in Higher Education: statistical report* in annual reports that gather together statistics across various social groups including *gender,* ethnicity, disability, and age, and bringing them together in what are referred to as 'multiple identities'. These statistics are presented separately for students and staff, and for the latter including but not only academics. These figures are a very useful source of evidence, and provide a source for government, in addition to its own Department for Business, Innovation and Skills (BIS), which also covers Universities, and the Department for Education that deals with schools.

Yet another potential source of statistical evidence is that of the Association of Commonwealth Universities (ACU), which brings together all 54 countries of the Commonwealth and its 500 universities. On its website, it argues that: 'Established in 1913, the Association of Commonwealth Universities (ACU) is the oldest international inter-university network in the world. Today's ACU

---

1   Sandra Acker notes that there are no such equivalent figures for Canada and I have not found evidence either about Australia.

combines the expertise and reputation of over ninety years' experience with new and innovative programmes designed to meet the needs of universities in the twenty-first century. HE is more international than ever before: the market for students and staff is a global one; research funds are increasingly allocated on an international, collaborative basis; academic reputations are based on global connections. Innovation and good practice do not stop at national borders. Moreover, at a time when tertiary education has never been higher on the development agenda, our experience in fostering collaboration between developed and developing country universities has never been more relevant or more important. Our 500 members are spread across five continents and, as you might expect, they represent a diverse range of institutions; but there are also many similarities – not least of which are a common language, common values and similarities in their organization and management. Commonwealth universities are therefore able, through the ACU, to network easily, extensively and fruitfully, sharing problems, solutions and good practice across a variety of higher education environments'.

Gender equality is not a prime objective of ACU but they do have a unit committed to developing gender equality in leadership and management in HE, established in 1985 as the ACU's Gender Programme 'to enhance and increase the participation and profile of women in the leadership and management of HE'. Three values of the programme are recognition first of the importance of having senior women as role models (not least to encourage more young women into science, engineering and technology); of the need for the ACU to play its part in equipping women with the skills and confidence to bid for and assume leadership and management positions and that the improved recruitment of women into all levels of leadership and management in HE is integral to the overall development of universities in terms of both equity and quality. Moreover, the ACU's Gender Programme set itself the two important objectives of assisting in the development of a Commonwealth-wide gender network whose members are encouraged to provide one another with professional and moral support, and developing a database of women who are already, or who have the potential to be, leaders. Several sources of data provide evidence of progress towards or achievement of the goal of gender equality in HE, whether amongst students or academe.

What *is* the Evidence through Numbers or Metrics of Gender Equality Amongst Students?

UNESCO's commitment to gender equality in education has a long history linked to political and feminist campaigning during the twentieth century. The specific achievement of getting these questions on an international agenda has an official story which is briefly recounted in the introduction where it dates back almost 25 years, to the UN's first *World Conference on Education for All* in Jomtien, Thailand in 1990: 'There, representatives from 155 countries launched the Education for All (EFA) movement by agreeing to make primary education accessible to all children and to massively reduce illiteracy by the end of the decade. They adopted a Framework for Action that defined targets and strategies aimed at meeting basic learning needs of all by the year 2000. Ten years later, in April 2000, 1,100 participants from 164 countries gathered at the world Economic Forum in Dakar, Senegal, to reaffirm their commitment to the notion of education as a fundamental human right and to the goals of EFA. The Forum reviewed progress up to that point and adopted a framework for action that sets updated targets. Another important development was the signing in September 2000 of a United Nations Millennium Declaration by all 192 United Nations member states and at least 23 international organizations that laid out a set of Millennium Development Goals (MDGs) to be reached by 2015 ... *A closely related theme running through all of these discussions has been that of gender equality in education.* From the outset, the global community has recognized that educating girls and women is an imperative, not only as a matter of respecting a basic human right for half the population but as a powerful and necessary first step to achieving the broader goals of EFA. Following the landmark Fourth World Conference on Women held in Beijing in September 1995, attended by representatives of 189 governments and 2,100 non-governmental organizations, the international community reached a consensus on achieving gender equality in education. The Dakar Framework for Action and the MDGs set the goal of eliminating gender disparities in primary and secondary education by 2005 and of achieving gender equality by 2015' (2012, p. 8; my emphasis).

The Atlas concentrates on providing both a global overview of the growth in educational opportunities and their gender specificities, focusing on both gender parity and gender equality: the former being defined as formal equality in terms of numbers, and the latter balances between men and women in terms of proportionality. Whilst there is little space for more than broad headlines, some attention is given to economic, geographical and regional differences, including between the 'global north' and the 'global south' and to the changing picture in relation to women's increasing involvement in education across the life-course. By way of general summary, it is argued that: 'The Atlas tells the story of enormous growth in educational opportunities and literacy levels throughout the world over the last four decades, especially since the Dakar Forum of 2000. During this period the capacity of the world's educational systems more than doubled – from 647 million students in 1970 to 1,397 million in 2009. Enrolments increased from 418 to 702 million pupils at the primary level, from 196 to 531 million at the secondary level, and from 33 to 164 million in higher education ... The Atlas pays special attention to the issue of gender equality. While educational opportunity expanded over the last four decades for both sexes (*sic*), the gains were particularly striking among girls in terms of access, retention and progression from primary to secondary and beyond. The maps and tables describe patterns of gender parity at all levels of education –

pre-primary, primary, secondary and tertiary – and show how these patterns are shaped by factors such as national wealth, geographic location and field of study. *An important theme is that although girls are still disadvantaged in terms of access to education in many countries and regions, they tend to persist and perform at higher rates than boys once they do make it into the education system.* Another theme is that all countries face gender equality issues of some sort, including situations where boys are disadvantaged in one way or another' (2012, p. 9; my emphasis).

Women Now Account for a Majority of Students in Most Countries

The headline story is that '*Women now account for a majority of students in most countries*' but this 'gender parity index' is expressed as if women were being favoured rather than given their basic human rights and indeed when subsequent employment is discussed it is clear that this has not happened. The authors report that: 'for 149 countries ... it shows that women are *favoured* in a sizeable majority of 93 countries while men are *favoured* in only 46. Ten countries have achieved gender parity at the tertiary level' (2012, p. 78; my emphasis). The authors of the Atlas go on to argue that: 'Although access to higher education remains problematic in many countries, the last four decades have brought a major expansion of higher education in every region of the world and *women have been the principal beneficiaries in all regions.* Female enrolment at the tertiary level has grown almost twice as fast as that of men over the last four decades for reasons that include social mobility, enhanced income potential and international pressure to narrow the gender gap. Nevertheless, enhanced access to higher education by women has not always translated into enhanced career opportunities, including the opportunity to use their doctorates in the field of research' (2012, p. 75; my emphasis).

An Increase of Around 500 Per Cent in Enrolments Over Less Than 40 years (1970–2009)

The discourses used about these dramatically increasing numbers are overly optimistic with notions of women being either 'favoured' or 'beneficiaries'. The Atlas argues that *Women are the biggest beneficiaries of rising tertiary enrolments* (2012, p. 77) but it is essential to contextualize and ensure a nuanced understanding. First, total enrolment at the tertiary level soared from 32 million students in 1970 to 165 million in 2009 – *an increase of around 500 per cent over less than 40 years*. In other words, education, and HE in particular, has become a larger part of the international or global 'knowledge' economy than in the twentieth century and known as 'academic capitalism' (Slaughter and Leslie, 1997; Slaughter and Rhoades, 2004): 'Of the 158 countries for which data are available, the gross enrolment ratio (GER) is below 20 per cent in 43 per cent of the countries and falls between 20 and 50 per cent in a quarter. Another quarter (26 per cent) of the countries fall between the 50 to 80 per cent range. The GER registers above 80 per cent in only nine nations' (2012, p. 76).

Secondly, they provide evidence of regional variation: 'Although every region of the world has experienced a surge in tertiary enrolment, the most dramatic gains have been recorded in regions that had the lowest levels of enrolment in 1970 and which continue to record modest enrolment levels to this day. Tertiary enrolments in 2009 were 24 times the 1970 figure in sub-Saharan Africa and 17 times in the Arab States. Enrolments multiplied 15-fold in East Asia and the Pacific, which now boasts the highest tertiary education enrolment of any region (52 million). Enrolments in North America and Western Europe rose by 250 per cent, but the region's share of total tertiary enrolment dropped from nearly half (45 per cent) in 1970 to less than a quarter (22 per cent) in 2009'.

Thus there is a growing shift in regional variation and involvement, with a delicate balance between the growth in the so-called 'global south' at the expense of 'the global north' (2012, p. 74). This detailed evidence is further elaborated to show that: 'The largest gains in enrolment have occurred in North America and Western Europe, in Latin America and the Caribbean and in Central and Eastern Europe – three areas where males also made lesser but still substantial gains. Females went from a position of disadvantage in 1970 to a majority position in 2009 in three regions: East Asia and the Pacific, Latin America and the Caribbean, and North America and Western Europe ... The global GPI as a whole rose dramatically from 0.74 favouring men in 1970 to 1.08 in 2009, which falls within the range of parity and slightly favours women. In 1970 only one region, Central and Eastern Europe, registered a GPI over 1.03 favouring women. By 2009 a majority of four regions had an index favouring women. While the GPI rose in all regions during this period, the relative position of some of the regions shifted. The largest gains occurred in Latin America and the Caribbean, where the GPI rose from 0.62 to 1.21 over the past four decades. North America and Western Europe moved from second to first place, while South and West Asia, which was at the bottom of the table in 1970, rose to seventh place. Sub-Saharan Africa dropped from sixth to eighth place' (2012, p. 75).

Globalization Has Led to More Attention to Gender Egalitarianism

These changing balances are also carefully elaborated, and presented in tables and maps, with evidence about how the rise in female enrolments has been more rapid in countries of Africa and Asia, given the lower base on which to develop. Moreover, some countries of the 'global north' may be said to have reached saturation and are unable to include more students. In drawing together an overarching conclusion for their Atlas, the authors conclude: 'Female enrolments have increased faster than those for males at all levels, most dramatically in tertiary education ... Whereas the challenge of gender equality was once seen as a simple matter of increasing female enrolments, the situation is now more nuanced, and every country, developed and developing alike, faces policy issues relating to gender equality. *Girls continue to face discrimination in access to primary education in some countries, and the female edge in tertiary enrolment up through the master's level disappears when it comes to PhDs and careers in research. On the other hand, once girls gain access to education their levels of persistence and attainment often surpass those of males. High repetition and dropout rates among males are significant problems'* (2012, p. 107; my emphasis).

The argument is that there are significant differences between men and women in their approaches to educational achievement and learning, with an emphasis on *girls' resilience through persistence and hard work*, whereas men tend to have a lower threshold of persistence and drop-out. However, it is also argued that the external environment rather than policy prescriptions *per se* account for women's dramatic increase in involvement with especially factors such as poverty and ambition to better themselves encouraging further participation: 'Over-representation of women in HE is not necessarily the result of affirmative action in their favour, for such legislation is rare. Rather, empirical research highlights several reasons for the growing participation of women in post-secondary education, beginning with the fact that higher levels of schooling are now required to attain social mobility and escape poverty. Even though HE leads to individual returns in the form of higher income, women often need to have more education than men to get the same jobs. *Globalization has led to more attention to gender egalitarianism.* Finally, once women gain access to HE they frequently exceed men in grades, evaluations and degree completion' (2012, p. 84; my emphasis).

They also conclude that whilst there has been an enormous increase in educational participation within and through HE, this has not been matched by greater participation in the labour market, especially not in academic or leadership terms. This is then one of the key paradoxes of gender equality in education: is it an indication of continuing forms of misogyny, sexism, or patriarchal relations in the wider society? 'It must also be noted that over-representation of women in HE has yet to translate into proportional representation in the labour market, especially in leadership and decision-making positions. Even though many women have started to benefit from their countries' improved education systems, they face barriers to the same work opportunities available to men. Women continue to confront discrimination in jobs, disparities in power, voice and political representation and the laws that are prejudicial on the basis of their gender. As a result, well-educated women often end up in jobs where they do not use their full potential and skills' (2012, ch. 5, p. 84).

'Significant differences exist in the extent to which men and women pursue education at the various levels ... women have reached parity with men in earning bachelor's degrees. They have an edge over men of 56 to 44 per cent in master's degrees, but this ratio is exactly reversed at the PhD level. Women receive more bachelor's degrees than men in three of the five regions and more master's degrees in two. *When it comes to PhDs, however, men have the advantage in all regions* ... Despite the narrowing of the gender gap in tertiary enrolment, significant differences are observed in the fields in which men and women choose to earn degrees ... the distribution of female graduates among various disciplines in science and in the social sciences, business and law in various regions ... The proportion of female graduates is much higher in the social sciences, business and law, where women are the majority of graduates in all but one region and in all of the sub-fields of social and behavioural science, journalism and information, business and administration, and law. The major regional exception to these patterns is Central Asia, which strongly favours women in science and where female graduates are a minority in the social sciences, business and law' (2012, pp. 80–82; my emphasis).

The fact remains that men predominate in jobs after the PhD and especially in relation to research posts. It is only the arts and social sciences that are dominated by women, including education: 'Among the four fields presented, *education is the most popular with women*. Women are more likely than men to graduate in this field in 77 of the 84 countries with data. They account for more than nine in ten graduates in several countries, including Aruba, Bermuda, Croatia, Estonia, Lebanon and Latvia' (2012, p. 82; my emphasis).

The final argument presented by way of conclusion in the Atlas is that: 'Despite ... achievements however, most of the developing regions still fall behind on several aspects of gender equality. It is often the case where a better level of education doesn't necessarily translate into better employment opportunities. Even though women outperform men in education, they still face significant shortfalls and discrimination in the labour market and end up in jobs where they don't use any of their skills. However, *even though education is not the only input into women's empowerment it is nonetheless a central one*' (2012, p. 107).

Much of this evidence can be shown in more detail both for the UK and the USA, and for aspects of the EU or EC. Given that the Atlas is short on evidence about employment and detailed data about students, I turn first to present a more detailed picture for students, both undergraduate and postgraduate and then move into more details about gender and academic employment, where the situation remains as it always has been – male domination.

The UK, USA and European Metrics of Gender Equality Amongst Students

There are several sources of evidence providing the detail that confirm the overall picture of moves towards gender equality amongst students in the UK. However, much of that evidence has to be picked out from amongst other data, given for example, the mission statement of the ECU in the UK: 'ECU works to further and support equality and diversity for staff and students in HE and seeks to ensure that staff and students are not unfairly excluded, marginalized or disadvantaged because of age, disability, gender identity, marital or civil partnership status, pregnancy or maternity status, race, religion or belief, sex, sexual orientation, or through any combination of these characteristics or other unfair treatment'. In announcing the ECU's *Equality in higher education: statistical report 2011* (December 2011) on the website it is argued that: 'This report presents an equality-focused analysis of information on staff and students during the 2009/10 academic year, plus a year-on-year comparison showing the progress of equality across the sector over the last five years. For the first time the report looks at the interplay of multiple identities (for example female black staff, male disabled students). Covering England, Wales, Scotland and Northern Ireland, the report provides a useful benchmark for institutions to compare their local statistics. New legal requirements across England, Scotland and Wales mean that HE institutions need to set equality objectives or outcomes. The figures in this report, alongside information gathered at a local level, will provide an evidence base that will inform these objectives'. This is ECU's most detailed report so far, and has been split into two parts. Both parts cover the following equality areas: Gender, Ethnicity, Disability, Age and Multiple identities. Nevertheless, the report's *part 2 students* (2011) does not start with headline figures about gender equality or parity but provides detail on other equalities such as disabilities, with the comment that 'the statistic on the cover shows the difference between students declaring a disability in different subjects. 14.4 per cent of students studying creative arts and design declared a disability, compared with 4.5 per cent of students on business and administration studies courses' (2011, cover). Even examining the summary data provided as either 'Students: key facts and figures or Gender: key facts and figures' (2011, p. iii and p.1) does not immediately alert one to the changing balances. As regards the key facts and figures for gender, along with one from amongst 'multiple identities' they are stated as:

- More female first year students studied part-time than men across all degree levels.
- Despite an increase in the proportion of male students over the past four years, in 2009/10 there was still a gap of 13.3 per cent between female and male students' representation.
- Assumed unemployment rates were higher for male leavers (9.1 per cent) than for female leavers (6.1 per cent).
- Fifty-one per cent of the male population were aged 21 and under compared with 45.9 per cent of female students. However, 20.9 per cent of female students were aged 36 and over compared with 15.3 per cent of male students (2011, p. iii–iv).

The overwhelming impression from reading these introductory pages is that *gender equality has become so normalized that it hardly bears comment*, and that the policy assumption is that concern must focus primarily on the ensuing issues or problems for male students (Willetts, 2011, op.cit.). Indeed, the authors of the report argue that 'In the academic year 2009/10, women made up 56.6 per cent of the student population. Female students were in the majority across all four countries (England, Wales, Scotland and Northern Ireland)'.

Table 2.1   All students by country and gender across the UK

	Female		Male		Total
	No.	%	No.	%	No.
England	1188110	56.7	905520	43.3	2093635
Wales	68455	53.5	59430	46.5	127885
Scotland	125480	56.8	95430	43.2	220910
Northern Ireland	30140	59.1	20850	40.9	50990
UK	1412185	56.6	1081225	43.4	2493415

Source: ECU's 2011 Equality in higher education: statistical report 2011 (December 2011) Table 1.3 p. 2.

However, this fact is qualified, as was the case with the Atlas, although a similar gloss is not put on the figures, with the statement that 'Women were in the majority across all degree levels and modes with the exception of full-time postgraduates where 50.4 per cent were male … The proportion of female students was highest amongst other undergraduates (64.7 per cent)' This is clearly illustrated in the summary table below.

Table 2.2   All UK students by degree level, mode of study and gender

	Female %	Male %
Full-time postgraduate	49.3	50.7
All postgraduate	53.6	46.4
All full-time students	54.2	43.2
Full-time first degree UG	54.4	45.6
All first degree UG	55.1	44.9
All students	56.6	43.4
Part-time postgraduate	58.2	41.8
Part-time first degree UG	58.8	41.2
All part-time students	61.3	38.7
Full-time other UG	63.3	36.7
All other UG	64.7	35.3
Part-time other UG	65.1	34.9

Source: ECU's Equality in higher education: statistical report 2011 (December 2011) Table 1.4 p. 3.

The report then goes on to show changes over the last seven years, mentioning this as 'profile over time', but taking a very short time period. Gender parity is certainly not a concern, except as the reverse of the concern with the Atlas: *the focus is on men.* It states that 'Over the past seven years, there have consistently been more female than male students in HE in the UK ... Despite an increase in the proportion of male students over the past four years, in 2009/10 there was still a gap of 13.3 per cent between male and female students' representation'. This time frame is far too short to illustrate the large changes in gender balance but not necessarily achievements and occupational shifts over time.

The chief executive of ECU, David Ruebain, in a public presentation made the following summary comment that: 'Over the past seven years, there has been consistently more female than male students in HE; and males more likely to obtain 2nd or 3rd class honours; or withdraw but *52.4 per cent of postgraduate students studying SET are male*' (Sussex University, 16 April 2012). Whilst he described rather than drew particular implications, it is clear that, for the UK, gender has become just one of several inequalities for students and is certainly no longer a key issue for the key equality bodies concerned with the question.

Trends in Gender Equality in HE Amongst Students Over the Last 50 Years

If a longer view is taken, there has been a dramatic reversal of trends over the last 50 years. This is shown in the following summary table, although we do not have disaggregated figures for 1960–61, when figures were produced for the UK Robbins Report on HE (1963). The economist Lionel Robbins was asked to undertake a study for the then UK government and give considerations to the various arguments for expansion. The report facilitated the expansion of HE, around the so-called *Robbins principle* that university places 'should be available to all who were qualified for them by ability and attainment'. At that time, tiny proportions of the eligible population of 18 year olds in Britain went to university – there were 216,000 students overall then (Robbins Report, Cmnd 2154, 1963, p. 15). The numbers of women were not separated out except, in what are now very old-fashioned ways: how the Robbins committee argued against the implementation of student loans, especially as to the potential impact that they would have on parental decision-making about their daughters. They were opposed to student loans because: 'In particular, where women are concerned, the effect might well be either that British parents would be strengthened in their age-long disinclination to consider their daughters to be as deserving of higher education as their sons, or that the eligibility for marriage of the more educated would be diminished by the addition to their charms of what would be in effect *a negative dowry*' (Robbins Report, Cmnd 2154, 1963, paragraph 646; my emphasis).

They also added that: 'On balance we do not recommend immediate recourse to a system of financing students by loans. At a time when many parents are only just beginning to acquire the habit of contemplating higher education for such of their children, *especially girls*, as are capable of benefiting by it, we think it probable that it would have *undesirable disincentive effects*. But if, as time goes on, the habit is more firmly established, the arguments of justice in distribution and of the advantage of increasing individual responsibility may come to weigh more heavily and lead to some experiment in this direction' (ibid., Chapter 14; my emphasis). In *Robbins Revisited: Bigger and Better Higher Education* published especially for the fiftieth anniversary of the report, David Willetts, the UK Minister for Universities and Science, used the Robbins comments to illustrate both the changing gender balance amongst students, and how the Conservative Government was pursuing similar aims. He argued:

'Robbins said that everyone able to go to university should have a place. And this was before one adds in the cost to universities of educating their students. To pay for all this Robbins toyed with the idea of loans repayable as a percentage of future earnings. He decided not to go down this route as he was afraid that positive

Table 2.3   **Proportion of higher education undergraduate students, by gender, in the UK (percentage)**

Academic year	Men	Women	Total
1970–1971	67	33	100
2005–2006	43	57	100
2010–2011	44	56	100

Sources: Department for Education (DfE) and Higher Education Statistics Agency (HESA). 2011. Statistical First Release, 'Higher Education Initial Participation Rate (HEIPR)'.

Table 2.4   **Undergraduate students in higher education (full-time and part-time), by gender, in the UK (thousands)**

Academic year	Men	Women	Total
1962–1963*	N/A	N/A	216
1970–1971	241	173	414
1980–1981	277	196	473
1990–1991	345	319	664
2000–2001	510	602	1,112
2010–2011	820	1,092	1,912

Sources: Department for Education (DfE) and Higher Education Statistics Agency (HESA). 2011. Statistical First Release, 'Higher Education Initial Participation Rate (HEIPR)' and *Robbins Report. 1963, p. 16. Table 5, 'Percentage of the age group entering higher education, Great Britain, 1962'.

attitudes to higher education were not sufficiently widespread, especially amongst young women. Looking back he increasingly came to regret his caution. Eventually after over forty years, we have ended up with a financing model very close to the one Robbins really preferred' (Willetts, 2013, p. 70).

Thus as with the global figures there has been more than a 500 per cent increase in overall student numbers over 50 years. There are now over 2 million students in HE in the UK. France has also had a similar huge increase in overall student numbers from about 300,000 in 1961 to over 2 million in 2010–11, and with a similar shifting gender balance from women's inequality to parity during this period.

Table 2.5   **Proportion of 17–30 year-olds having entered higher education (full-time and part-time), by gender, in the UK (percentage)**

Academic year	Men	Women	Average
1960–1962*	5.6	2.5	4
1999–2000	37	41	40
2005–2006	37	47	42
2009–2010	41	52	47

Sources: Department for Education (DfE) and Higher Education Statistics Agency (HESA). 2011. Statistical First Release, 'Higher Education Initial Participation Rate (HEIPR)'; *Robbins Report. 1963, p. 16. Table 5, 'Percentage of the age group entering higher education, Great Britain, 1962'.

Similar trends can be shown for France as an example of another European country:

Table 2.6   **Proportion of higher education undergraduate students, by gender, in France (percentage)**

Academic year	Men	Women	Total
1960–1961	65	35	100
2005–2006	43.5	56.5	100
2009–2010	44	56	100

Sources: Vasconcellos, Maria. 2006. L'enseignement supérieur en France. Paris: La Découverte; MESR-DGESIP-DGRI SIES. 2012. Filles et garçons sur la marche de l'égalité de l'enseignement supérieur, p. 30.

Rampant Gender Inequalities in HE: The UK Academic Labour Market

The picture painted by the ECU for students is one of gender having become a *minor* issue in relation to student attainment and progression, across a range of subjects and disciplines. The ECU's report *Equality in higher education part 1: staff* (December 2011) paints an entirely different picture: it is one of *rampant gender inequalities*. The headline figures are prefigured on the cover with the caption: 16.3 per cent median gender pay gap and 20.3 per cent mean gender pay gap. 'The statistic on the front cover shows the median and mean pay gaps between male and female staff working in higher education across the UK (Figure 1.28)'. The headline figures also paint a similar story of gender inequalities with the following highlighted:

- Overall in 2009/10, 53.8 per cent of all staff were women.
- Female staff made up 46.8 per cent of full-time staff and 67.1 per cent of part-time staff.
- While there has been relatively little change in professional and support roles in relation to gender since 2003/2004, there has been a marked increase in female academics (40.0 per cent to 44.0 per cent).
- *A higher proportion of staff in professorial roles were male (80.9 per cent) than female (19.1 per cent).*
- *Men comprised 55.7 per cent of academic staff in non-manager roles and 72.0 per cent of academic staff in senior management roles.*
- *The median salary of female staff was £29,853 compared with £35,646 for male staff, an overall median pay gap of 16.3 per cent.*
- *The mean salary of female staff was £31,116 compared with £39,021 for male staff, an overall mean pay gap of 20.3 per cent.*
- *76.1 per cent of UK national staff in professorial roles and 67.4 per cent of non-UK national staff in professorial roles were white males* (my emphasis).

The report elaborates on these points, namely that 'the highest proportion of men were found within full-time academics (61.7 per cent) and the highest proportion of women were found within part-time professional and support staff (78.7 per cent)'. It also comments about change over 7 years 'there has been a marked increase in female academics (40 per cent to 44 per cent) but a higher proportion of staff in professorial roles were male (80.9 per cent) than female (19.1 per cent). The difference was most noticeable within SET departments where 84.9 per cent of staff in professor roles were male and 15.1 per cent female ... Men predominate in teaching and research roles (56.3 per cent) with 51.7 per cent of teaching-only roles, 46.8 per cent of research-only roles and 39.0 per cent of teaching and research roles were held by women'. These differences are reflected in salary with the proportion of men earning over £50,000 was around double that of women (31.9 per cent against 16.3 per cent for academic staff). The gender pay gaps differed across the four nations quite dramatically:

Table 2.7   Median and mean pay gap by country of institution in the UK

	Median %	Mean %
London	11.6	15.8
England excluding London	18.7	20.6
All England	16.3	19.6
Wales	21.1	23.2
Scotland	21.3	23.8
Northern Ireland	21.0	21.1
UK	16.3	20.3

Source: ECU's *Equality in higher education part 1: staff* (December 2011) Table 1.31 p. 1.

It is a measure of how contradictory evidence-based policies are that these two reports on *Equality in HE* can be written and published together without any overarching comment about the *dissonance between the two* in terms of gender equity. It is abundantly clear that despite the huge increases in educational opportunities up to postgraduate research where women have been sufficiently ambitious to attain as much if not more than men, that they remain subordinate across all sectors of academic employment.

UK Gender and Academic Labour Market: The Masquerade of Misogyny?

I interviewed Professor Sir Adrian Smith, who, at the time (February 2012), worked directly to the UK Minister for Universities and Science, David Willetts, and was the UK government Department of Business, Innovation & Sciences (BIS)'s *Equalities and Diversities champion* to provide evidence about current UK government gender equality policies in HE. (He has subsequently become Vice-Chancellor of the University of London [September 2012]). He argued that the UK government wanted to advance women's position in universities amongst other inequalities and had at his fingertips all the latest figures about gender and HE. Most of this is unsurprising but some is worth repeating for the light it sheds on the orientation of the UK BIS Department and its policy focus within its equalities and diversities agenda. Sir Adrian came armed with all the most up-to-date data, largely from the UK Higher Education Statistical Authority (HESA) and other Government sources. He produced trend data about the changing balances between men and women as full-time academic staff in all UK institutions. In 1995–96 women constituted about 30 per cent (32,554 out of 111,458) although their proportions varied across types of institution and region. By 2003–2004, whilst the numbers of full-time academic staff in all UK institutions had gone down slightly (106,900) women had increased their share of the total to 35 per cent (37,525). Women, of course, held the lion's share of part-time posts having almost 60 per cent. By 2009–10 the proportions of women in full-time posts had increased to 38 per cent (45,195 out of 117,930).

Less Than a Quarter of Women Are (full) Professors (2905) Out of a Total of 15,320

It is important to note that women remain in relatively subordinate positions relative to men, and have not increased their share of senior positions, as we have already seen from ECU figures. For example, *less than a quarter of women are (full) professors (2905) out of a total of 15,320* and proportionately more are on fixed-term rather than open-ended or permanent contracts. There remain far more women on part-time contracts than men viz., almost two-thirds or 34,705 out of 63,665. Thus, over the last 15 years, whilst the proportion of academics in UK institutions has barely increased, women have increased relative to men, although largely remaining in subordinate roles. (http://www.jobs.ac.uk/careers-advice/working-in-higher-education/1379/statistical-overview/)

Given the number and proportion of women obtaining doctorates in 2010–11 these trends could, with Government will, be altered. Out of the full-time doctorates for UK domiciled students women now are almost reaching parity with men (3815 out of 7870) and for part-time students have already done so (1325 out of 2655). However, if we include in other EU or non-EU domiciled full-time and part-time students the picture changes dramatically. For non-EU domiciled women are less than 2/5ths of the full-time total (1880 out of 4940) and similarly for part-time (235 out of 555). So the widening of participation to doctorates to students from the EU and, more importantly, the non-EU is having effects on *increasing gender inequality in doctoral studies* … The current policy of widening the diversity programme to focus on other groups rather than just gender is better value for money. This clearly illustrates the lukewarm commitment to gender equality!

In his evidence about diversity in academic careers, taken from the Research Council UK (RCUK)'s report *Sustainability of the UK Research Workforce: Annual Report to the UK Research Base Funders Forum 2009* (RCUK 2009), in most career disciplines the proportion of women has increased at each career stage over time. For example, the number of female professors in the Arts and Humanities were up from 10 per cent in 1994 to 25 per cent in 2007 and he added that 'the Department has launched a consultation on narrative reporting which considers ways to achieve greater disclosure of the numbers of women at various levels within organizations … The Coalition have made a commitment to have 50 per cent of all public appointments to be held by women by the end of this Parliament'. He ended by drawing attention to 'Further Government Action on Diversity, especially The Public Sector Equality Duty (PSED)'. He elaborated that this meant that public bodies, including those receiving funding from a public body, must have due regard to the need to i. Eliminate unlawful discrimination, harassment, victimization and any other conduct prohibited by the Equality Act; ii. Advance equality of opportunity between people who share a protected characteristic and people who do not share it; iii. Foster good relations between people who share a protected characteristic and those who do not. He even added that 'within BIS we will be developing our equality objectives (in compliance with the specific duties of the PSED) in consultation with stakeholders, partners and staff'.[2]

What is crystal clear from this array of facts, figures and policy statements about the future is that the UK Coalition Government has a rhetorical commitment to a very weak definition of equality of opportunity for women within and across HE but absolutely no understanding, let alone interest, in altering the balances in the subsequent labour markets, and certainly not the academic labour market. Moreover, interestingly, all the key spokesmen for diversity and equality remain white middle class men, perhaps with vested interests in maintaining the status quo.

All of this is not surprising given that David Willetts is British Minister for HE and had stated publicly in April 2011 that 'feminism had trumped egalitarianism' and university-educated women were to blame for taking working class men's jobs drawing on his book published in April 2011 in paperback with a new justifying afterword which restates the book's purpose: to deal with *injustice between generations* rather than social or ethnic groups, while gender relations are taken for granted. He wants to ensure that working class men are encouraged into HE, at the expense of middle class women, albeit that the overall numbers of students applying for HE are declining, given the imposition of tuition fees. Willetts, and the Coalition Government, also through Michael Gove as Secretary of State for Education, want to ensure traditional Conservative values including traditional roles for men and women. This was called patriarchal relations by feminists but can now be known by the more explicit term misogyny, as mentioned by the Australian Prime Minister, Julia Gillard, in her Parliament in Autumn 2012.[3] She has since suffered at the hands of misogyny in being voted out of office on a vote of confidence amongst the Australian Labor MPs (26 June 2013).

'SHE FIGURES': Science in the European Academic Labour Market

She Figures 2009 published by the EC paints a rather different picture: in the preface to the report Janez Potočnik, a Slovenian politician who serves as European Commissioner for Science and Research, states that 'while there are equivalent numbers of women and men working in the field of Humanities, only 27 per cent of researchers in Engineering and Technology are female. And what about

---

2 It should be noted that the Government Equality Office (GEO) set up a review of the workings of the PSED in the spring of 2013 in the light of the Government's Red Tape Challenge. The report was published on 6 September 2013 and recommended numerous modifications to the regulations, which equality groups considered would water the law down.

3 The UK's *The Guardian* editorial in its assessment of her time in office regarded this as Julia Gillard's finest speech.

researchers' career progression? *Women account for 59 per cent of graduates, whereas men account for 82 per cent of full professors. Do you find that hard to believe? Check out chapter 3'* (my emphasis).

He then presents the case for more action by policy-makers: '*She Figures 2009* tells us that the proportion of female researchers is actually growing faster than that of men (over the period 2002–2006, +6.3% for women and +3.7% for men) ... The figures are encouraging but the gender imbalance is not self-correcting. *She Figures* is recommended reading for all policy-makers, researchers, teachers, students, and for parents who share a vision of a democratic, competitive and technologically advanced Europe'. The headline figures and trends are not dissimilar to those in the UK, but the report argues for serious action to make gender equality across all science and research more of a reality. Apart from the aforementioned figures others for women include:

- In the EU, their proportion is growing faster than that of men (6.3 per cent annually over 2002–2006 compared with 3.7 per cent for men); the same goes for the proportion of women among scientists and engineers (6.2 per cent annually compared with 3.7 per cent for men).
- On average in the EU-27, women represent 37 per cent of all researchers in the Higher Education Sector, 39 per cent in the Government Sector and 19 per cent in the Business Enterprise Sector, but in all three sectors there is a move towards a more gender-balanced research population.
- In the EU-27, 45 per cent of all PhD graduates were women in 2006; they equal or outnumber men in all broad fields of study, except for science, mathematics and computing (41 per cent), and engineering, manufacturing and construction (25 per cent).
- Over the period 2002–2006, there has been an increase in the overall number of female researchers in almost all fields of science in the EU-27.
- Women's academic career (*sic*) remains markedly characterized by strong vertical segregation: the proportion of female students (55 per cent) and graduates (59 per cent) exceeds that of male students, but men outnumber women among PhD students and graduates (the proportion of female students drops back to 48 per cent and that of PhD graduates to 45 per cent). Furthermore, women represent only 44 per cent of grade C academic staff, 36 per cent of grade B academic staff and 18 per cent of grade A academic staff.
- The proportion of *women among full professors is highest in the humanities and the social sciences (respectively 27.0 per cent and 18.6 per cent)* (my emphasis) and lowest in engineering and technology, at 7.2 per cent.
- At the level of the EU-27, women account for 23 per cent of grade A academics among 35 to 44-year-olds, 21 per cent among 45 to 54-year-olds and 18 per cent among those aged over 55. The situation thus appears more favourable for the youngest generations of female academics but *the gender gap is still persistent* (my emphasis).

- *The official measure of the overall gender pay gap covering the entire economy stood at 25 per cent in the EU-27 in 2006, a slight improvement from 2002 when it stood at 26 per cent* (my emphasis).
- On average throughout the EU-27, 13 per cent of institutions in the HE Sector are headed by women and just 9 per cent of universities have a female head ... .

The authors of *She Figures 2009* are clearly committed to gender equality and they argue strongly for *proactive policies*, such as 'A gender-mixed composition of nominating commissions, an increase in the objectivity of the applied selection criteria, tutoring of women, or even the fixing of quotas' are all policies that are generally evoked to balance out the unequal situation that continues to prevail in the academic sector and to work against the discriminatory snowball effect. The gender pay gap is the highest in those occupations that are most open to high-level female researchers, even though it is large everywhere, particularly in public enterprise. It also deepens as the age of the researcher increases. There is no spontaneous reduction of the gender pay gap over time, a conclusion that holds up for all gender inequalities that were set forth and analyzed throughout *She Figures* 2009.

Gender-blind or Antagonistic International Debates About Gender Equality?

Given this political framework, it is hardly surprising that the ECU reports could be so contradictory and that others in policy arenas such as the then head of the UK's HEPI (Bahram Bekhradnia, 2009) would not want to develop strong policies for gender equality. Even sophisticated sociological researchers tend not to include gender equality as a key variable: Phil Brown, Hugh Lauder and David Ashton (2012) in their acclaimed book *The Global Auction* do not provide much evidence of the role of gender in the international transformations of the knowledge economy and nor do other international researchers as I argued (David, 2011, pp. 147–65).

European policies are frequently strongly in favour of gender equality not on social grounds but for economic competition and business innovation, such as a recent gender summit about research in Europe with Mr Robert-Jan Smits, EC Director General for Research and Innovation arguing that: 'The promotion of *gender equality is part of the European Commission's strategic approach* in the field of research and innovation. It contributes to the enhancement of European competitiveness and the full realisation of European innovation potential' (2011, p. iv).

Similarly, the evidence presented in *The Chronicle of Higher Education* (2012, November section B) about gender equality in the USA provides a nuanced understanding of the changing trends. It provides detailed data about the race, ethnicity and gender of students at more than 1,500 Institutions, using 'final figures from the [Federal] Education Department' in the US for 2010. A summary states that: 'That fall [2010], 21.6 million undergraduate and graduate students were enrolled at less-than-two-year, two-year, and four-year postsecondary institutions eligible to participate in Title IV federal student financial aid programs. Of those, 57.2 per cent were female, and 55.3 per cent were white. Among minority groups, blacks made up the largest share, representing 13.4 per cent of all students enrolled, followed by Hispanics, 12.2 per cent, and Asians, 5.3 per cent. More than 60 per cent were attending full-time ... The list is limited to degree-granting institutions with enrolments of 4,500 or more as well as all colleges, regardless of enrolment size, that were categorized as "Baccalaureate Colleges-Arts and Sciences" by the Carnegie Foundation for the Advancement of Teaching in 2010' (2012, B36).

There is also commentary on the figures with Katherine Mangan arguing that 'Despite efforts to close gender gaps, some disciplines remain lopsided' and presented evidence of the degrees conferred by discipline and sex (*sic*) of student in 2009–10 for both bachelors and doctorate degrees. Overall, in terms of Bachelors degrees for 1.6 million students, the share is 57 per cent for women (943,381 students) and for doctorates out of almost 160,000 students, 52 per cent for women (81,953) (ibid., B6). It is also argued that there remains a very strong gender gap in degree attainment among African-Americans in 2009–10 with over 1.3 million African Americans attending college in 2009–10. The author of the article therefore discusses why 'black men are not graduating in high numbers', although they are going to college and considers the numbers of black men in prison or jail by comparison. The gender gap amongst African-Americans is even higher than the overall per cents, so that 66 per cent of African-American women compared to 34 per cent of African-American men gained a Bachelors degree, whilst there was a very slight reversal for doctorates with 65 per cent of African-American women compared with 35 per cent for African-American men (ibid., pp. B9–13). Similarly it is argued that student 'engagement can be a bit more eye-opening for men than for women' across the board (ibid., pp. B15).

Lady Academe and Labor-Market Segmentation in the US

There is also commentary about the changing nature of the academic profession, with one article provocatively entitled 'Lady Academe and Labor-Market Segmentation. The narrative of women's success via HE rests on a house of cards' (2012, B18). The male author, Marc Bousquet, argues that 'scholars of globalization generally attribute a worldwide feminization of the labor force to neoliberal trade policy and a political assault on workers' rights ... [but] the role of gender in the global economy isn't represented particularly well by old-school pipeline theories of women entering particular industries whether it's ... college teaching ... American college campuses exhibit a markedly gendered distribution of power, prestige, and pay closely related to the feminization of certain disciplines'. He then demonstrates that despite women's successes in attainment they remain severely disadvantaged in power and prestige in academia. He goes on to mock those who argue that academic feminists are now very well off, asserting that 'Because of the widespread normalization and feminization of contingency, the segmentation of the academic labor market is far worse than in management, law and clinical medicine. The gap between return on education investment is commonly worse for academic women than for women in other professions'. He concludes that 'the academy is one of the few places where an "other-than-bourgeois" feminism survives, and in some places, thrives. The best traditions of intersectional analysis and of socialist, materialist, working-class, anarchist, and radical feminisms live in academe and through it. But as in the sociologist Johanna Brenner's apt characterization of the labor movement itself, that bigger-picture feminism is today a "survivor project", a figure of trauma and mourning, and not generally a vital mode of opposition and change' (2012, B20).

Feminist Research on Global HE: Changing the [patriarchal] Rules of the Game?

The question of feminism, gender and HE is both the subject of much debate, and highly charged and contested. What is the evidence about the changing gendered nature of leadership amongst academics in HE? Barbara Bagilhole (one of my participants) and Kate White have conducted two research studies on this theme, the first of which is an edited collection (Bagilhole and White, 2011) and the second of which is a book, taking forward these ideas (Bagilhole and White, 2013). In *Gender, Power and Management: A Cross-Cultural Analysis of Higher Education* they put together a most exciting and innovative study of women as feminists in global HE. The book had a long gestation since Barbara first met Kate White, an Australian gender researcher, at the turn of the twenty-first century, at a European Gender Equality in Higher Education conference. They decided to collaborate on research and, having developed an initial study of skills for effective HE management, they recruited feminist researchers from six other countries to join their network, from across a range of social science disciplinary backgrounds. The resultant network drew only on countries in the global north although they extended beyond an Anglophone or American domination. Two further former British Commonwealth countries were added, namely New Zealand and South Africa, as well as Ireland, and two southern European countries, viz. Portugal and Turkey. And finally Sweden, as representative of a European country committed to gender equality was added. This eventually became the Women in Higher Education Management (WHEM) network, which gained funding from the Swedish research council for the production of this study and edited book, which drew upon and developed the collaborative network to analyse gender and power in senior management in universities, using feminist perspectives and methods. What they were specifically interested in were the dynamics of women and men working together in HE management teams and how these dynamics operated cross-culturally. Taking an explicitly 'feminist standpoint theory' approach

(Harding, 1987) and locating themselves clearly in the study, they are able to tease out women's experiences in the different universities they studied. Kate White provides an excellent contextual analysis of legislative frameworks for equal opportunities, including employment and issues around the overarching gender pay gaps, including the impact and influence of specific frameworks on the careers of women within comparative countries. Whilst it is extremely exciting that the WHEM network have collaborated to produce this nuanced and carefully executed study, it is also disheartening to find that the picture remains quite bleak for women in senior management. This is largely because there have been contradictory trends both in HE and in the developing economies of which they have become a more critical and central part. So women are now far more in evidence in HE and in senior management but the effects of neo-liberalism and managerialism have been to confine women to relatively limited roles, and not the most senior leadership positions. Bagilhole and White are to be congratulated for the vigour and passion of their continuing collaborative work and it is to be hoped that they are able to make more substantial in-roads into university senior management of the future.

Louise Morley (2013) argues trenchantly about how new managerialism and the so-called 'leaderist turn' in HE, are subverting and reinforcing the 'rules of the game' in patriarchal ways. She provides 'an international review of feminist knowledge on how gender and power interact with leadership in HE ... to unmask the "rules of the game" that lurk beneath the surface rationality of academic meritocracy'. She argues that: 'curiously, in a culture of measurement and audit in HE, women's representation in different roles and grades is not always perceived as sufficiently important to measure, monitor or map comparatively. The Centre for Higher Education and Equity Research (CHEER) at the University of Sussex had to construct its own tables. The data that do exist suggest that women disappear in the higher grades i.e. when power, resources, rewards and influence increase (ECU, 2011; Lund, 1998; Singh, 2002, 2008; *She Figures*, 2003, 2006, 2009). The highest shares of female rectors (vice-chancellors) were recorded in Sweden, Iceland, Norway, Finland, and Israel. In contrast, in Denmark, Cyprus, Lithuania, Luxembourg and Hungary, no single university was headed by a woman when *She Figures* reported in 2009. Women's proportion of rectors was also very low (7 per cent at most) in Romania, Austria, Slovakia, Italy, the Netherlands, the Czech Republic, Belgium and Germany. This under-representation reflects not only continued inequalities between men and women, but missed opportunities for women to influence and contribute to the universities of the future'.

Morley concludes that 'we need new rules for a very different game', and I will return to these changing 'rules' in Chapter 8. It is abundantly clear that gender equality is a highly politicized and contested notion in HE today, given the changes towards neo-liberalism and its impacts upon women's participation in global [and academic] labour markets. Whilst there has been huge transformation in women's participation as students in HE across the globe, this is *not* matched by significant change in women's participation in academic labour markets as this brief trip through the various statistics for Europe, through the EC and EU, the UK through

ECU and official government figures and the USA amply illustrate. What role have women, feminists especially, played in these changes and how do they now reflect back on them, and think about the future? I turn now to consider the origins of a feminist perspective in HE, or as academic feminism enters universities.

Chapter 3
A Life History of Academic Feminism

Introduction: What is Academic Feminism?

Whilst there has been a massive growth in women's participation as global HE has become a fundamental component of knowledge economies, the culture of HE remains sexist and indeed misogynistic. Gender equality in HE is about students: the global academic labour market remains riddled with patriarchal relations, as we have seen in the previous chapter. For instance, gender equality is not a criterion for academic posts overall in the UK but has become a criterion for applications for research funding for British *academic scientists* as noted in *The Guardian* (29 January 2013, p. 30). As we have seen the question of leadership in global HE remains patriarchal and so problematic, as evidenced by the international conference in Dubai on gender equality in HE leadership (*The Guardian*, 6 March 2013). I now want to explore what lies behind these transformations over the last 50 years, focusing on what role women collectively have played in developing political, social *and* educational agendas for change. Were these agendas for political action or activism rooted in education, or an understanding of the past to argue for change towards a fairer and more equal society? What kinds of knowledge about past political and social action were important for formulating a gender agenda? These are fundamentally moral or ethical questions about social and gender justice: feminist values, in short.

In this chapter, I discuss how I collected my evidence through life histories, narratives and stories to create a collective biography of academic feminists around their values and knowledge. This is a form of participatory action research. I then discuss how these academic feminists now see themselves, and whether or not, as they reflect upon their contributions to academic life, they think of themselves as 'second-wave' feminists. This term was coined, in the last few decades, in the literature (including Wikipedia) for the collective actions of the women's movement. Whilst often contested, it is used to distinguish the political activities of women during the last third of the twentieth century, as they were creating an innovative feminist pedagogical approach. Just what was meant by feminism and is it possible to name this collective endeavour as 'second-wave' or is this term inappropriate either theoretically or descriptively? Does it capture this new and innovative approach to women's equality within higher education and universities? How useful is the 'wave analogy' and what do my participants think of it as a concept?

It is also increasingly used in public arenas to depict the kinds of campaigns developed by the women's movements around the world, and, in particular, in countries of the global north. As the renowned feminist historian, Sheila Rowbotham argued in a public lecture entitled *Discovering the Other America*

(22 October 2012) at the British Library, the learning between American and British political activists and scholars was of vital importance to the developments of feminist political activities in the 1960s and 1970s. Certainly much of the literature on this, and debates about so-called 'second-wave' feminism, comes from HE or from women who had been students in universities, if not having taken an academic career path subsequently. This is a point made frequently by feminist historians, and was repeated by Professor Rowbotham.

In the *Handbook of Gender & Women's Studies* (Davis, Evans and Lorber, 2006) there are several biographic reflections on aspects of *academic feminism* across the global north: from women's studies, to culture, knowledge, the state, work and family, sexualities, technologies and change. The reflective and autobiographic focus is similar to the more recent publication *Transatlantic Conversations* edited by the joint editors of the *European Journal of Women's Studies* (Davis and Evans, 2011). Clare Hemmings thinks through a life history of academic feminism in her essay called 'The Life and Times of Academic Feminism' (Hemmings, 2006 pp. 13–35). She argues that 'we need to start our histories of academic feminism from an assumption of difference and contest, an attention to subordinate as well as dominant knowledge in the present, to open up a range of possible futures rather than predictable outcomes ... we must adopt a reflexive approach that openly interrogates the relationship between the histories of feminist theory that we tell and our own intellectual biographies. Nostalgia cannot be the ground of any meaningful life, still less one committed to political and collective transformation ...' (2006, pp. 28–9). It is precisely this academic feminism and the feminists who sought to create it that I want now to reflect upon.

Reflecting on a Collective Biography of Academic Feminism

Using feminist methodologies, such as biographies, life histories, narratives and story-telling, I want to look at how international networks of feminist educators, activist academics and social scientists, developed new feminist knowledge, pedagogies, courses and curricula within universities or for adult education. I know of no such reflexive and collective account, based around the biographies and/or stories of the women reflecting back upon their practices, although there are many individual intellectual biographies and life histories. As Hemmings argues, these are also vital for how we, as feminists, might want to create new pedagogies, knowledge, courses and curricula in the transformed and now neo-liberal global university.

Through a collective biography, or what is sometimes now called 'prosopography' (Townsend and Weiner, 2011, 141–9) I consider the explicit activities of women seeking to transform the academy through feminist politics and practices. I searched for an appropriate method, whilst also asking my participants about their own meanings and approaches to feminism in academe. As Weiner notes (2011, pp. 142ff) '*prosopography* is yet another designation for the systematic quantification (*sic*) of lives. Inspired predominantly by the noted French sociologist Pierre Bourdieu, it has become a powerful research approach … Interest in prosopography has also paralleled the increased interest in biography as a research source, and the wish to connect individual action with social structure' (2011, p. 142).

Prosopography is clearly related to, but distinct from, biography and the similar but largely family-based approach of genealogy, which itself draws from the work of another French sociologist Michel Foucault who has also been taken up by many feminist scholars, particularly of the 'third-wave' or those interested in post-structuralism. Prosopography is about the details of individuals' lives, and is more than the plural of biography: it is not just the sum of any collection of biographies. The important point is not the quantification but the ways that the individual lives have developed from common roots and values, both culturally and educationally. It is precisely the ideas and interconnections of the biographies, especially through formal and informal education, politics and activism, pedagogies and practices that I want to make explicit: in other words a collective genealogy or life history.

Weiner also mentions pertinently Olive Banks' work on British feminism and especially her attempt to develop a biographical approach to 'first wave' feminism (Banks, 1985; 1986). Banks created an account based upon feminist *activists* rather than sympathizers (Townsend and Weiner, 2011, p. 144) making her own broad but socially contextualized definition of feminism. Weiner (2008) had previously written engagingly and warmly about Olive Banks and 'her least "fashionable" work – her engagement with collective biography and narrative … this research was indeed "pioneering" – not least because it used biography systematically as *a method of reversing historians' amnesia on women's participation in social and political movements*' (2008, p. 403) (my emphasis). Whilst I have created a collective biography, I did not do so through leafing through other biographies and accounts, nor by quantification, except by using the conversations and written replies to my questions. I developed the collective biography through conversations with women academics who are still alive, and willing to reflect upon their own academic and educational lives, rather than through their own writing.

I too took a broad definition of feminism in finding out about the women who were *actively* involved in changing women's social and political lives through developing new pedagogies. Building upon Banks' important legacy within the sociology of education as well as her work on British feminism, I talked with academic feminists in the humanities and social sciences, drawing on international networks of scholars in the 'global north'. I used feminist approaches, linked with the 'biographic' turn within the humanities and social sciences to reflect upon individual biographies, life histories and narratives. My study is not based upon a traditional 'sample', even of a qualitative kind but more about network analysis. A recent example of a qualitative approach using similar (and perhaps some of the same) participants is that of Kate Hoskins' (2012) study of 20 'successful' women education professors in UK universities.

I also want to problematise the point that Szreter (2006) makes in his obituary, namely that Banks 'demonstrated that Victorian feminism was composed of many strands and that there were continuities between "first" and "second wave".

It is her achievement that both of these are now commonplaces of historical knowledge' (Simon Szreter, *The Guardian*, 12 December 2006). What Szreter calls 'commonplaces of historical knowledge', are now 'received wisdom' or the 'feminist cannon' (Davis and Evans, 2011) and are more complex. The question of the relations between first, second and indeed third wave feminism is also in dispute, as Banks herself, like many of the other feminists born in the first three decades of the twentieth century (such as de Beauvoir, Friedan, Myrdal) do not fall easily into the waves or generations as Banks defined them in terms of their birth dates. It was indeed their education, writings and dates of publication that were the more important, with both de Beauvoir (born 1908) and Friedan (born 1921) being seen as foundational to 'second-wave' feminism although not born in that generation and Banks (born 1923) together with Alva Myrdal (born 1902), the Swedish sociologist and policy analyst, foundational to feminist sociology.

Banks (1968) develops a cohort analysis of first-wave feminists: 'The data on which this study is based is, therefore, mainly biographical in nature although the method of analysis is primarily sociological ... Feminism like socialism, is in many ways impossible to define in any really objective way so that, in the last resort, the choice ... is, and must be, a very personal one' (Banks, 1986, p. 2). Using her personal values she selected the women to include in her feminist biography (Banks, 1985). Most of the women included were long deceased, whilst my study relies on the women's own reflections taking seriously the issue of self-selection. Banks also mentions that 'another decision that influenced the nature of the selection of entries was that it should be a dictionary of feminist activists rather than the very much larger number of individuals who might be described as feminist sympathisers ... those included had all been involved actively one way or another in working for the attainment of feminist goals' (1986, p. 2).

My definition is also of feminist activists but activists within education and academe rather than just in the political sphere as a way of 'achieving feminist goals'. This is another definition of activism, although educational activism may differ across the cohorts because of the huge expansions of HE during the period of my study. The women I spoke with were all products of the global transformations of HE, becoming academic feminists and aiming to further transform academe and wider society. Banks also included a small number of men 'who were active in 'first-wave' feminism' arguing that whilst contentious, they had special significance since they 'uncover the process by which a man becomes a feminist' but she excluded them from the main analysis (1986, p. 3). I took the opposite decision that, whilst being equally contentious, has the simplicity of a wider analysis of my international women participants.

Banks also argues that 'the sample of feminists which make up this study, cannot claim to be based on a truly objective definition of feminism or feminists. Nor can it have claims to completeness. Indeed, it is difficult to see how such a claim could be fulfilled ... If, however, it is prudent to recognise the limitations of the sample, it would be wrong to assume it is in any sense random or arbitrary. It includes the great majority of the leaders of the women's movement during the period of the study ... ' My study is also not arbitrary or random, focusing on those who see themselves as feminist educators and activist academics. Whilst it may be even less complete or comprehensive than Banks', it gives a flavour of the power of the feminist ideas, ideologies and theories, as well as the knowledge as they have developed in academe of the global north, what many of my participants call their *passions* or their lives as we shall see.

My women were virtually all known to me prior to our conversations, through a variety of international networks, ranging from women's studies, sociology and social policy, through to sociology of education, including gender and education, and research reflecting on gender and HE. Very few of the women who replied did so through other contacts and connections, and in some respects, it reflects the *associational* nature of my own networks. Similarly, the contributions from other countries of Europe, or Asia, and the women from the Antipodes are rather scarce in number but their accounts make up for their lack of quantity.

There is also no sense in which my study has captured the voices of those who might be considered, as Banks notes, the *leaders* of the women's movement or even academic feminism. Rather, I have a rich and diverse spread of feminist educators and academics, including ones who saw the obstacles rather than opportunities for creative endeavour in HE. This has also meant a rather uneven set of cohorts in terms of culture, but it demonstrates the rapidly changing landscape of HE over the last 50 years, especially in terms of women's involvement and being either first-in-the-family and/or working class. I have let the women decide whether or not they considered themselves feminists, and the meanings that they attributed to this and the now commonly used notion of gender equality and gender justice.

Banks defined the 'main unit of analysis as the cohort or generation, based upon *year of birth* and designated four cohorts:

- Cohort 1 consisting of all those born before 1828 and so representing the first generation of the women's movement.
- Second 1828 and 1848; most of the leaders of nineteenth century feminism once it had emerged as an organised social movement ... including *Emily Davies, born in 1830, who did perhaps more than anyone else to open higher education to women* (my emphasis) ...
- Those in the third cohort were born between 1849 and 1871 and came into the women's movement only during the last decades of the nineteenth century ... suffrage ...
- Cohort iv, born between 1872 and 1891, represent the last generation of first-wave feminism' (1986, p. 5).

These four cohorts were the basis of her analysis of social origin, education, religious affiliation, political values and how beliefs match family background and childhood experiences, reaction and responses (1986, p. 6). My analytical approach is similar. Jane Martin (2013, pp. 58–9) also uses this approach for her study of feminist activists in local government over time and space, using selectively from first to second-wave feminists, arguing that: 'Banks ... explore[d] the common background characteristics of those who *led the "first wave" of British feminism defined as a movement to end sexist oppression* (my emphasis) ... By following Banks I am looking at how feminist actions, ideologies and practices articulate together over time ... In [my] study *five linear cohorts* have been designated to explore (a) intergenerational changes and (b) three broad phases of political involvement understood in relation to the ... London education service ... '

Martin has disregarded the differences between first and second-wave feminism, by designating five age cohorts for her study of municipal socialist feminism across the twentieth century. She is interested in the changing political values and campaigning of these cohorts, the last of which falls clearly into my definition of 'second-wave feminism', representing 'the impact of distinct feminist perspectives in the 1970s and 80s on state education in London' seeing them as part of '*the breakthrough generation*' (ibid., p. 68, my emphasis). 'In a range of ways, in diverse projects [they] ... made their voices heard ... Within the academy, Diana Leonard was ... outward facing ... They introduced new issues into education politics that troubled the patriarchal norm in a period ... Collective memory was crucial to the 1960s wave of women's liberation seeking to establish a legitimising tradition, a heritage to impart' (ibid., p. 72).

Following Banks, I grouped the women into broad age cohorts, to understand their origins, actions and activities in becoming feminists in academe: what were their values and lives? They were from what Martin calls *the breakthrough generation* and beyond and it is this *heritage to impart* that I am capturing by drawing on the voices of the three age cohorts, all of which capture both the years of birth and some 20 years later, involvement in university or college education. Unlike either Banks or Martin's studies, all of the women I talked to were involved in universities, and it is important to capture not only their birth dates, but also the timings with respect to types of HE, as it was part of an expanding system. Of course, the transformation of HE in relation to the changing international economy is a major context for this as is the rise of feminist sociology and education across the globe.

A Cohort Analysis of Academic Feminists

My women fall into three cohorts whereby they were involved in university whether undergraduate, postgraduate or doctoral education approximately twenty years after their births. This grouping allows me to analyse their replies around family, education and feminist influences, literatures and knowledge, including intergenerational influences, and writings, and reflections on experiences in academe for thinking about the future. As I analysed my data I found that these three age/HE cohorts presented themselves, rather than an arbitrary division into those women still working within HE, and those who had retired. I had originally grouped my women into those still active in academe and those who were largely or semi-retired, thinking that this would influence their perspectives, with a much smaller grouping of younger feminist women in academia, who might ostensibly be 'third-wave'. Intriguingly, along with all the other social and political transformations taking place, changes in the age of retirement are also affecting the consciousness and values of these cohorts. Moreover, the age of retirement has become much more flexible in most of the countries from which my participants were drawn, and thus there were overlaps between the generations and cohorts. My set of cohorts of age of birth and age of initial entry into HE creates three relatively distinctive groupings. The most important factor is that the first cohort entered HE in the period of the initial expansion of equality of educational opportunity, including HE. They were indeed 'the breakthrough generation' (Martin, 2013).

Cohort 1 – Born Between 1935 and 1950 and Entering HE After 1950

The first is a very broad cohort of those whose birth spans the Second World War born between 1935 and 1950. Whilst for many of these this is not a particular consideration, for some the intervention of WW2 has the effect on them of having been children of refugees (second generation), or of being refugees themselves (first generation) and this may influence their educational values. What is important here is the fact that all of these women, whilst they may have experienced the privations of schooling during the wartime, all are eligible to be of university age between 1955 and 1970. And 1970 has become a critical moment for this study in terms of the kinds of political and radical publications (Figes, Firestone, Greer, Millett, for example) that 'inaugurate' a kind of activist and academic feminism through baby boomers and others.

Cohort 2 – Born Between 1950 and 1965

The second cohort is made up of women who were born in the early days of expanding university opportunities, beyond the baby-boomers and bulge generation. Born between 1950 and 1965 this group of women are able to come of university or college age between 1970 and 1985. These are the days of major educational opportunities and expansionary zeal across countries, and the heyday of social democracy, a period rich in possibilities, and drawing upon the opening up of educational opportunities internationally. These women are able to articulate with passion and solidarity the aims and values of academic feminism and are not in effect sandwiched between the pioneering women of the first cohort, and the transformative generation of those who may be third-wave feminists.

Cohort 3 – Born Between 1965 and 1980

The third cohort comprises those women young enough to be the children, and, possibly, the grandchildren, of the first cohort, born as they are between 1965 and 1980. Interestingly, this final cohort of feminists is of the generation of women to come of university age between 1985 and 2000, and just before the turn of the twenty-first century – they are the products of Thatcherism and Reaganism, the heyday of economic liberalism beginning to move into neo-liberalism and how it began to influence HE policies and practices. They are both solidly part of the transformed university, and beneficiaries of the major expansions globally, but they are also much more subject to the obstacles, impediments and obfuscations of an increasingly neo-liberal global university, with all of its performative culture and managerial forms of control through metrics.

Table 3.1   Participants from networks of international feminists

Current Country of Residence	Totals	Cohort 1 (1935–1950)	Cohort 2 (1950–1965)	Cohort 3 (1965–1980)
AUSTRALIA & NEW ZEALAND	5	4+1	–	–
CANADA	7	6	1	–
INDIA/ISRAEL/ SPAIN	*3*	*1*	*1*	*1*
IRELAND	2		1	1
UK:	83	45	28	10
ENGLAND	*76*	*41*	*26*	*9*
SCOTLAND	*2*	*1*	*1*	*–*
WALES	*5*	*3*	*1*	*1*
USA	10	9	1	–
TOTALS	110	66	32	12

I did not target key figures or *leaders*, but rather used my networks of feminist educators and, assuming that my participants would broadly subscribe to the designation 'second-wave' feminist, I asked them about this in how I approached them. As can be seen from the table, the vast majority of my participants are, like myself, born in the shadows of the Second World War, with about a third born in the heyday of social democracy, a tiny number of the targeted younger generation being potential 'third wavers'.

'No Permanent Waves': Reflections on the Wave Analogy for Academic Feminists

Do the women subscribe to the notion of 'second-wave' feminism or *on reflection* do they have a more nuanced understanding of the developments of feminist knowledge and pedagogies in the global academy? Is it still possible to classify feminist thinking amongst these networks in terms of age and or political and theoretical approaches? And can the most recent generations of feminist activists or pedagogues be termed third-wave or fourth? I wanted to capture notions of feminism as they began to permeate academe internationally. My question is similar to the task that Nancy Hewitt (2010, p. xi) set herself in her 'symposium ... thinking about histories of feminism and women's activism over many years. This project ... allowed me the freedom to re-imagine narratives of women's history, women's rights and feminism'. Hewitt was interested in getting colleagues in the US to reconsider the *wave analogy* as a way of thinking about the long-term historical developments in US feminism: in her resulting edited book – *No Permanent Waves: Recasting Histories of US Feminism* – she argues that it 'engages the ongoing debates about the adequacy of the "wave" metaphor for capturing the complex history of women's rights and feminism in the United States. But it also moves beyond those debates to offer fresh perspectives on the diverse movements that constitute U.S. feminism, past and present ... The contributors, from different generations and backgrounds, argue for new chronologies, more inclusive conceptualizations of feminist agendas and participants ... The concepts of waves surging and receding cannot fully capture these multiple and overlapping movements, chronologies, issues and sites' (2010, p. 1).

Like Banks, she is clear that the notion of 'wave' was commonly used from the late 1960s, and had been used prior to that. I also assumed that the term had contemporary resonances despite some of the critiques. My email to these women colleagues, starting in the early autumn of 2011, had a list of eight questions (see Appendix), with the following comments: 'I am writing to you about my latest book ... which is about *second wave feminism* (sic) and HE and especially feminism in education/social policy/sociology/social sciences. It is entitled ... *Feminism, Gender and Universities*. I am trying to review the impacts that forms of feminism had on the emerging and changing academy and gender in HE ... I look forward to hearing from you on what is beginning to be an exciting reflexive project and developing critical conversations about HE now and the future of the neo-liberal academy'.

As I saw this task as being both about reflecting back on feminist activism and pedagogies within academe, and thinking about the future in the now neo-liberal university I realized that I needed to draw upon wider networks and to specifically interrogate the notion of 'second-wave' feminism. I also wanted to think through how useful this analogy with waves has become in the massively expanded university. To what extent is the contemporary neo-liberal university at all akin to the university that previous generations or networks encountered and entered? This kind of consideration of current practices and pedagogies sets the context for reflecting back. Feminist practices are now endemic in some universities, although there is still major resistance to women, let alone feminists, in senior positions.

One of my broad questions was about changes in universities and the influences of feminism, with a specific question: Do you now consider yourself a second-wave feminist? This has raised interesting issues about the meanings of feminism for the women within and across the cohorts. Reflecting upon the responses of my participants, I would say that most subscribed to this idea although there were some controversies about whether 'second-wave' was sufficient for many of the differences, and whether it was a term about political action or activism rather than developing feminist knowledge, pedagogies or theories. And indeed it was here that most of the doubts crept into the comments; was 'third wave' feminism distinctive and if so how? Did it lie in the developments of theories rather than actions, and transformations in how to approach feminist knowledge and teach it?

As might have been expected when conversing with academics, I had a range of replies raising debatable and controversial issues. My participants mostly positioned themselves in relation to feminist politics outside academe as well as to their own passionate interests in their own curricula, pedagogies and practices inside. There were clear differences in relation to when they entered the academy and in what capacity, as well as related to subject or discipline, including involvement with women's studies and within the social sciences or humanities. In developing a collective biography of academic feminists in the following chapters, each details the cohorts of academic feminists.

Before discussing the detail, feminist values today are my starting point. Whilst there was questioning of the 'wave analogy' there was some general recognition of its utility but for what? Does its usefulness lie in thinking about an international network of academic feminists, seeking political and social changes through political activism, or is it a useful way of thinking about different kinds of feminist knowledge, pedagogies and theories as they have developed in academia? Certainly, it is now an important part of the literature on the history of the women's movement and feminism that the late 1960s and 1970s were seen as the period for the development of 'second-wave' feminism by contrast with the 'first-wave' feminism of the turn of the twentieth century, as discussed by Banks (1986) and by Martin (2013) as 'the break-through generation'.[1]

WLM Hitting the Air-waves of Academe: Cohort 1's Feminism

Sara Delamont uniquely remonstrated with me for an inaccurate definition of 'second wave' feminism in typical academic fashion: 'second-wave went up to 1968, and anything after that was "third-wave" – so Social Feminism was 1919–1968 – so no, I'm 3rd Wave 1969 … ' Her notion was taken from the assumption that Banks was second-wave and that she was beyond, given her own account of feminist sociology (Delamont, 2003). Most others subscribed to my version of the 'second-wave' as being the international women's political movements in the 1960s and 1970s.

---

1   And this notion of 1960s and 1970s 'Sisters' is quickly catching on again as the email networks from the Feminist Library grow since the reunion in January 2014.

One of my participants from this 'international feminist group', imaginatively thought of *waves as not being about hair, but air,* as in her comment that 'WLM hit the air-waves just as I was entering graduate school'. Many of my participants saw Stevie Smith's poem *Not Waving But Drowning* as being a major critique of one of the several ideas behind waves rather than it being a singular notion. A small minority agreed with the retired British social policy feminist: 'No I don't put a label on it. I don't know, maybe not at all. But age and cohort effects are hard to disentangle'. One American feminist wrote: 'Because I consider first-wave feminism to be the nineteenth century women's movement (i.e. pre-1920), I would identify myself as a second-wave feminist, i.e. a product of the 1960s and 1970s, along with my age cohort (or at least those of us who attended university and graduate school in that era) … Since I haven't really been a fan of most feminist theory and have a problem with post-modern/post-structural vocabulary, I haven't found a lot of more recent methodology and theory useful for my teaching or my research. Feminism, especially Jewish feminism, has helped to shape my life and my career. I consider myself to be a moderate 'equal-rights' feminist, not an activist. I live my life as a Jewish feminist in my home, my synagogue and my community, as well as in my professional life as professor of Jewish history and of European women's history … '

The American feminist pedagogue, Frinde Maher, provided a clear and succinct summary: 'Yes … whom younger women call "The Second Wave". In spite of many of us having spent years diversifying and deconstructing our definitions of the falsely unifying term "woman" "Third Wavers" tend to accuse us of racism for not seeing differences among women. Also, it seems to me, they are not fighting those fights for inclusion the way we did. But I could be wrong. The challenge is to use feminism as a constant tool to fight increasing inequalities across the globe, against women but also against their families and their communities. Second Wave feminism is against inequalities in a way that I feel Third Wave feminists, with their concern for "the body" and transgender issues, are not always … '

The Canadian feminist scholar, Alison Griffith wrote: 'Yes. Not many of the new generation of academic women call themselves feminists. *It is both assumed and subsumed.* For me, it means that the feminist academic conversation has moved away from its political roots. I see the influence of feminism as waning, overtaken by other social justice issues. Given that gender seems to be the most difficult social distinction to moderate, and given the shift to neo-liberal social conditions, I don't find this surprising, just depressing'.

On the other hand, for example, another more radical American feminist wrote: 'I have always been a feminist in my daily living. If by that you mean of the 1970s, yes … Postmodern feminists are much more daring on a personal level than we are or were'.

However, even if the women did not necessarily subscribe to the second-wave epithet, their critiques of third-wave or post-modern or post-structural feminism tended to be very critical, usually negatively but not always and some claimed no longer to be just a second-wave feminist. However, that also depends upon the political position taken in respect of types of feminism, so for instance a British feminist wrote: I think there is a kind of 'third wave' developing now, after a period when young women seemed to feel there wasn't a problem and when various vacuous ideas, such as pole dancing is empowering, were gaining ground. Sadly, in hard times women are again finding that life is very unequal. I also sense a difference, but this is quite anecdotal, between the generation of women who are now over 30, and women in their 20s who seem to be more militant. But there is a focus once more on issues relating to sexuality, I would say less Trade Union consciousness (not surprisingly) and little understanding of class ... And another Canadian feminist said that she wasn't a second wave feminist but a *socialist-feminist* ... this differs politically from people with other politics.

Amongst my participants was a loose network of largely British feminist activists in Bristol when we were developing feminist pedagogies in the 1970s. Several of us put together the first British reader for women's studies (BWSG, 1979) and I discussed these issues with them and others involved in the women's movement in both the social sciences and the arts in Bristol. Many have dispersed to other places and countries, and developed different agendas, although all having remained in academe. Many have retired too, and engaged in different activities and yet they all, interestingly, still subscribe to being feminists, if not second-wave. Two of the Bristol feminists have now settled in Canada, having spent a formative period in Bristol and gave similar discursive answers to those of their former colleagues in critiquing developments in feminist sociology and theory. Most felt, as Liz Bird did: Yes firmly still in the 1970s, and as Ellen Malos put it: '*More passionate than third wave?*' However, Helen Haste firmly contradicted the rest by saying that: 'I am not sure what this means. I regard myself as a "cultural" rather than a "socialist" feminist and this links with post-modernism'. She was contradicted by another saying that she was 'only interested in the more political perspective, with "less lipstick" and around critical realism rather than the post-modern ideas'. Helen Taylor perhaps expressed our sentiments about subsequent waves most clearly: 'Yes ... That's a difficult question! I think that my commitment to women and to women's issues is rather different from subsequent generations' commitment to gender issues, queer theory and such like. I still feel a gut response to the original demands of the WLM [none granted, as far as I can see, though several better than they were] and *anger at patriarchal attitudes, assumptions and sheer power*. I feel political and social power relations have been forgotten somewhat, and can't get as interested in issues around the body and sexuality as younger feminists, though *I do share frustration with the way older women are marginalized and desexualized within our culture*'.

Jackie West was also clear about her difference: 'Yes. Much of the academic feminism I now encounter [or at least the kind that gets publicity] seems to have got increasingly preoccupied with the cultural turn, with materialist questions sidelined ... or perhaps I attend the wrong events? Within my discipline [sociology], there has been a growing interest in identity and subjectivities to the exclusion of broader economic and political questions (other than rag-bag "globalisation")'.

Hilary Land was also clear: 'I would consider myself a second-wave feminist not least because the issues that the WLM was concerned about are still important and likely to become more so as we enter this age of austerity. I am still concerned with women and children's poverty – material issues are just as important as ideological ones i.e. we have bodies which need nurturing as well as minds – *we need bread as well as roses*. My research interest concerns care as much as financial [in]dependence and perhaps – an effect of ageing – more interested in relationships between the generations and how these are gendered. This raises global questions not least because with Europe becoming an ageing society we will be even more dependent on migrant care workers'.

Marilyn Porter now resident in Canada made the complex point that: 'Generationally, yes; politically resist that naming I am not really sure about the "wave" metaphor. While it is a useful shorthand, especially as between first wave [early suffragettes and others] and second wave [us], I am less happy with the designation third wave, as either simply generational [our daughters and subsequent young women] or as representing what we see as significant changes in the political content of feminism. Certainly, incoming groups of younger feminists have to both challenge the way older feminists cling to the high ground [and actual positions] and suggest new theoretical framings for new issues, and talking about themselves as a new "wave" may help. But it also polarizes debates, and risks denigrating any of the old thinking as also "outmoded". I do not think that this is the case, especially in terms of the postmodern turn. In many ways I think the newer thinking is either wrong or weaker than the positions we took. I find the shift to a preoccupation with "the body" to the exclusion of trying to understand the broader social and economic problems that face women disturbing; and I tend to associate the most recondite postmodern theorizing with an abandonment of engaged and politically relevant feminism'.

Sandra Acker also now resident in Canada agreed that she was a second-wave feminist and went on: 'Interesting question. We positioned gender/women more centrally. We drew from liberal, socialist and radical feminisms, with their various sub-groups, and often worked pragmatically, for example, espousing liberal feminist standpoints rather than more radical ones so that something would get done. Newer feminisms seem less action-oriented. Sexuality has always been contentious and while second-wave feminism accepted or embraced lesbian feminism, the idea of playing with or troubling the idea of gender is a newer phase ... intersectionality has taken a greater role, so that the category of "women" is often challenged. With that challenge, it is difficult to do the kind of work second-wave feminism did in educational circles in raising consciousness and working for changes in representation and curriculum and classroom experience. Another challenge has been the idea that feminism has done its work and it is now underachieving boys that educators need to be concerned about'.

Another member of the Bristolian network, the renowned feminist of intersectionality, Avtar Brah commented: 'Yes. I consider myself as a "second wave" feminist, although sometimes I do not know what this means, apart from age. Of course the struggles were different whereas the gains of some of those struggles are taken for granted today by younger feminists. There are few women's studies courses these days. The emphasis is much more on gender as a relational category. Sexuality studies are often now part of gender studies. Perhaps, the impact on the neo-liberal university is much less'.

Fiona Williams, a social policy feminist, wrote: 'Yes but these days I consider myself more of a "global feminist" that is concerned with how geo-political relations affect women ... . This is a big question. In my own experience, I have *moved both with the new waves* (especially in taking on an intersectional approach to social division and difference) but held on to the old in that I see gender as still a critical lens with which to view the world ... The Centre of Interdisciplinary Gender Studies at Leeds when Sasha Roseneil, Jean Gardiner, Grizelda Pollock, and I, amongst others, set it up were heady days and its inter-disciplinarity felt like the apotheosis of feminism in the academy'.

These replies chimed in well with others from cohort 1 who considered themselves to be firmly but critically from a second-wave perspective, so that another leading British education professor said: 'I am a second wave feminist and sociologist; I have always been concerned to help make girls' voices heard in the public domain especially heard by teachers and so I do appreciate the skills of those who are able to uncover female identities and experiences. However nowadays it is worrying that teachers are no longer really our audience. In the 1970s and 1980s we validated teachers as agents of change. Gaby Weiner used to call them "insider reformers". In the 1980s we spoke directly to the teaching profession and showed them our research findings. Now it seems as if the audience for gender and education is ourselves. We have lost a lot of our audience in the profession and the worry is that we are speaking to ourselves about ourselves. I am definitely a second-waver!'

Another leading British education professor was more equivocal about being of the second wave: 'I suppose I do because that is where I started but I have a lot of time for younger feminists' ideas, enthusiasm, energy and hope ... My view is that newer feminisms are much more individualistic, and hedonistic than when I started, but that is due largely to changes in society that we are living through'. The Australian feminist Lyn Yates was also equivocal: 'Yes. I did see feminism as both "modernist" in the sense of allied to movements like Marxism, but also post-modernist, in the deconstructive aspects of it being particularly important and having value. I think that some of the further elaborations of deconstructive or poststructuralist work, and the endless taking up of Foucault, have got more jargon-laden and moved further away from practical engagement ... . I've been through many of the debates about women's studies in universities and the different forms (and names) these might take. Currently the humanities and social sciences in Australia are being financially squeezed and there is much less opportunity to mount interest-driven subjects compared with big and combined ones. But I think some attention to feminist issues is quite mainstream in history, sociology'.

Whilst the American liberal feminist Catherine Marshall tried to have it both ways: 'Yeah. I mean, no. I mean I consider myself grabbing at anything that works, to tell you the truth! I don't care what the label is, you know. I definitely am of the feminism that says it's about leadership and policy and power, wherever that falls. And that includes, you know, the women's ways which says it is power issues that decide that women's lives don't have anything special about them or that women's voices don't have anything special to say. It is power, the politics of knowledge issue, questions that say that. And so that's kind of a blend between women's ways and politics, *wherever that falls in the waves in the ocean* ... Good question. At the time that I discovered liberal feminism and was an enacting liberal feminism, I knew nothing of critical theory. And critical theory knew nothing of gender, as it was developing ... I sort of discovered critical theory and feminist theory, not at the same time, but they came together as I was recognizing the politics of gender and the politics of knowledge. All these are terms that I never knew in graduate school. They just weren't there. So, when I looked at critical theory, I thought: This is really interesting! Because critical theory is basically saying there are oppressive forces built into institutions, including the institutions of policy and politics and power – and, you know, universities and schools and churches, and every place! And said Yeah! No kidding! and they're oppressive to, critical theory mostly developed originally around class issues, particularly in England. And then it became critical race theory, and somewhere along the line I recognized that critical theorists weren't talking about gender. And so, that's when I came up with this term feminist critical policy analysis as a way of saying: let's pull all of this together, and look at how policies, unpack how policies are oppressive and excluding issues around gender. And create a more powerful way to look at those things both theoretically and methodologically. ... And there aren't any requests for proposals for research using feminist critical policy analysis. So it hasn't exactly taken over, but ... '

Several other international feminists have also changed their theoretical and political perspectives, whilst also remaining committed feminists in academe. Two Australians, Bronwyn Davies and Jane Kenway both have changed their thinking: Bronwyn Davies said: 'No. I find it hard to think in generational terms. I'd like to think my work is somewhere near the forefront of current thinking even though I am quite 'old'. Jane Kenway said: 'Second-wave as it is, is not a useful analogy for me. My main concern has always been about which feminist modes of thought and practice are most powerful for the purposes and politics at hand ... . I would probably be considered "second wave" but frankly that implies a linear and even generational approach to feminist history that I don't subscribe to and don't apply to myself ... .'

Several British feminists agreed such as Maggie Humm: 'Perhaps simply in terms of my age but I'm very interested in post-feminist art ... I find that any young student relishes the chance to discover what might be called feminist ideas (as long as they are not introduced with that nomenclature initially)'. And perhaps the worries about academic feminism are well expressed by Mary Stiasny: 'I probably do ... but

I hate to think that this might mean that we are "over" … I think we still have a voice because too many younger women think that the battle is won … I think that we had less self-confidence about the rights we had, and more anger which was necessary to make a stand since we were less confident – we were learning and realizing our Voice; but I fear that this means that while we were therefore less convinced by the changes and cosmetic effects we saw around us, now women are less aware that things are not as changed as we are told they are … (does this make sense? Our conscientisation meant that we saw the smoke screens – now women may not see them …)'.

Finally, Sue Middleton also expressed the changes well: 'I don't think of it this way, although I accept that the younger women's issues, needs, ideas and modes of operating are quite different from those of our generation – and so they should be. Personally, I felt a huge change at menopause (after hysterectomy at 46) as personal questions of reproduction, career "stage" and motherhood (my daughter left home) were personally less immediate. My focus shifted away from gender *per se* and more into issues concerning the fate of educational theory in the amalgamating universities and teachers' colleges. I began researching the lives and ideas of "old" teachers (… did our oral history) – including feminists. I became assistant dean graduate studies developing a research culture and an EdD. I had a feminist dean … and a largely female student and staff body. Students were repelled by feminism (it was their mothers' thing) through the late 1990s. But now things have changed again. Present students are enthralled by "old feminism" but sometimes think the battles have been won. It doesn't take much though to get them worked up about the gender pay gap, sexualisation of children, and the work–life [im]balance. It's not up to "us" though to fight their battles for them – they have to do it themselves in their own way. WE will have enough problems fighting for the remnants of public health care in our dotage!'

Riding the Wave: Mid-career Feminists (Cohort 2)?

As we move through the cohorts of feminists entering the academy and becoming feminists in the 1980s and 1990s, the trends seem to shift slightly and move possibly more towards 'third-wave' feminism. This can perhaps best be summarized by Jocey Quinn, the British feminist, who sees herself as 'riding the waves': 'I consider myself a feminist, many of my beliefs were strongly formed through feminist activism in the 80s which I guess may be historically second wave but I am alive now and contributing and *so still riding the wave I hope* … I can see broad distinctions in terms of campaigns about violence against women for example where to my mind feminists used to hold stronger positions and be more rigorous in seeing connections across all aspects of life. Subsequent generations are more global in their outlook and in this they are stronger'.

And another international feminist Gabriele Griffin said that: 'Yes resistance from diverse groups of women to women as a category … politics has changed massively and birth of third-wave feminism is the heterosexual version of queer theory and defends a consumption politics. Yes I am a second wave feminist because of my politics; third wave is more neo-liberal and I am against that kind of politics. I am rooted in the second wave but not uncritical towards the ideas ... the concept of wave is just a shorthand' ... Lucy Bland also said that she was a second-wave feminist and that third wave feminism has second wave feminism to build on. 'We had first wave feminism, but it seemed so "old" that initially at least, we reinvented the wheel. I hope that third wave feminism isn't doing the same'.

Yet others were also anxious about the relations between second and third wave feminists, as the British academic Audrey Mullender put it: 'I'm old-fashioned and I regard everything "post-" as a bit of a backlash against the real anti-oppressive practices we were managing in the late 80s and early 90s'. Whereas others were more sanguine, like the British educator, Carrie Paechter: 'I consider myself a feminist. Waves don't interest me ... 'On the other hand, the American feminist, Wendy Luttrell claimed that: '*I am a* feminist BUT second wave I guess you would say that I was part of the "women-centered service" movement that grew up out of the initial second wave activities ... saw myself as an "activist" who would return to the community with my new found knowledge to improve the organization, its curriculum and pedagogical practices (which I did do)'.

Interestingly, the question of where those feminists or women of colour position themselves in relation to the wave analogy is yet another perspective as is evident from Heidi Mirza's trenchant comments: 'I consider myself a "third wave black/ postcolonial feminist". I belong to a small but important community of women scholars of colour in Britain. There is a generation of postcolonial women who have struggled together in the academe since the 1970s, and some of us are now professors! Black British Feminism in the early 90s was a very powerful because it brought together women of colour who were writing and doing brilliant work but in isolated little "pockets" in different universities in the UK. Independently we were writing on similar themes. Some were just finishing their PhDs, some were already established. Black British Feminism opened up a moment of possibilities and brought us together to make such a powerful statement. It created a new subject area based on our collaborative writing. It was such an energetic and vibrant time. I'm very proud to have been part of this'.

Her colleague and collaborator, the black feminist Ann Phoenix also mentioned the differences in the moves from second wave feminism which she saw as different in terms of 'the rebalancing of collectivity and individualism – they forged their careers through doing their [academic] work so now careers are upfront; stops people thinking of joining the union'. Gemma Moss agreed: 'I do identify very much as a feminist within the left and TU politics, though my most active period was as a teacher ... . I do think professional third wave feminism has turned feminism into a private language you more or less have to do a doctorate to speak. If feminism means something then it means something in the real world, not as a theoretical object in the knowledge-making factory of the academy. This doesn't mean not holding on to base principles – but I think something odd has happened to knowledge-making too. So it's a question of sorting out what has really shifted, what stays the same'. The Irish feminist Maria Slowey also felt that: 'Yes ... I lost connection (and patience) with feminist theory in the 1990s when it seemed to me to have retreated into the academy, to have distanced itself from practice, and, in certain respects not only became trivialized, but even dangerous (for example, revisionist perspectives on pornography which do not take account of the underpinning commercial, neo-colonial and – literally – life threatening implications of the industry) ...'

The international feminist Kari Dehli also criticized the wave analogy: 'I don't think the "wave" analogy works that well as it implies too much of a linear movement from one era or form of feminism to the next. So no for the reasons suggested I don't think this label is useful or accurate'. And so did the Indian professor of women's studies, Nirupama Prakash: 'I believe not so much in theories/ waves as much as changing perceptions of men as and where required'. And again the international feminist Corinne Squire said that: 'Perhaps because I've worked for a long time around HIV issues, I don't tend to define myself as a second wave feminist – whose waves are those? – but simply as a feminist. Certainly working on this topic has made me think more transnationally about feminisms, as has working in South Africa and other international contexts around HIV ...'.

Amongst the 'education feminists' most closely associated with colleagues in the third cohort there was some perplexity as Gabrielle Ivinson said: 'Probably yes. There are fewer consensuses about what we are doing. There are few theoretical or ideological positions that we agree on. So, diversity and the lack of pride in calling ourselves "feminist" make for a diaspora. However, globally we see women rising up and facing up to their oppressors in the most dramatic and impressive ways. I think these movements have been possible because of the history of feminism in the West. I think globally feminism is alive, and that locally it is hidden [gone underground in Vygotsky's sense of the term] ...'. Whilst Chris Skelton was far more positive: 'Yes. Third wave feminist theory seems to be much more sophisticated and insightful than second wave. It enables us to recognize gender as disembodied (sometimes too much so and the most recent work of Becky Francis is helping to "put the body back" into theory). It facilitates research so that we are able to see how and where masculinity and femininity are constantly in flux in the lives of school children'.

Neatly linking cohorts 2 and 3 are the partners Penny Tinkler and Carolyn Jackson: 'We probably would just consider ourselves to be feminists, rather than second wave feminists *per se*. While many of the ideas of "second-wave" feminists have been very influential for both of us, we're uneasy with such distinctions (which can be divisive)'.

A Second and a Half Waver: Feminists of the Third Cohort

The feminists of the third cohort (i.e. those born after 1965) are also more questioning of the wave analogy, with some of the younger more international women doubting the uses of the term at all any more, if ever. Those who remain committed to feminism can perhaps be seen to be somewhat ambivalent about which generation or cohort they belong to, and this is perhaps well articulated by the following two comments:

Fin Cullen, probably the youngest of my study and a British feminist, said: 'I think I am probably a second and a half waver. Generationally speaking, I should probably be a third waver, but as my early entry into feminism attests the key theoretical thinkers that shaped my baby feminist years were distinctly second wave (and before, I found a copy of Mary Wollstencraft at 16 which opened my eye to the earlier history). However, I did spend some time reading riot grrrl fanzines, and pogoing at riot grrl gigs (see Bikini Kill; Hole; Babes in Toyland) but really I preferred the earlier non-riot grrl and more implicitly feminism of The Slits ... The generation tussles between the "right" focus and approach that feminism should adopt is intriguing. I think some third wave approaches might be dismissed as not "beefy" enough. By that I mean it could be seen to be more concerned with fripperies, and that the deeper questions raised by second wave movement need returning to'.

Her colleague, the British feminist Pam Alldred also claimed that: 'Erm complicated. No to another feminist, rather as an academic feminist I would specify more of a third wave position, but outside in the world, I often feel like a second wave feminist and it's enough to be arguing from there (what I call, wrongly probably, first principles)'.

Penny-Jane Burke said: 'No I feel I don't have the right to do that as I didn't come to feminism until the early 90s. However ... I identify most strongly with the insights of second-wave feminism ... I think those women younger than myself who might see themselves as third-wavers would understand the context of their concerns in a different way as to second-wavers – perhaps it is largely generational and differences are also due to the successes and achievements of second-wavers which younger feminists are then able to build upon and critique'. Similarly, Kelly Coate wrote that: 'The theory of course inevitably begins spilling into practice, but discovering feminist politics at the end of the second wave of the women's movement was like showing up to the party a few days late. Those of us who were young feminists in the early 1990s were caught in between the second and the third wave, trying to figure out in which direction to look. Looking backwards was always done with some envy, through hearing stories of the events that had taken place. My favourite anecdote was about the first feminist caucus meeting of the BSA, where the men had to be physically locked out of the room so that they would stop interrupting the women. As it was explained, women's role at the BSA conferences up to that point had largely been one of acknowledging the genius of the men. The idea that the women were finding a room of their own and locking the men out was hugely threatening. We all found out later what happens when the men are let back in, which is why we looked back on that history of feminist scholarship with envy and looked forward with some trepidation ... ' (in Davis and Evans, 2011, pp. 81–2).

Amanda Coffey wrote: I am not sure that I fit the second or third wave – my generation benefitted and was influenced by second wave feminism, and perhaps had an influence on third wave feminism ... We can leave the concluding comment of this section to one of cohort 3, Heather Mendick who neatly expresses the ambiguities of the term second-wave feminism in the following crisp comment: 'I guess so – though I was too young for the second wave proper I feel strong continuities with it. I'm not convinced there's been subsequent generations'.

Conclusions About the Permanency of Feminist Values

Whilst the wave metaphor was heavily debated, all my participants across the three cohorts subscribed to a notion of *feminism*, at very least being about forms of gender equality within society and academe. Many of them were still working through its meanings for their scholarly work as well as for their political and academic practice. I turn now to consider who all these academic feminists are by looking more closely at the educational, family and social backgrounds of the women participants across the 3 cohorts to shed more light on the meanings and development of feminist pedagogies, and their passionate embrace by all three cohorts. One of the most complex issues here is the relation between social class and family background and educational or university participation. These questions illustrate the complexities of the socio-economic and political transformations over the last half century and the place of women, and feminists especially within them.

The American feminist of cohort 1, Kathleen Weiler's musings about these questions, help us to move into a wider consideration of the nuances of the educational, social class and familial backgrounds of these women becoming feminists: 'I consider myself as having been shaped by second wave feminism. I am part of that generation of women who attended college in the early sixties before the women's movement when expectations for women graduates were very low, at least so it seemed to me. Very few women went into law or medicine and those who went on to get PhDs found it hard to get jobs. There were no tenured or tenure-track women professors in the history department at Stanford where I was an undergraduate, for example. I think I had two women professors in all my undergraduate courses – one in Spanish and one in creative writing. My family had no expectations that I would go beyond a BA or any knowledge of what graduate school meant. So when I graduated in 1963, I couldn't imagine a future as an academic. Instead, I got married and later taught high school for fifteen years. In those years, what we then called the women's movement – what I consider the second wave of feminism – emerged, along with the other social movements of the 1960s and 1970s. Like many other women of my generation I was shaped by the political concerns of this movement, which focused on analyzing sexism and building institutions and a culture that would be equitable and responsive to women's needs. I was part of a consciousness-raising group and began to read feminist works and tried to introduce women's issues into my high school classes ... but in terms of waves, I must say I am uneasy with the whole concept – it assumes a kind of linear development of ideas with sharp breaks that I don't think captures the instabilities and tensions within feminism as both a movement and a theoretical perspective. The reality is much more complex than this. I feel most comfortable claiming feminism as a political movement emerging at particular historical moments. Those of us who claim the term feminist are shaped by the historical context in which we work – both those who have gone before, those who are working contemporaneously, and those in opposition to feminist ideas. Second wave feminism, for example, emerged from an activist social movement with clear political goals. This was a very different context than the acutely self-conscious feminist academic world of the 1990s, deeply influenced by poststructuralism and the challenges of queer theorists and women theorists of color. And the global financial/political/moral crisis we are living through now in the aftermath of 2008 sets out a different context yet again – one that calls feminists back to an engagement with ongoing political struggles, not just arguments over theory. As a political stance, I think that feminism is greatly strengthened when it calls into question the concept of gender itself and considers both men and women to be positioned within a gender system of meaning and power. At the same time, I feel feminist scholars should not lose sight of "women" as the focus of our research – the flesh and blood people who live through/against the category of woman. As a feminist, I think one asserts the value of women's lives and takes a stance in favor of equality and justice. Because of this political stance, I see feminist scholarship as calling for the articulation of the feminist researcher's interests and social location "on the same side" as the women we identify as our "subjects". But if we don't consider our own and other's social locations and identities – around race, class, sexuality, to name the most recognized – in our stance of being on the same side, then obviously we will just repeat the same asymmetrical and potentially damaging kind of scholarship we seek to avoid ... .'

Chapter 4

A Collective Biography of Academic Feminism: University Pioneers?

Introduction

This collective biography is about the educational, family and social class origins of my participants: were they pioneers in changing university times? Whilst they are in no way representative of academic feminists, let alone women academics, they are illustrative of the manifold changes in both education and the wider socio-economic systems over the last 50 years. They show how the exclusion of women from HE has changed over their lifetime as HE has expanded globally as part of the knowledge economy. I elaborate on the women's professional and educational positions to illustrate how these global transformations have impacted upon their educational and academic lives, as students and academics. What are the women's positions now in terms of seniority and professorial status, and what of their research through doctorates? What are their social, familial and educational origins and do they change as we move through the three cohorts?

Current public policy debates about social mobility and notions of either 'first-in-the-family' (the British concept) or first generation (the American concept) to go to university are framed in gender-neutral terms. In the UK, as we saw in Chapter 2, now that gender equity amongst students is assumed, debates focus on the educational needs of working-class men as compared to middle-class women (Ringrose, 2012; Willetts, 2010). What my study reveals dramatically is that the majority of my participants across the three cohorts were 'first-in-the-family' but not all from working-class backgrounds. The expansion of global HE has impacted on a diversity of women. Many of cohort 1 were 'first-in-the-family' but from the growing middle classes, since they had previously been denied educational opportunities and rights, but over time, and in association with educational expansion, more women from lower-middle and working-class families began to 'benefit' (in cohorts 2 and 3). It is not only middle-class women who have 'benefitted' from university expansion, nor is it only middle-class women who have become feminists. In the process, of course, and by definition becoming a graduate makes one middle class!

These are linked as forms of social and geographic mobility, across the various countries of the 'global north', together with socio-cultural questions, such as black and minority ethnicity (BME) and religion. I also signal how education and universities influenced their lives together with feminist or equality values, although inevitably as HE changes so do the women's lives. All the women, from across the three cohorts, are proudly committed to gender equality and/or feminism, making similar comments to Kathleen Weiler's, despite their diversity of backgrounds and origins. I start with the professors from across the cohorts,[1] focusing especially on cohort 1.

Academic Feminists as Professors

The majority of my participants are *full* professors, in the US sense of the term, as already mentioned in Chapter 1, and the majority are in cohort 1, given how skewed my study is towards older women. All the women living in Australia, Canada, New Zealand and the USA, who are in cohorts 1 and 2 are full professors, with only two women from overseas in cohort 3 who are not [yet] full professors. It is only British women in the three cohorts who may not be full professors, and indeed for cohort 1, may no longer be in HE, either having retired or moved out to other positions, such as public policy activists. Given the neo-liberal moves, especially in the UK, very few of the women professors in British universities are 'tenured' in that US sense, that is holding permanent appointments. The British system of 'tenure', which was in any event looser than in the USA, was abolished through the 1988 Education Reform Act – and few of the women in my study had reached that stage in their lives and careers by 1988. (Indeed one of the participants from cohort 1, by no means the eldest, spearheaded the campaign not to abolish tenure and resisted ever being made a professor in the aftermath of the Act! Sara Delamont remains a reader [not a full but possibly an associate professor] today).

Interestingly, only a little over three-quarters of cohort 1 are full professors, despite all of them having reached the end of their professional academic lives, whereas almost nine out of ten of cohort 2 are full professors, with the other four still having the possibilities of becoming a full professor (with one promoted appointment since my study), and only a third of cohort 3 having been appointed or promoted to a professorship (see Table 4.1 below) (although again there have been three promotions to professorships since). Even though this is not at all representative it appears that the trends are increasing towards more promoted positions amongst the women academics involved over time, although the kinds of women promoted tend still to be confined to white rather than BME women.

Taking just the British women who hold chairs, there are 57 (well over two-thirds) who are called professors overall and in each cohort there are substantial numbers: almost two-thirds in cohort 1 (29 out of 45), and in cohort 2 there are 24 out of 28 women (or 6/7ths) and in cohort 3 only a third yet. It is probably not just chance that means that amongst cohort 2 the majority are women holding chairs, since this is the age range for promotions in the UK, namely being between the ages of about 40 to about 60. This is also indicative of the moves

---

1   One of these two has just been made a professor – Rajani Naidoo.

towards professionalization of the academic profession, and the entry of women, including feminists into academe and the professoriate. There is a question about why more of cohort 1, have not become professors, having reached the end of their careers in the UK.

Table 4.1   Participant (full) professors

Country	Cohort 1	Cohort 2	Cohort 3	Totals
AUSTRALIA/NEW ZEALAND	5			5
CANADA	6	1		7
INDIA/IRELAND/ ISRAEL/ SPAIN	1	2		3
USA	9	1		10
UK	29	24	4	57/83 (69%)
TOTALS	50/66(76%)	28/32 (88%)	4/12 (33%)	82/110 (75%)

Why Are So Many of Cohort 1 Not Professors?

This question about becoming a [full] professor has to do with the changing nature of HE. It was not the obvious or possible progression for all of cohort 1 in the UK. Quite clearly this was not an expectation for many of those who agreed to participate, and particularly not for those older participants, born before the Second World War. Opportunities for women in academe were scarce. Some indeed, whilst very intellectually able and academically successful as undergraduates, may have taken different career paths, most particularly for those [heterosexual] women, marrying and raising a family, as was then conventional, before returning to academic work. Some became schoolteachers and others researchers before marriage, or combining with rearing children. As we have seen the American feminist Kathleen Weiler, on graduation from an elite private university, trained as a schoolteacher at Harvard Graduate School of Education and returned to academe much later in life, having married and raised her family. This is also true for others of the American, Australian and British participants, although curiously not for most of the Canadians.

Whilst sexuality has been a key issue for feminists, there were few across my participants who openly raised the issue in relation to their formation, whilst others refer to it as their kind of personal and academic feminism, particularly women in cohorts 2 and 3 (to be discussed later). One distinguished professor in cohort 1 wrote that: 'I formed a relationship with another woman whose family had been Communists, so I was exposed to a completely different attitude to women and politics generally than that which I had obtained in my very conservative family'.

Some of the women only became feminists later in their family and working lives, and, in some cases, as a result of the discriminatory processes within academic workplaces which meant that having entered the profession after child rearing they did not advance very far and left to pursue other more public feminist activities. For example, Annette Lawson, a distinguished British public policy feminist and sociologist who won an Order of the British Empire (OBE) in 2004 for services to diversity wrote that she did not become a feminist: 'until I was 50! I thought you could do anything if you worked hard enough – the merit view of life. But was rudely awakened by the way [Uni] treated me. It was wonderful American colleagues and friends who helped me into feminism between 1985–88 when we lived in Berkeley and I was a visiting scholar to the then CROW – Centre for Research on Women at Stanford, and at the Institute for Human Development at Berkeley. On the other hand, I have a memory from when I was about six or seven in Somerset which is significant – I ran in the 100 yards race at the school sports day – remember it was a boys' school. I won with a lot of support from my brother and cousin who ran alongside cheering me on ... But when I was called up for my prize, I heard one of the fathers of one of the boys say "what is a girl doing even running in this race, never mind winning it?" And I always knew my brother as the first born and only son was the favourite and my younger sister who was learning disabled – "slow" was another because of her vulnerability. So I was a typical middle child ... [Annette had already mentioned that she] 'went to university and won the studentship for the best student in the year in the University of London, two years running, and went straight on to do *a doctorate which was immediately published* ... After early marriage and childbearing until the youngest of three was three years old, I did not work for money. But in 1976 I became a Lecturer at Uni. This was an appalling step because I should have negotiated re-entry at, at least Senior Lecturer level, as a male colleague did at the same time. Never occurred to me and I was never promoted yet given huge admin responsibility – Senior Tutor, Graduate Studies and Chair of Department. After the fiasco of leaving Uni, I was never successful in getting another academic job (not even called for interview). Partly it was because I had not been promoted and so had the age and kind of career that should have got me a chair but I imagine my applications were binned as soon as they saw "Lecturer". Hence I set up a consultancy mainly focused upon gender equality but also diversity more generally ... I became an activist and was successful at that – chair of the Fawcett Society, and then National Association of Women's Organizations (NAWO), a Commissioner of the Women's National Commission (WNC) and its chair ... .'

Of course, there is also a question about the institutional locations of the professorships as well as the subjects (especially education) and academic backgrounds. Several have held posts in what are now considered 'research-intensive universities' in Australia, Canada, the USA and the UK; what used to be considered Ivy League universities in the USA, and what are called the elite Russell Group universities in the UK. Equally, there are many who have pioneered feminist and women's studies in the newer universities of the UK, Canada and the US. It is a tribute to the women's persistence and resilience in the changing academic profession that women academics have achieved promotions and the status of professors, albeit that not all are linked explicitly to feminist or gender studies.

Some of the women mentioned how important it was to them explicitly to mention doing feminist work across their careers. The distinguished Canadian feminist Margrit Eichler wrote: 'My entire life has been shaped by feminism ... [beginning] at university ... It was the beginning of the feminist movement, and I joined a women's liberation group ... We women were a small minority ... .' Her colleague, and co-editor, the distinguished Canadian women's studies professor Meg Luxton wrote: '[beginning] at university late 1960s ... . My whole adult life is lived as a feminist and has shaped everything I have studied and written. I have been an activist in the WLM and continue to be involved as an activist. As a scholar, I write from a feminist perspective'.

There is also no clear connection between the universities where the women have become professors and their universities of origin in terms of undergraduate degrees, interestingly, although there is more of a link in terms of type of university, in which they studied as undergraduate or even as graduate students and social class origins. Few participants from cohort 1 went to newer universities as undergraduates although there are exceptions such as Jane Kenway from Australia and Carol Smart in the UK. This is partly because these universities were only being established when the women were going to university – the 1960s and 1970s, as part of the expansion of HE. So the vast majority of cohort 1 across all countries went to what are nowadays the more elite universities, unless they went to teacher education colleges prior to gaining higher degrees (and there are a substantial number of these). More of cohort 2 and 3 went to new universities by explicit 'class' choice.

Doctorates as An Important Criterion for Cohort 1

Whilst all the participants are highly educated, as well as mainly being professors, inevitably perhaps because it is a study of women academics, there are also some interesting features about precisely what that means in terms of official qualifications and the gaining of a doctorate at a particular stage in an academic career, across subjects, especially education, the social sciences and humanities. The majority of my participants are involved in some aspect of education and therefore the stage at which they may have obtained their doctorate tends to be later than the traditional male student, involved in full-time research study, straight after graduation.

Although the vast majority of my participants have got doctorates, either a PhD or DPhil, or an education doctorate (EdD), or PhD by publication, this also varies across the three cohorts. All of cohort 3 has some kind of doctorate, only one of cohort 2 does not have a doctorate but is a professor, but there are 10 of cohort 1 who do not have doctorates (including both professors and non-professors, or senior researchers) (see Table 4.2 below). The reasons for this are, indeed, to do with both the changing nature of HE, and women's changing place within it, as well as the subjects taken, and the fact that a large proportion of my participants are in education. For several of cohorts 1 and 2, gaining a doctorate occurred later in life, either on returning to HE or because other social and family factors intervened. Indeed, it is quite clear that these trajectories are rather typical of women's lives for this generation.

Table 4.2   Participants with doctorates

Country	Cohort 1	Cohort 2	Cohort 3	Totals
AUSTRALIA/NEW ZEALAND	5			5
CANADA	6	1		7
INDIA/IRELAND/ ISRAEL/ SPAIN	1	1	2	4
USA	9	1		10
UK	35/45	28/28	10/10	73/83 (88%)
TOTALS	56/66 (83%)	31/32 (97%)	12/12 (100%)	99/110 (90%)

Doctorates and Professorships: Both, Either or Neither?

All the participants outside of the British Isles have doctorates and are 'full' professors. In the case of the British Isles there are several participants who do not have doctorates. Of course this is partly a function of my selection of women to speak with. It is important to consider, however, who the women are who do not have doctorates, before going on to consider the nature of the doctorates. All those who originated from the USA, Africa, and Asia and are now resident in the British Isles, across the three cohorts do, indicating country as well as cohort differences and time of arrival in the UK. This does not necessarily extend to those from the Antipodes. Ellen Malos, the distinguished researcher on family policy and domestic violence, is one of the four from cohort 1 who is neither a professor nor a doctor (although she has an honorary doctorate from Bristol), and hails from Australia. She wrote that: 'I worked as a teacher while doing an MA on a left wing Australian novelist. I came to Bristol because my husband was offered a fellowship in the Physics Department. Here I started an ambitious MPhil/PhD on "The Tyranny of History in the works of James Joyce and William Faulkner" which failed to survive the difficulty of combining research, writing and motherhood in the rather hostile environment of the University of Bristol in the heyday of early Bowlbyism.[2] There was a period I went back to school-teaching which was made exciting by the advent of the WLM ... I have been pretty well immersed in feminism (and left wing socialism) for most of my life and have always combined learning and activism, and learning THROUGH activism ...'.

Her story is mirrored by others of the cohort, who are neither professors nor have a doctorate with, for example, Pam, a feminist child-care advocate, writing: 'I was enrolled for a PhD, grant from the Medical Research Council (MRC) for three years, topic the father's role in family with John Newson ... completed tape recorded interviews, transcribed and coded but did not write up. (It was personally a difficult time for me while in Leeds and meant to be writing up). I later completed an MSc in the Psychology of Education at the IOE ... .' The housing and social policy expert Ruth wrote: 'I did one year taught MA course in the sociology of professional organizations (or something like that) at Leeds University. I did two years of a PhD in Community Studies at Leeds, which I never finished. I went on to a three year research job after that ... ' Another wrote: 'I gained an MA in Vocational Education and Training in the IOE in the 90s through evening study. I began a PhD through part-time study but never completed. I later decided to apply for a PhD through publication but never got beyond getting the agreement of the *University to proceed*'. Several of cohort 1 who are professors have similar stories of disinclination or failure to complete theses with one saying that she 'started a PhD but wrote it up as a Masters (Research) when both supervisors left and I got a full-time job at a new university ... later did another MA as part of a sabbatical on politics ... .'

On the other hand, for some of the senior members of cohort 1 a doctorate was not at all expected: three very distinguished British professors of social policy, Heather Joshi, Hilary Land and Elizabeth Wilson do not have doctorates, and did not consider embarking upon them. *Heather* was awarded an OBE in New Year's Honours, 2002 for services to Women's Issues and described how she went from obtaining a very distinguished undergraduate degree and postgraduate Masters (MLitt) in economics to academic research posts, Elizabeth wrote simply No, and Hilary described her early immersion in social policy research: 'Summer 1964 Brian Abel Smith and Peter Townsend got grant from Joseph Rowntree Foundation to do poverty survey. I got one of the research assistantships (Brian had been my tutor and he was a very inspiring teacher, and I was thoroughly enjoying an introduction to the social sciences and studying issues that were relevant – otherwise I'd have gone into social work'.

---

2   A philosophical position, taken by the childcare expert John Bowlby in the early post-war period, about a commitment to mothers staying at home to care for babies (see New and David, 1985).

For others of this British cohort it was a belated realization of the necessity of a doctorate with a professor of feminist literature, writing that she only started working on a thesis: 'Much later (eight years) when it became clear that *I could not progress as an academic without a PhD*. And also because I had embarked upon a very early form of infertility treatment and fearing a lack of success felt that the PhD could become a substitute (to stop people continually asking about my lack of children). I was still an activist and chose to study the US polymath Paul Goodman (poet, anarchist, activist, town planner, novelist, educator, psychiatrist, playwright, political essayist etc.) who had been very influential in the left especially in education. My university paid the fees if I registered as a CNAA PhD so I had an "internal" supervisor … '

One professor of cohort 2 was also on the cusp of change, so that she did not undertake a PhD, saying: 'yes I took a year working abroad after my first degree and then did conversion course to Sociology and social research at University College Dublin … I then travelled again. A new National Research Fellowship was advertised, I applied and was appointed – at the same time registered for a Masters by Research in Trinity College Dublin (MLitt – I never considered doing a PhD as the funding was for two years only and I needed to work)'.

Diverse Doctorates as a Sign of Changing Forms of HE, Especially for Women

Another older professor in cohort 1 who was a mature undergraduate student wrote that she: 'didn't get very far with the PhD. Supervision was lax and I was involved in loads of activism. I also separated from my husband and moved house … I wrote quite a lot however throughout the 1980s and was awarded a PhD by publication in 1990 – seven years after getting a permanent job at a new university' … And another participant in cohort 2 wrote: 'I started a doctorate when I got my first academic post at 34, but withdrew from it because of family problems. I didn't complete my doctorate (by publication) until I was 55'.

Several from cohorts 1 and 2 have doctorates by publication such as those who are professors. One wrote: 'I did a Masters at LSE and then much later got a PhD by publication under "staff regulations" – i.e. through my publications which had begun to be feminist. I had no supervision or advice – just did it on my own'. Madeleine, like Fiona, embarked upon a PhD but was not able to complete it, and so wrote papers that subsequently became a PhD by publication. Fiona had 'started a PhD at Ibadan University in Nigeria but fell critically ill and had to return to the UK after two years … There was total lack of support for my attempt to do a thesis on Nigerian women as political agents. The anti-colonialist white teaching staff were only interested in the formation of male Trade Unions in West Africa and the radical Nigerian academics were very much influenced by Stokeley Carmichael's politics at this time which were often demeaning to women … .'

Finding My More Self-confident Voice

Jackie West's account (a participant from cohort 1) of her doctoral work from very early promise through despondency to finding her 'more self-confident voice' on retirement is most inspirational: 'this is a long story. I was appointed without even having started one and found myself initially directed towards topics such as female/male offenders in young people's institutions or women in the police service, the latter resulting in a good deal of participant observation (very interesting in fact). But my socialist feminist politics took over and I began a study of factory work in south Bristol, aided by a close friend made through WLM connections who was a shop steward. I did participant observation on the line making Golden Virginia. I had great support from a professorial colleague and again much later when the topic switched to the proletarianisation of clerical workers, but my heart wasn't in it and when access was refused by an insurance company I was more than happy to let it go ... who needed a doctorate anyway, I thought ... then. But I began to regret that decision, as increasing numbers of my own doctoral students graduated and gained chairs, while I became almost the sole colleague without this title. So I am delighted to have, at last, put this esteem issue to rest by very recently having completed one by publication. *A swansong, almost certainly, but important.* Esther Dermott was my formal adviser, the link with the university after I had officially retired. Her wise and astute suggestions in response to what I thought was my final draft of the commentary were fantastic – they helped me to *find a more self-confident voice*!'

Some Doctoral [and Educational] Origins of the 'Education Feminists' in Cohorts 1 and 2

One of the education professors trained and worked as a teacher, and returned to academe much later, and '*didn't graduate*' as she put it but 'went to Teacher Training College – needed to stay near home/ensure I could get a well-paid job so it was the 'natural' route for a young woman like myself ... [Instead] did 2 MAs and a PhD and a Dip Ed which was fabulous ... .'

Another education professor similarly went to a 'College of Education to do a B.Ed. to become a primary school teacher which I was for three years. Then I decided to do an MA ... and thought about in the evening but decided not, as I had two young children and it was too far away. I lived in north London then ... after my MA it was suggested that I do a PhD and I was so flattered that I started part-time PhD on girls and maths ... However, I couldn't sustain it, and it was only later when I was asked by Dale Spender to write an article on Harriet Martineau (published in 1983) that I decided to do a PhD. It took me eight years to complete part-time ... but eventually I got my PhD after some difficulty ... .'

Overall, and across all the countries, one fifth of the participants (22 women), all now professors, *initially trained as teachers*. The majority is from cohort 1 with less than a third from cohort 2. The older women who trained as teachers had varied routes into and from teaching, although for the most part they undertook undergraduate studies, followed by teacher education. Twelve from cohort 1 trained as graduates such as the ones from the Antipodes, from Israel, the USA and the UK.

Some in England trained initially at college, because much teacher education, at that time, was not included in universities, teaching and later moving into teacher education. This was also, as one put it, a *class* choice, being from a working class family. Whether trained initially at college or university, several from cohort 1 started off as primary schoolteachers. Chris, in cohort 2, from a working class family, did primary teacher training, taught and then obtained a degree from the Open University, before doing her doctorate.

Making It Up as I Went Along

Kathleen Weiler elaborates this picture of schoolteacher becoming teacher educator: 'When I did go to graduate school to get a doctorate in education, I decided I would write a thesis that would address feminist issues. The topic of my doctoral thesis (which was later published) was on a topic dear to my heart as a feminist high school teacher – I studied feminist high school teachers! Politically and theoretically, I was drawn to this research because I hadn't found anything like it in the theory I was reading. I did my doctoral thesis with Henry Giroux at Boston University in the early 1980s when Giroux was himself deeply engaged with European cultural and critical theory. I found this theory exciting and Giroux was very supportive of my interests, but I still wasn't clear how to connect critical theory with my feminist concerns. In my graduate program, there were no courses addressing gender, let alone feminist educational theory, *so like many other feminist education scholars in the early 1980s I was sort of making it up as I went along*. I was aware of some education scholars who were developing a feminist analysis. [I met Madeleine Arnot while in graduate school and knew the early work of Miriam David, Rosemary Deem, Angela McRobbie, and Jane Gaskell, but was unfamiliar with the research of such scholars as Sari Biklen in the United States, Lyn Yates in Australia, or Sue Middleton in New Zealand. In fact Sue was conducting the research for her book *Educating Feminists* at almost exactly the same time that I was doing the field work for what became *Women Teaching for Change*, but we were unaware of one another at the time. I felt I was alone with my research. I thought my task was to reconcile my feminist politics (a broad but random reading of feminist theory) with the more structured reading and analysis I was doing of (male) critical social theory and neo-Marxist educational theory. As I carried out the research, I became much less sure about my ability to reconcile these. I also came to see the work of the women teachers I was "studying" as also more complex, particularly around questions of race and institutional power. So things became decidedly more muddied the more I hung around the schools doing fieldwork and particularly when I began to write. I think this process of seeing greater complexity was typical of second wave feminists at this time who moved from a commitment to the political activism of the women's movement to the complexities of studying individuals in institutions and social structures ... .'

Three Australians have very similar trajectories and discuss how their doctorates were feminist in focus – with Bronwyn writing: 'I went to a small rural university in part because "the city" was regarded as too dangerous by my father for girls (1961). I enrolled in a BA and Dip Ed as I got a "Teachers College Scholarship" which carried with it the obligation to do five years' teaching. I wanted to study science but having been to a small girls' private school I had not studied Physics and Chemistry, which were pre-requisites ... My first jobs were teaching in school and then later I became an academic ... I had found my BA utterly demoralizing and did not enrol in the Dip Ed until after my marriage was over. I had thought the only thing I was competent to do was marry and take care of husband and children ... *After I was widowed at age 25 I completed a Dip Ed while teaching in school and then a BEd and a PhD while teaching at university full-time and raising my 3 kids.* For my PhD I had a few nominal male PhD supervisors who claimed they couldn't understand what I was writing as it was qualitative research. I was blocked from submitting my PhD for examination when it was completed on the grounds that they could not assess its quality. I negotiated that it would be submitted to a high status outsider for evaluation. His evaluation was so positive that I was able to submit it. It was later published as a book with Routledge'.

Another American also took time to become an academic feminist, saying that: 'When I went to college I went to the female arm of Harvard University. We took all our classes with the men and Radcliffe, our college, was mainly a residential entity and a place where there were some programs, some athletics, some theater. The main setting of our education was Harvard, although "girls" were not allowed to use the main Harvard undergraduate library. The Radcliffe library was much smaller ... The mission was clear and unambiguous – Harvard existed to train society's leaders and their wives ... I did a doctorate in Education at Boston University where I got an EdD. My dissertation was on discussions in high school History classrooms, showing that the teacher, not the students, was responsible for the level of discussion in the class. (That is, "lower track" students could have as sophisticated and as critical discussions as honours track students.) There was nothing in my dissertation about gender although I could easily have controlled for gender in my analyses of classroom discourse. My supervisor was a Boston Uni professor who was a statistician. After ten years of high school history teaching ... I began my college teaching career [and] became a feminist ... .'

The Professor is Almost Always White

There were only tiny numbers of BME or 'visible' (to use a Canadian expression) minority participants in my study, with one professor in cohort 1 and four BME professors in cohort 2, with one other BME participant in cohort 3. Headed '*the professor is almost always white*' and featuring a photograph of Heidi Mirza (one of my BME cohort 2 participants), the main feature article in *The Guardian's Education* section (29 January 2013, p. 30) was about promotions of female and BME academics to so-called 'top jobs'. She became one of the UK's first black female professors in the 1990s – the bye-line for the feature was 'Campaigners say universities will appoint more minority ethnic and female academics to the top jobs only when their funding depends upon it'. The article's main focus was on senior women in the sciences and argued that although there is now an initiative for gender equality here (the Athena scheme, mentioned in Chapter 2), there is no such similar scheme for BME staff. It also discussed a recent survey by the University and College Union (UCU) which showed that 'figures released by the Higher Education Statistical Agency ... reveal that the numbers of women and BME professors in our universities remain woefully low; just one in five professors are women (20.5 per cent), despite the fact that they make up almost half (47.3 per cent) of the non-professorial academic workforce. Only one in 13 (7.7 per cent) of professors are from BME backgrounds: BME academics fill 13.2 per cent of other posts'. The article examined why women don't apply for senior posts: 'Some might argue that they must be applying for positions for positions they are not qualified for. But that seems unlikely at such a high level, says Heidi Mirza ... It has to be a "discriminatory process". HE is about peer review and has a fundamentally nepotistic way of operating. It's about networking and people supporting people they know who are like themselves, who they feel will mirror their own areas of interest. BME people often don't fit into that. Universities in the UK are still very much white, male institutions of privilege and self-reproduction'.

Clearly, women professors in the social sciences in the UK remain a disproportionately small number, and BME even smaller. Sally Tomlinson, another education professor, wrote a reply to *The Guardian* article, in the Higher Education Network series, about *My university life as a woman professor* which chimes in beautifully with my stories. 'Learning ... that support and disparagement came in equal measure from male and female colleagues. Where some males can be ambitious and strong, some women are egotistical and bitchy. Particular help from Professor Miriam David, who organized a series of meetings for women professors and heads of department ... Women and minority applicants for professorships still face overt and covert discrimination in HE ... (www.guardian.co.uk/higher-education-network/blog/2013/Jan/31/female-professoir-university-life-equality)

The Social and Educational Origins of These Academic Feminists

What are the social class origins of the women, and what are the differences across the cohorts, especially as the expansion of HE has begun to percolate through to generations of women? The notion of social class that I am using is drawn from the women's accounts of themselves, rather than any objective notion, based upon, for example, a sustained analysis of their fathers' occupations or education, as was the convention in sociology until quite recently. Given that all my participants are social scientists and have been involved in considerations of social class in all of their own work they have a sophisticated and nuanced understanding of these questions. The relationship between social class and other social factors such as socio-economic disadvantage, socio-cultural identities and the workings of privilege versus poverty is one with which they are all familiar. Recent theorizations of class have included a complex mix of parental education as well as occupations, but most usually with a focus on fathers' occupation and education. Mothers' education has begun to play an important part in feminist analysis, as shown in the material that I have gathered.

In reply to a set of prompts about providing 'some contextual material' in which I asked about 'where and when you were born, and into what kind of family – class, siblings, parents to university and their employment' most did mention their parents' education, as well as their occupations or employment, and the kinds of families that they grew up in. Many of them also mentioned their own education before college or university. Their self-definitions of social class are interesting especially in terms of the fractions of both the middle and working classes. There is a range of responses in relation to upper and upper middle class, and as to whether or not families who were working class were aspirant for education, for example through involvement in trade unions. Definitions of social class also vary across the US and UK, with the term working class having a more pejorative meaning in the US.

Family backgrounds are defined not only by parents' social class as being about income (or means) but by also their occupations, with many of the women having parents who were either schoolteachers or university professors. This turned out to be significantly higher than expected, especially related to those feminists involved in so-called 'education feminism', rather than those who might see themselves academic feminists *per se*. Given the changes in HE, over the last 50 years, and the fact that teacher education has been transformed from being mainly in colleges to being in universities, as we have seen for many of my participants, many of them also had parents, mothers especially, who had participated in teacher education not then named as HE, and so were not (technically) 'first in-the-family' or 'first generation', though they felt it was so. Because HE, in the UK at least, was for a very narrow segment of the middle classes, until the Robbins expansion of the 1960s as we saw in Chapter 2, many from rather privileged middle-class backgrounds were 'first-in-the-family'. Many of my participants volunteered this information from across the three cohorts.

How are we to assess the educational and social backgrounds, given that what we have are the women's reports of their families and schooling, rather than the traditional emphasis on parental or father's occupation, which is how Olive Banks (1986) arrived at her classifications of the first-wave feminists? She argued: 'It is often assumed that "first-wave" feminism was essentially a middle class movement, appealing predominantly to middle-class women and in fact an examination of the social origin of the female sample suggests that this assumption is largely if not wholly true. For the purpose of measuring the social origin the sample was divided into four groups, according to father's occupation ... It should be recalled that this sample represents the *best-known of the feminists*, and that many women in relatively humble positions in the movement have not been included (1986, p. 10)'.

Whilst I have used a similar method to Banks in terms of cohorts for the analysis, they differ in several crucial respects. All of my participants are, or were, gainfully employed, whereas many of Banks' women were not. This indicates the sea change in socio-economic contexts between the nineteenth and twentieth centuries in women's working lives. Banks (1986, p. 12) pointed out that: 'The proportion of the women who had been gainfully employed rose throughout the period of the study, reflecting changes over time in the pattern of employment of women in the middle classes as well as the rising number of working-class women in the sample who would normally expect to work at least in the years before marriage ... The occupations followed were more varied too, although *teachers were still the largest group* (my emphasis)'. Teaching remained a key profession for Banks' cohorts and this is a clear similarity, although types of education and teaching differ markedly. Given that my participants have all remained in, or returned to, HE, and that HE globally has remained relatively elite despite policies to widen participation, just how middle class are my participants? There are obvious continuities, given the origins of first-wave feminism in college education, as Banks (1986, pp. 13–14) makes clear: 'By cohort IV however, the majority of women in the sample were college educated, reflecting not simply a change in educational provision, although that was a part of it, but also the attractions of feminism to the girl who had been to college, as well as college, to the girl who was already a feminist. Educational level, as might be expected, was closely related to social origin. Only one (6 per cent) of the 16 women of working class origin had been to college compared to 45 per cent of the professional and 36 per cent of the business category. This renders even more remarkable the high level of college education in cohort IV, since almost a quarter of the women in that cohort are of working-class origin. Indeed, of the middle-class women in that cohort all but two had been to college or university. It is entirely fair, therefore, to argue that, as far as this sample is concerned, *active feminists were not only predominantly middle class, they were also, even for their class and period, unusually well educated* (my emphasis)'.

Jane Martin (2013) followed Banks in constructing her cohorts of twentieth-century metropolitan feminists, as we saw in Chapter 3, also using Stacey and Price (1981) to think about how they succeeded: 'To make sense of political careers I reconstruct the stories/social action dialectic with the help of frameworks from a 1981 publication, *Women, Power and Politics* ... [who] talk in terms of five "success" factors. *These are growing up in politically active, middle-or-upper class families, a good education, the ability to rely on the resources and support of their families and to avoid or minimize family commitments* (my emphasis) ...' (Martin, 2013, p. 60).

Are My Academic Feminists Predominantly Middle Class?

My participants diverge quite remarkably from these five success factors since not all from middle-or-upper class families, nor do they all have a 'good' formal education, and, most importantly, the range of domestic resources and [reduced] familial responsibilities that Stacey and Price (1981) assumed were necessary. Stacey and Price, like Banks herself, stood on the cusp of first to second wave feminism, and were early British feminist sociologists in academe. They probably all did have these social factors in their backgrounds, but my academic feminists differ markedly, as they are all born from the 1930s, and came of age as feminism and the WLM were re-awakening in the 1960s. The pace of change of education, and global HE especially, was rapid during the twentieth century.

I have summarized the social class backgrounds across all participants in the three cohorts in Table 4.3 below. One criterion that I used is one that those who mentioned mother and/or father being a teacher, as a way to distinguish within the middle classes: from upper middle to middle or perhaps lower middle. This was often how they themselves mentioned their class backgrounds. I also included having academic parents in the upper middle class designation, as some of the women from the USA, mentioned this. Notions of social class vary slightly across the countries, with working class not common in the US, but the American feminist Wendy Luttrell (cohort 2) uses it for her father whereas her mother was a teacher: 'My father was a construction worker, and my mother was a teacher before she became pregnant with me (I was told that when she married, she was told by the principal of her school that were she to get pregnant she would lose her job, which indeed she did) ... *My parents' marriage "crossed" class* in this sense, and religion (my father raised a Catholic and mother raised a Baptist)'.

The participants in my study overall are skewed towards the middle classes with almost three quarters of the participants seeing themselves as from upper middle-class to lower middle-class families, and about a quarter claiming to be from the working classes. There is an odd pattern across the three cohorts, which is *not* towards a more equal social class family background. In cohort 1 the vast majority are middle class, with little over one in five being working class, whereas in cohort 2, well over a third (38 per cent) say they are working class, dropping back to a third in cohort 3. In cohort 1 a third say they are upper middle class, whereas it is only a quarter in cohorts 2 and 3. This may be an artefact of the selection of the cohorts and grouping together of all the participants, across countries, where there are very few from countries other than the UK in cohorts 2 and 3. It is clear that there is a trend towards more lower middle and working class families in HE, from these data and given the changing forms of global HE, especially the daughters of mother-teachers.

Table 4.3   **Social class families (including parental education) across the 3 cohorts**

Social Class Distribution	Cohort 1 (1935–1950)	Cohort 2 (1950–1965)	Cohort 3 (1965–1980)	Totals
Upper/Upper Middle Class	22 (33%)	7 (25%)	3 (25%)	32 (29%)
Middle/Lower Middle class	30 (45%)	13 (40%)	5 (42%)	48 (45%)
Working class	14 (21%)	12 (38%)	4 (33%)	30 (27%)
TOTALS	66	32	12	110

Cohort 1 has most of the upper middle-class participants, although they are very diverse, and fewest of the working class. These fine class distinctions, especially amongst the middle classes, in cohort 1 are illustrated in the following. Two women from very upper middle-class families show how daughters were relatively excluded from university education on a par with their brothers, in the early twentieth century. By chance these two women were born a couple of months apart and are now both aged over 70 and living in North America. One account is by the now Canadian feminist, Marilyn: 'born in north Wales in May 1942 – wartime and when my father went off to the navy my mother retreated thankfully to a sheep farm belonging to my maternal grandfather, where she was free of the constraints of middle-class sociability in Liverpool and could work hard running the farm and raising her children. My grandparents were solid middle-class professionals in Liverpool (at least the men were: women were "just wives"). My father, when he returned from the war was a moderately unenthusiastic accountant … .My mother was taken out of school at 16 because her father saw no point in educating her further or of her working as he didn't approve of "rich men's daughters taking money out of poor men's mouths". The only member of my family who had ever been to university was an uncle, who obtained a miserable 4th at Oxford, thus confirming the general family (and class) conviction that university was a waste of time – much better to get stuck into an apprenticeship in a profession … .'

The American Frinde: 'born in Marblehead, Massachusetts, USA in August 1942 and grew up in an upper-class family with connections in Boston society. (I "came out" as a debutante in Boston!) My father was an architect with a BA and an Architecture degree from Harvard and practiced architecture in Boston. My mother had one year of college at Bryn Mawr because her college career began during the Depression. Her father, an engineer, could only afford four-year college for their son. Thus their three daughters could only have one year of college apiece … .' Those with 'academic' parents can also be classified as privileged and/or upper middle class, with the late Jean Anyon from the USA saying: 'My parents were labor organizers in the factories of the northeastern US. My father later became a professor at the University of Pennsylvania; my mother was a post-abstract expressionist painter ... .'

The British academic, Heather Joshi, also had highly educated parents: 'I was born to parents who were both Cambridge-educated scientists. My mother had a PhD in Zoology. My father just had a polymathic reputation, which took him into the codebreaker team at Bletchley, although his day job was as a marine biologist. My mother gave up paid work in 1945, although she never stopped being a scientist. Apart from a couple of years when she taught sixth formers Biology on a part-time basis, she did not "return to work" until 1967. This was precipitated by the wreck of the Torrey Canyon, from which she emerged as a leading international expert on biological and practical aspects of marine oil pollution. She stopped this work soon after my father retired in 1972, but was awarded an MBE for her work. My maternal grandmother was one of the first women to graduate from the London School of Economics circa 1905, but her career in paid work was mostly before that. She was a saintly figure who envied me the opportunities my generation had. My paternal grandmother was a conventional upper middle class lady who doted on my father and objected to my mother taking paid work ... .'

Sandra, now a Canadian citizen, is originally from the United States, and her mother is like Wendy's: 'My parents were teachers, although my mother stopped work when she was pregnant with me, and did not go back to teaching. She was a physical education teacher and my dad was an art teacher. He taught in elementary and junior high schools when I was young, then moved into high school teaching for most of his career ... Both of my parents had bachelor's degrees ... Additionally my father had a master's degree in educational administration ... for which he took courses part-time at night ... I also remember him teaching summer school courses in English and history, as teachers in those days did not make much money. "Teachers' salaries' were always bemoaned as low ... My dad had been upwardly mobile by becoming a teacher, as his parents were Jewish immigrants from Poland and his father worked in a factory. My mother was slightly downwardly mobile, as her family was well-established in Detroit and her father and grandfather were businessmen. The Depression affected both their families and their own lives as young people ... .'

Another Canadian, Alison, wrote about her 'working class family': 'My father worked for the government. I remember that money was short but my mother couldn't work outside our home – government policy. When I was six, she returned as a bookkeeper ... My mother graduated from high school but my father had had to go into "service" when he was approx. 16 ("under-footman"), then immigrated to Canada. Dad had been offered a scholarship for high school but his mother (much married, often single parent, housekeeper) told him, according to family myth, that "his family was working class, always had been working class and always would be working class". Dad finished high school in Canada, rode the rails to Vancouver, and was unemployed for several years. It was the height of the Depression. Money was available for training as a radio operator, so he became a radio operator. Finally he got a job and he and Mum could get married'.

Sue is from a New Zealand working class family: 'Mum and Dad didn't believe in married women working, but she took occasional temporary work such as supervising the exams at the local district High School. My mother saw herself as a city girl (from Auckland). She had to leave school at 14 after one year in the commercial course at a technical school. She would love to have done an academic course and wanted to be a librarian. Her own mother had spent three years in a mental institution and left the family and country (when Mum was about ten) after discharge from the asylum. Mum had to move from Auckland to Palmerston North to support her father's new taxi business, but soon found herself nursing him as he was dying of cancer. She met my father when he was still at high school. Dad was from a working class family of six and grew up in Palmerston North. His mother was of Danish descent and from a hardworking farming family ... she was determined that all six of her children would finish secondary school, despite having a husband (formerly a dairy factory labourer and door-to-door salesman) who was out of work throughout the Depression. My Dad completed secondary school and wanted to follow his sister and three brothers to primary teacher training college ... but the college (in Wellington) was closed during the Depression. So he became an office junior at a stock and station firm (selling farm supplies) ... He remained in this rural work all his life ... .'

'First-in-the-family' to Go to University

One way to try to establish the changing class trends across the three cohorts is somewhat different from the processes that Banks used for her four cohorts. Although I did not specifically ask my participants whether they were 'first-in-the-family' to go to university they volunteered the information for me. This is produced in the table below, adding some of the social class information from the table above, to complete the picture. Overall, only a little over a quarter claimed to be from working-class families whereas nearly double said they were 'first-in-the-family'. This clearly illustrates how the expansion of HE, specifically to include women's professions such as teacher education and social work, has become part of the expanded university. It also produces very interesting class trends across the three cohorts, with proportionately more from the working class in cohorts 2 and 3 than in cohort 1. Equally there has been a growth in the proportions from of 'first-in-the-family' middle class in cohorts 2 and 3.

Only one in five of cohort 1 participants said they were working class (14/66) whereas two out of five said they were 'first-in-the-family', although occasionally this refers only to being the *'first-**girl**-in-the-family'*. This latter includes 12 upper middle class women such as Marilyn and Annette, who said: 'I was the *first girl*

Table 4.4   First-in-the-family or first generation to go to university

'First-in-the-family' with working or middle class family	Cohort 1 (1935–1950)	Cohort 2 (1950–1965)	Cohort 3 (1965–1980)	Totals
'First-in-the-family'	26 (39%)	21 (66%)	8 (75%)	55 (50%)
Working Class	14 (21%)	12 (38%)	4 (33%)	30 (27%)
Middle Class 'First-in-the-family'	12 (18%)	9 (28%)	4 (33%)	25 (23%)

in my family to go to university [but] I was born in London to a prosperous landed gentry Jewish family of Sephardi origins ... .' It also includes people like Nira: 'born in Tel Aviv ... I was *the first in the direct family to go to university* although my parents had cousins who went to university in Lithuania'. And Maggie who said that she was '"first-in-the family" to uni. but as far away as possible as I had to escape from home due to my stepmother'. Linda also said that she was: 'Lower middle class. One sister, 5 years older. First in my family (including the extended family) to go to uni. Mother had got matriculation; worked in a bank until forced to retire on marriage (because of the then "marriage bar"). Father was a buyer of menswear in a department store (left school at 13 to support widowed mother)'. Fiona said that her 'parents were working class who became middle class after the war by virtue of my father's progression at work as a design engineer. I had two elder brothers but I was first to go to University across the whole extended family. Mother was a housewife/artist. My parents were proud that I went to university but they also thought that it would provide me with a good marriage'. And there are several shades in-between even in this cohort, with Ruth, whose conception of 'first-in-the-family' implies to full-time HE: 'My father was a school teacher in a secondary modern school (teaching English, and also drama as an extra-curricular activity) having done emergency teacher training after the war. His family were Jewish immigrants ... My father had left school at 14 when the family moved to London. When I was 10 he achieved a degree in Sociology from Birkbeck studying part-time ... My mother was a piano teacher, and taught music in schools, when I was growing up. Effectively, as far as any of us knew, *I was the first in the family* and the first amongst cousins to go to University. There was no economic support from family from the point when I left school ... .'

The working class 'first-in-the-family' are more clear cut, with examples like those already mentioned planning to be teachers. Lyn: (12 years after Ellen from Ballarat, Australia) said: 'mine is definitely a working class family ... father was a milkman (brought up on a small diary farm) mother a mender in a woollen mill (or full time housewife). Both left school at minimum age (14)'. Diane also said that she was from a: 'Working class family, oldest of 8 siblings. Father left school at 13 to become a coalminer, mother left school at 16 to work in the office of a factory but became a housewife on marriage ... .' Val also mentioned her working class background: 'Born in late 1947 and so I was a babyboomer in a Rochdale slum, spending my first 5 years of life in a Victorian slum with an outside toilet ... Mother was 20–21 when I was born – very young parents who had a shotgun wedding'; Carol told of her: 'upper (aspiring) working class parents, both hairdressers, one brother three years older. I was first to go to Uni although my brother did later ... ' and finally Vaneeta said that she was 'born into a second generation working class Italian-Franco-American family where neither of my parents completed high school'.

Two-thirds of cohort 2 said they were 'first-in-the-family' whilst only a third said they were working class. Examples of the range of middle-class families are: 'Neither of my parents went to university, but both had full secondary education. In a different generation my mother would certainly have progressed to university – after taking the Leaving Certificate she worked in the civil service until she got married. Later in life, she attended university extra-mural courses in a range of subjects (including philosophy) and took some pride in being a "university student"' ... 'No-one had been to university before me ... father worked in a small flooring company; mother a primary school teacher ... ': 'My parents were shopkeepers and wealthy enough for us to have a comfortable childhood. Mine was a large family and schooling was important. My parents didn't go to university but there was a strong emphasis on being successful at school. I was however the only person in my family to make it to university proper'. ... 'My adopted parents were self-employed (newsagents and sub-post office businesses) and *I was the "first-in-my-family" to uni*' and yet another said: 'I was the eldest girl and in the end my parents had six children (in the space of seven years!) ... My father trained to be a priest ... but decided against it the year he was due to be ordained ... my mother was from a large Catholic family. *Neither parent went to university but my mum trained to be a primary school teacher.* My father used wireless skills learned at the end of the war to get into computer engineering. He worked for IBM for most of his life'. And also another said that she was from a 'marginally middle class, father foundry manager, mother housewife' family ... .'

Working class families in cohort 2 include: 'Parents were both working class, but aspirational middle class. *Neither went to HE.* Father wanted to and gained entrance qualifications, but his parents sent him out to work as they needed his income. It was a lifelong hurt for him that he wasn't able to be a lawyer. He was an insurance manager, but also did very well during the war and rose to the rank of major. My mother was half Maltese and immigrated to the UK when she was 13 – very bright, but absolutely no educational opportunities. She married young and had my sister when she was 20. All my mother's creativity went into the home – cooking, gardening, dress-making etc. – very Catholic!' ... 'Eldest daughter (of two) of a postman. Mum stayed at home and did occasional waitressing or factory work to supplement income. We lived in council housing throughout my ... adolescence. Neither parent had any form of education post 14'. ... 'Skilled working class family – I was the *first to go to University.* My father was a toolmaker and my mother was a bus conductor and then owned a café (she came from a family of shop owners). My brother was expelled from school at 15, married and emigrated to Australia, divorced and returned ... My sister also left school at 15 and went into a factory' ... 'Working class background in Cheshire with 5 siblings. My parents left school at 14 and dad began as a farm labourer and lived on a farm in a tied cottage, and three of my siblings were born in wartime' and: 'Very poor working class family, eldest of five siblings. My father left school at 14 and worked as an unskilled labourer for most of his life – his longest job was in an abattoir. My mother left school at 15, married at 19, and worked first as a factory worker and then a secretary. We lived in rented flats and then on a rough council estate. No-one in my family had been to grammar school, let alone university ... .' ... 'Born ... to young parents (mum 19 and dad 21). Mother's background upper working class; father's lower working class. We all lived with my grandparents until I was five when my parents got a council flat ... both parents left school at minimum age ... ' ... 'an upper working class family ... nobody in the family had been to university'; ... 'I was born into a working class family. My father was a manual worker in an oil refinery, my mother a housewife ... ' Finally two of the BME women told of their similar Caribbean influences: Ann was 'born to a peasant family (mother a nurse and midwife; father an electrician; *neither parent went to university*) in the Caribbean' and whereas Heidi's is more mixed with Trinidadian teachers: 'My mum is Austrian and my father was Indo-Caribbean. They met in London ... I was born in 1958 ... and my brother is a year older than me. It was the 1950s, the whole period of no dogs, no Irish, no blacks – it was a very difficult time for both of them. So we went to live in Trinidad when I was 4 years old. I was schooled up until 16 in Trinidad'.

To conclude, from cohort 3 a quarter said they were working class, whilst three quarters were 'first-in-the-family'. Examples of working class families are: 'My father was a first generation Irish immigrant (Catholic) who worked in the wholesale fruit and veg trade. My mother was a protestant, born in the English midlands to market traders ... My mother worked all her working life as a seamstress in a factory ... My parents separated when I was 6. *I was the first and am still the only member of my family to go to university*'. Another was also 'first-in-the-family' and working class: 'the third child of three ... My father, around that time worked as a labourer for his father who owned a quarry. Later my dad became a hospital porter ... My mum did not undertake when I was a small child ... I'd describe my family as working class, although partly because of my grandfather's relative wealth from his business, we lived in what was a middle class area, in a relatively large house, with a large garden, large car etc. So, overall, I'd say definitely working class in terms of "cultural capital" but with a middle class home etc. My parents placed a lot of value on education for us as children. Both parents left school at the end of compulsory schooling ... ' And: 'father a police officer/mother a nurse so, I guess, working class and I was the first-in-the-family to go to university. My elder brother became successful in sales after leaving school at 16 and entering a YTS. My middle brother attended a number of universities before returning as a mature student, and successfully completing a business studies degree. My youngest brother works in telesales after completing a vocational qualification at a further education (FE) college'. More ambiguous is her colleague, when she explains her class background: 'my slightly conservative and deeply dutiful parents – although the fact that I know which (one) of my mum's friends went on the pill *before* getting married (gasp!) is a hint of another story. First of two children ... born to a (full-time) mother who gave up work (in a Manchester department store) to have me, and long hours working, self-employed (family business) father. Dad was/is a printer and was first to go to university if we're generous with the definitions ... he studied printing and design at a college that subsequently became part of Manchester Uni. Gerry and the Pacemakers were there too, I think. My dad was living with his Grandmother and had a scooter ... My mum's family were respectable working class. My Dad's family were either the same or possibly lower (and newly) middle class. His dad was a printer's apprentice, a night – school addict and worked his way to the head of the company, then had a very middle class retirement playing golf and fishing on the Isle of Man (not only for tax reasons though as my gran was from there) ... .' And finally Delia from Spain said that she was: 'Working class – I am "first generation" in my family at university except an aunt (mother's sister) who is a doctor ... .' Whilst Penny-Jane, from the US, simply said that her parents were artists with *no university* ...

Concluding Thoughts About These Feminist University Pioneers

All this shows that the global expansion of HE has indeed allowed for *more opportunities for women as students*. The women themselves tell nuanced stories about the education and social transformations and of their formation in for example, Catholic, Protestant, Jewish and/or BME families. It is clear from this brief analysis that over the three cohorts most participants are not from privileged social and family backgrounds, but have been *pioneers in creating HE for themselves and subsequent generations*. We turn now to hear these stories from the three different cohorts, all of whom have been affected by these global transformations. This has not necessarily been a simple or easy path, as is illustrated by the following comment of the distinguished US professor *Lois Weis* from a privileged and Jewish family: 'I began to self-identify as a feminist when I was a graduate student in 1970 ... I went into the academy after completing my PhD in Education Policy Studies. Feminism is woven through every fiber of my being and has been since the early 1970s ... I began to be pulled by feminist theories and research to some extent when I was a graduate student, but became more involved with this work as a faculty member. As a faculty member I was pulled by socialist feminist theories and associated empirical research. My family was not impressed with my move towards radical politics in general nor feminism more specifically. They in fact took issue with who I was becoming both intellectually and personally'.

Chapter 5

Second-Wave Feminism Breaks
on the Shores of Academe

Introduction: 'The Zeitgeist' of the 1960s and 1970s

The diverse and international women from cohort 1 (66 in all) are our focus
in this chapter, to get a sense of their reflections, from the vantage point of the
second decade of the twenty-first century, on their passions and politics, but
perhaps most importantly, their pedagogical approaches. How did ideas from the
WLM and 'second-wave' feminism begin to influence academe, creating feminist
knowledge and values? What were the particular ideas that slowly morphed into
more academic feminism as the generations developed from the 1950s? My
participants' replies to my questions about *contextual material* on becoming a
feminist *(at university, before or after)* and the influences of feminism on learning
across the life course *(activism versus theories; influential writers)* are the basis of
this collective biography.

Cohort one is distinctive in that their university education, whilst opening up
opportunities for women as students, was also very traditional. For some of the
older participants in this cohort, they were going to university (or college) at the
same time as the older members of cohort 2 were born, namely the 1950s. The
similarities between the younger participants (those born after the Second World
War) – the 'baby boomers' – and those of cohort 2 who are born during the early
part of the 1950s are considerable, given the expansion of university education and
its gradual involvement of women as students. Many of these women are 'first-in-
the-family' to go to university, crossing class and culture.

The women varied about whether they became feminists before, during
or after university but it was mainly *after university*, although glimmerings or
early ripples may have been felt at university, and indeed, for some well before
university. Several mentioned that they had always been feminists and this had to
do with their upbringing and especially their mothers' commitments to forms of
equality. Others said that it was their reaction to their mothers' work and role in
the home. Whilst they all mentioned personal aspects of their biographies, such
as their cultural and social class backgrounds, and relationships to their parents or
partners, above all, interestingly, a number of key texts came up as influences on
their budding consciousness, and desires to change women's situation, wherever
they found themselves.

Few of this generation of women mentioned materials from their university
courses. It was only the 'education feminists' who might have returned to

education after a spell of school teaching that mentioned the growing importance of academic feminist works, as Kathleen and Lois had done. Several mentioned how they themselves had written autobiographically about becoming a feminist and how it influenced their subsequent work (Delamont, 1989, 2003; Evans, 2011; Fine, 2011; Nava, 1992, 2007) whilst others mentioned how hard it was to separate out the process from their total biography.

For the budding academic feminists of cohort 1, it was the development of materials outside the university, and often part of a wider political project – the WLM – that first captured their imaginations and became their passions: '*it was the zeitgeist*'. Leaders or 'best-known' second-wave feminists were often cited: names mentioned before such as Simone de Beauvoir, Betty Friedan, Germaine Greer, Kate Millett, Juliet Mitchell, Ann Oakley and Sheila Rowbotham, including some who had passed away in 2012: Eva Figes, Shulamith Firestone, Adrienne Rich to name a few. This is also the case for those who could have been included here as participants: most recently Mary McIntosh (13 March 1936–5 January 2013), 'an influential sociologist known for her work on gender and sociology' as *The Guardian* obituary (11 February 2013) headline announced died. Ken Plummer's obituary stated that she was 'a prominent second-wave feminist, a founder member of the modern lesbian and gay movement in Britain, and one of the most influential feminist sociologists between the 1960s and 1990s'.

The Moving Women of Cohort 1: Women's Movements

How did second-wave feminism begin to 'break on the shores' of academe, to use the lovely term coined by the Canadian feminist, Lorna Marsden (Robbins et al., 2008)? What were the ripple effects of the growing wave as it moved into academe? Cohort 1 consists of women born between 1935 and 1950. Of the 66 women their birthplaces are even more varied than their current countries of residence, although there are clear movements between particular countries especially of the former commonwealth of the UK. Five are now resident in the Antipodes, six in Canada, one in Israel, nine in the USA and forty-five in the UK (with forty-one in England, one in Scotland and three in Wales). These women were not all born in the countries in which they reside and this is significant for their stories *but* the early stirrings of a feminist consciousness were being felt everywhere.

Some of the most intriguing movements are of the six women now in Canada, since only one was born there (Alison Griffith), whilst three were born in the UK (Jane Gaskell, Meg Luxton and Marilyn Porter) one in the USA (Sandra Acker) and one in Germany (Margrit Eichler). The one woman in the USA who was not born there was born in Canada (Harriet Freidenreich). By contrast, almost all of the US women were born there (Jean Anyon, Michelle Fine, Frinde Maher, Catherine Marshall, Judith Raymo, Maxine Seller, Kathleen Weiler, Lois Weis) and two others – one now resident in England and one in Canada (Vaneeta D'Andrea and Sandra Acker). There are ten women from the USA and another two from Canada.

Similarly all the five women from the Antipodes were born there as was Ellen Malos now in England. This is also the case for the majority of the women in the UK, with forty-five born there, including the Israeli woman (born in England Judith Abrahami), and the three now resident in Canada (Jane Gaskell, Meg Luxton, Marilyn Porter). There is also the interesting question about the women's movements (in both senses) and forms of migration. Although there are clearly movements across the country for both those of the USA and the UK, there are not many movements in the UK between England, Scotland and Wales with only one born in Scotland (Gail Wilson) and three in Wales (and all now resident in either England [Dulcie Groves and Caroline New] or Canada).

There are earlier migrations too with one woman born in Italy to refugees from Poland at the end of the Second World War, coming to England as a baby and those daughters of recent refugees from Europe. Most have Jewish family backgrounds as does one Israeli woman now in England born in the then Palestine and one who came from South Africa. There are twelve Jewish women (four from the USA) in this cohort although this may affect their views differently since their socio-economic backgrounds are rather varied.

There is but one (BME) woman from India who spent her childhood in Uganda and was educated in the US before migrating to the UK. Avtar exemplifies how my participants melded together their personal and educational journeys especially through feminist or women's literature to create new lives for themselves. Her education crossed continents, cultures and subjects with an initial desire to be an agricultural economist in a developing country, given that she had spent much of her childhood as an Asian living in East Africa, and studied in the USA, before coming to the UK for further studies. Her becoming a feminist predated her university education: 'I went to university in California (UC-Davis). I studied agriculture for my BSc and Adult Ed for MSc in Madison Wisconsin. I took these subjects because I wanted to return to Uganda to work in the agricultural sector. But during my studies, I found that I enjoyed social and humanities courses much more than my major subjects ... I became a feminist when I was about twelve when I read novels by a Punjabi writer called Nanak Singh. I was also influenced by Amrita Pritam, a Punjabi poet and novelist and Waris Shah, another renowned Punjabi writer. They all critiqued women's position in Punjabi society. I have been deeply influenced by feminism, and have contributed to it both through activism as well as theory ... I did a PhD at Bristol University on intergenerational continuity and change among Asian and white respondents, and questions of marriage, family and gender were part of it'.

Another woman also migrated from Germany to the USA for her graduate education before settling in Canada. Margrit Eichler went from studies at the Free University of Berlin, Germany to graduate studies at Duke University in the USA. When she applied for her first teaching post, in 1971, she 'applied ... saying I wanted to teach on women'. Stories of a US sojourn for graduate education were a key to becoming feminists for this cohort.

Becoming Feminists through US Graduate Studies: A Sign of the Times?

Several spent time in the US where they became feminists, it being the late 1960s–1970s. Their US studies were critically important though they may have had earlier presentiments about becoming feminists around their mothers' views and roles, but few stayed on in the US. *Helen* said: 'I went to the States after a rather conventional English degree out of a sense of excitement about American literary and popular culture and discovered there a radicalism I'd not shared in Britain (despite '68 and all that). Feeling personally freer in the States allowed me to discover my feminism and participate in the early WLM. *I became a feminist when I undertook an MA at Louisiana State University from 1969 to 1971.* I read Betty Friedan's *The Feminine Mystique* and immediately joined the National Organization of Women (NOW) and CR and campaign groups'.

Liz, going to university in the 1960s in England went on to the USA to do a Masters, writing that she went to 'Oxford in the mid-1960s to do PPE (Politics, Philosophy and Economics) but the why is interesting: I did Oxbridge entrance in English but got called for interview for PPE as the admissions tutor decided that I would make a good social scientist from reading my entrance exam essay – she was probably right but I have always been somewhere between arts and social science. From Oxford I went to the University of Sussex to do a doctorate in the Sociology of Art and Literature but spent a year at Cornell University whilst doing my studies. *I was there from 1969–70 and joined the first ever women's group – we marched, sat in, and campaigned for abortion rights* (my emphasis) I returned to the UK and went to Scotland in 1971 but did not really get involved in feminist politics there – made some good friends in the "Women in Action" group and did march in favour of abortion rights – SPUC off. This was more of a big step for my partner with whom I started living in 1972 as he was raised a Catholic but still joined in the march … By listening to Ellen I've been reminded that I too was a "tomboy" and preferred playing with my brother to my sister as I regarded her as unbelievably wet but am now much closer to her than to my brother – this could be partly the influence of feminism and indeed "sisterhood"?'

Two Canadian women went to college [university] in the US where they '*found feminism*' with one deciding to stay on living in the US, as *Harriet* said: 'I became a feminist while I was at graduate school at Columbia University (1968–73) when I participated in a CR group together with other grad students. Feminism, especially Jewish feminism, has helped to shape my life and career. I consider myself to be a moderate "equal rights" feminist, not an activist. I live my life as a Jewish feminist in my home, my synagogue and my community, as well as in my professional life as a professor of Jewish history and European women's history … '.

Jane Gaskell, a Canadian academic who went on to write about feminism's impact on education, and to be Dean of the Ontario Institute for Studies in Education, now part of the University of Toronto, went to college in the US, including graduate work, before returning to Canada: 'In 1968 I graduated with a major in sociology from Swarthmore College, a Quaker, liberal arts college outside Philadelphia. I received an excellent academic education, and a strong introduction to activist politics, but never had a female professor and never discussed feminism. The next year I moved to Harvard to study in the Graduate School of Education. In the student paper, I saw an advert ... for a women's liberation group. Looking for political action and extra-curricular activities, I went to the address mentioned in the ad. There must have been 60 women gathered in someone's apartment. We were formed into CR groups of about 15, and I stayed with my CR group, attending meetings once a week, until I left Cambridge 3 years later. *This is the group that taught me feminism* ... most of us were white ... We read feminist texts, often photocopied, ephemeral material ... We shared tales of orgasms, rapes, housework and men and we discussed what it all meant for a theory of feminism and political action. This reading was by far the most exciting reading I was doing as a grad student, although I took some classes that discussed women's issues, e.g. Talcott Parsons and a ... seminar with Matina Horner ... She was a model of feminist intellectual challenge and became president of Radcliffe. She was also pregnant, and talked about it in class'.

Nira Yuval-Davis, the renowned feminist theorist of inter-sectionality, *became a feminist in the US*, also in Cambridge and through her sociological fieldwork on new Jewish movements about the same time: 'I was born in Tel Aviv in Yeshuv Palestine ... My mother was a housewife and fulltime mother and was one of reasons I did not want to live life just via and through family. My initial studies at the Hebrew University in Jerusalem were in sociology and psychology. My parents were proud of my school achievements. All this was pre my becoming feminist although my gut feeling was as a feminist, and my mother said Golda Meir should be my role model. *I only became a feminist (and socialist) in the US.* I married in 1965 and Uri went to the US to do a PhD at Brandeis ... it was at a time when wives followed husbands ... I started to do a distance PhD at the Hebrew University on '*Different Ways of being a Radical Jew in the Diaspora*' and attended classes at Harvard and so I was exposed more to feminist activism and ideology. I became a mother and interviewed Jewish feminists ... one told me a joke that a non-Jewish woman was a sex object but *a Jewish woman is a good sex object with a brain* ... Uri decided to settle in Britain because his father was born here so we moved here in 1973 and I finished my PhD at Sussex. I was conflicted about Harvard positivism (such as Talcott Parsons) but sociology extended my world – I loved it so much ... Britain also extended my world and sociology and another key moment was the 1974 BSA conference on feminist sociology – with Diana Leonard and Sheila Allen ... and outside sociology the European Socialist-Feminist Forum and other feminist and socialist organizations. When I came to Britain I realized fully how sociology extended visions ... Feminism has been very influential in my learning, and from PhD work, shortly after finished my PhD I started to study feminist aspects of the Zionist project, and the role of women in Israeli military and in national reproduction ... '.

Maggie also became a feminist in the US, but later in the 1970s: 'Partly with experience of discrimination, partly teaching at the University of Massachusetts in 1977 with a lively feminist studies programme. Feminism was very influential (but not more than class). It took me eventually into founding women's studies, attending feminist events both academic and activist. And, above all, in my general life and family experiences'.

Two women who were born in the USA left, although their feminist stirrings also were in US graduate school and before. Vaneeta D'Andrea said that: 'I studied secondary education and social science at college [university] on the advice of a high school guidance counselor who told me that my dream of being an archeologist was not possible because "girls are not archeologists" but that I could be a history teacher "which was much the same thing". I became a feminist in the early 70s after completing a master's degree and while I was in my first university level teaching post. I was involved in the development of a group of courses on women's issues during this employment in a community college and it was this group of women who raised my consciousness. I also took this community college to court on the basis of sex discrimination and won the case in the Federal court in Maryland ... I then worked on my doctorate which was also on a feminist issue. I have tried to influence feminism both through my research, my teaching practices and by being an activist ... I took on responsibility to organize the regional chapter of Sociologists for Women in Society (SWS) while in the USA and was involved in American Sociological Association (ASA) from the 1970s until I came to UK 20 years ago. Since the 1970s feminism has always influenced how I understand materials and pedagogies ... and any work that I do ... SWS was a regional group part of ASA and grew out of its work ... it was national and got to be so big we started to organizing regionally and based on a support group concept and all academic women get-together monthly ... presentation on recent research ... or group be critical friends. This was very important because many of the women were the only woman in their department in 1980s ... so for most it was the only chance for real feedback ... It was really important for me. So I put some effort into it ... When I moved to London I joined a group at City University and LSE with Sylvia Walby and Michelle Barrett when Sylvia was at LSE and met there ... monthly ... pretty heavy duty theoretical analysis of women's issues. It was different from an activist orientation ... and then I left City and learnt later that it all disintegrated ... '.

Sandra also melded together her personal reasons for becoming a feminist – her views of her mother's life – with the early stirrings of feminism in the USA in the late 1960s and the literature, especially Betty Friedan's work: 'In one sense I was always a feminist. I did not see why my mother, who was so intelligent, was a housewife and devoted to her children (us) without directly using her education. My parents encouraged all of us to do well in school and go on to higher education and into careers (though we were also to get married). I think my first exposure to feminism *per se* was reading Betty Friedan's *The Feminine Mystique*, which I loved. However, I can't remember when I read it. I think it must have been when I was at graduate school, not undergraduate. The late 60s were such a time of upheaval and feminism came along with student protest and civil rights and anti-Vietnam protests. Students formed CR groups and I belonged to one of them. It was exhilarating … . I think I have approached most of my scholarly pursuits through the lens of feminism – both research and teaching. I also have a feminist way of looking at relationships, family, media, and everyday life. I have never been an activist in the usual sense but have tried to change people's thinking through my teaching and writing. Earlier in my career I did quite a lot of organizing of seminars and workshops and so forth on various aspects of gender and education … '.

Other US Stories of Becoming Feminists in Graduate School as *Incredibly Cathartic'!*

Several US feminists mentioned how important graduate school was, along with more personal factors, such as family disapproval, divorce and having children. Lois Weis's comments at the end of Chapter 4 show the complexities although she remained resolute, adding that 'Gail Kelly and Maxine Seller, close friends and colleagues, introduced me to a wider range of intellectual feminists from a number of countries: Miriam David, Madeleine Arnot, Gaby Weiner and Jane Gaskell. Later I met Jane Kenway, Jill Blackmore and Sue Middleton … '. Her colleague, Maxine, from an upper middle-class family, said that she 'became a feminist after university. I lost my fellowship in 1957 when I became visibly pregnant – didn't understand the connection at the time. *I became a feminist during my first work experiences*, in the late 1960s. As soon as I started to hear and read about feminism I said "o yes". With a colleague I started a "Women in Society" course at the community college where we were teaching. I also helped to set up a day care center there for returning "mature" working class students. Began adding material on women to the European and US history courses I was teaching. Started reading Gerda Lerner, Alice Kessler Harris and other women historians and began rethinking the whole structure and method of my teaching. Had been at a women's college (Bryn Mawr) but my history instructors rarely mentioned women except as anti-liquor fanatics and slightly ridiculous "suffragettes". For my profs in grad school, women did not exist … '.

Similarly the late Jean Anyon said: 'I was always a Marxist/Socialist. And then during the 1970s, when the US women's movement was strong, *I became a feminist and left my husband for graduate school* … my [academic] work doesn't focus on women; it focuses on macro-economic structural/regulatory framework that constrains the lives and opportunities of women and people of color … '. Another also from an upper middle-class family, having been to Smith College (a women's college), and married before going to grad school, Judy Raymo said that she too became a feminist: 'In 1970, when women's organizations became more active. I began in community organizing and was very active in politics while residing in Westchester county, particularly women's issues. My interests became more academic when I obtained my PhD (2 decades after I got my BA). I have sought to influence feminism through my writing and speaking as well as through leadership positions in AERA and ASHE – I was Vice President of Division J (Postsecondary Education) of AERA and chair of SAGE (Standing Committee on Gender Equity) of AERA. For ASHE, I served on the Board as chair of the Publications Committee … '.

Frinde said that it was a while to become: 'a feminist after university and after 10 years of high school history teaching, at the same time that I began my college teaching career. Although I had been in a CR group in the late 1960s, it didn't really take – I spent the 60s as an anti-Vietnam war activist and a socialist revolutionary who thought that the women's movement was secondary to the workers' movement to overthrow capitalism. Since the early 1980s, until 2008, I was a college professor of both Education (which meant that I trained secondary school teachers) and Women's Studies. My college, Wheaton College, was an all-women's college until 1988, and the faculty benefitted from grants from the government and private foundations to include study of women into the curriculum. The study groups that these grants sponsored for faculty became *my introduction to feminism as theory, history, pedagogy and activist practice.* I joined the ranks of academic feminists as soon as I came to Wheaton and because my field was pedagogy, or classroom practice, my research field became feminist pedagogy … *The Feminist Classroom* sought to influence fellow academic feminists to see the classroom as a site of feminist activism and feminist knowledge-making … .'

Catherine, who was born after the Second World War, in an educated middle-class family and who married young as an undergraduate student had a rather different trajectory. She ruminated about *key moments* although she saw feminism as *incredibly cathartic*: 'Boy this is – that's such an interesting question. Probably around three. Watching, you know, not consciously but sort of watching what my brothers could do and what I could do and how that changed – was different, but more consciously … In actions, around age 18 or so *when I was starting college and a young mother and wife.* And active, in an activist way, around, just *while I was in graduate school*, while I was a teacher, and I became more activist and intellectual around that time too. It became more of both an activist and an intellectual pursuit around that time. So that would be around 22–4, or something like that … The word feminist was not used in any of my coursework or in any of the readings. It was, the 19, the late 1970s while I, when I was searching for a university program, I was, every place I went to look, I always asked whether there was a Women's Studies program, and went to look at the women's center, and things like that. So I was already on this quest independently, but that, there was no marriage between Educational Administration and Feminism at that time … . *Incredibly cathartic*, I think is a good word for it. In that feminism, both as activism and as intellectual pursuit, and as research and scholarship, have been, has been THE way in which I've been able to integrate what I know and sense about myself, about my life, about my excitement in asking questions about politics. And being able to integrate politics, qualitative inquiry, and leadership into one fell swoop, and that really came together, in my mind in several key points. One is when I was putting together my materials for tenure. And at that point you have to basically kind of make a case that of your current, your past and your current research, and teaching, and service and in the process of writing all that, putting all that together, I came to realize who I was. You know. And that was one key point. And another key point was when I, in this, subsequently began to search for other scholars who were doing the same kind of thing, or at least integrating feminist insights with policy and politics and power questions. And when I found those women, and their writing, – that was another key turning point, and *I pursued essentially my, I'll have to say, my second doctorate on my own.* I just labeled it that, but. You know, my own reading of the kinds of things, and my own research and writing, on the kinds of things that had not been there in my university preparation at all … .'

Early Stirrings During University: 'Out-of-fashion' Feminism or 'Real Turning Points'?

Several of the British women went to Oxford, like Liz, all from middle class, privileged and educated backgrounds *not* 'first-in-the-family'. Elizabeth Wilson said that: 'I went to Oxford University in the late 1950s, when there was (as I only later discovered) a debate about why women were being sent to university. In the words of the principal of my college we were being educated to be "diplomats" wives' (she actually meant civil servants' wives, but "diplomat" sounded more glamorous I suppose). There were women dons of course, but they were largely treated as bizarre eccentrics, even Iris Murdoch – and I feel many of the faults in her novels are partly due to the Oxford atmosphere in which she lived … *I read Simone de Beauvoir at university, so in that sense I was a feminist, but it was very out of fashion then* … As I became an academic at the height of the women's movement in the 70s, feminism has been very influential in my teaching and I was also involved in various campaigning groups … I still think that de Beauvoir probably influenced me more than any other writer, because I was so young when I read *The Second Sex*. I was actually more interested in general Marxist theories in the 70s. Having worked in a very conservative psycho-analytical set up I was much less impressed by all the Freudian stuff, although I do still think some of Freud's concepts are important. I taught women's studies, among other things, for a time, but was actually more interested in developing cultural studies during the latter part of my teaching career and actually was most interested in women artists, painters e.g. the Surrealists, most of whom weren't really very feminist … .'

Elizabeth's conservative family background can be contrasted with that of Sue Himmelweit's. She went to Oxford a decade later and also felt that it was at university she became a feminist although there had been earlier ripples from her mother's positive influence. 'My mother was clearly a feminist too but probably wouldn't have thought about using the term – though wouldn't have rejected it either'. Sue had initially gone to 'Cambridge to read Maths as an undergraduate because I loved it and was very good at it. But once I became politically active just before and at university, (I was vice-chair of the Labour Club in Cambridge) I didn't consider the maths I liked doing (very pure) politically relevant. Thought I ought to do something more useful, thought about various other things during my undergraduate career, but still went to Oxford to do a DPhil in maths. But after the first year doing maths courses, when my supervisor didn't help me find a DPhil topic, I switched to economics. I chose economics rather than any other social sciences because with my maths qualifications, I could change to it without doing any further exams. I became a feminist during my time at Oxford, but probably was one before without knowing the term. I had not been unsympathetic to feminism but had not seen it as terribly important ... We didn't use the term feminist but talked about the women's movement ... The *real turning point for me* was *the first women's conference at Ruskin* in June or July 1970. I wasn't going to go because there was a sit-in on at the university and that was more important. There were four to five big burly Trade Unionists blocking the entrance ... and I was furious and I asked what they thought they were doing and I walked in all fired up about it ... I never finished a PhD and did a Masters ... and none of that had anything to do with gender, nor had much to do with my other politics ... same with economics ... and but then the miners' strike in 1974 was another turning point ... .'

Another awakening at Oxford: 'I was an embryonic feminist at Oxford though I didn't call it that. I just hated the male-dominated and public school culture of the place and found the male politicos really off putting. I had gone up to do PPE with early ambitions to go into politics. That's when I realized politics was not for me. When I graduated I went to LSE to do social admin as I thought would be social worker ... I first identified with the women's movement in the late 1960s when living and working in London. Feminism has been the focus of all my academic work since the mid-1970s. Somewhat to my regret my activism got diverted into Women's Studies and to a smaller and smaller segment of academic thinking. Becoming a feminist was really intuitive. I remember going to a left wing bookshop in Camden Town (can't remember its name) and just buying everything feminist I could lay my hands on. And then I started going to meetings, usually of the socialist variety, and CR groups. I don't remember any specific campaigns until the mid-1970s when I campaigned for a women's refuge in ... But very quickly my energies were taken up with developing Women's Studies in HE.'

Heather Joshi, at Oxford with Liz: 'I got increasingly interested in the gender angle after university. It has been a great support and influence with quantitative evidence ... as an undergraduate I remember being moved by Hannah Gavron's *The Captive Wife*, Ester Boserup's *Women's Role in Economic Development*, and Germaine Greer's *The Female Eunuch* ... .' Caroline, from a lower middle-class family, became a feminist 'after studying Moral Sciences at Cambridge and a BPhil conversion course to sociology at Nuffield College, Oxford (because I couldn't think what else to do) (from 1967–69) ... *I became a feminist in 1970*. Someone talked to me about it in 1969 (about the Miss World protests) and it sounded a bit silly to me ... but I then got heavily involved in socialist feminist politics ... I have been an activist mostly in child care and recently with other older women. I set up a Women's Network at Bath Spa when teaching there. I have taught and written a lot about gender ... I read the realists, not postmodernists or reductionists like Mary Daly. Oh and Chris Cuomo, the ecological feminist ... .'

'First-in-the-family' Becoming Feminists Through their 'Readings'

Many participants from fractions of the middle classes were 'first-in-the-family' as beneficiaries of widening educational opportunities for women in this expansive post-war period. Many women had both very privileged education, including in elite and private schools, as well as for their undergraduate education. For the British women, going to Oxford or Cambridge is the case for almost a quarter (nine of the forty-three). Ellen is both 'first-in-the-family' and working class going to the elite University of Melbourne, Australia in the 1950s. On her immigration to the UK, she studied at Bristol University in the second half of the 1960s: 'I wanted to go to University because I had decided when I was about ten that I wanted to stay on at school and did not want to leave school at fourteen, get married and have children (which at that time and place meant to be a full time housewife and mother). I was always a voracious reader of just about anything I could get my hands on. This involved first convincing my father to let me go to the High School (six years possibly leading to matriculation) rather than the Girl's School five years, culminating in the School Leaving Certificate, working in an office or nursing etc.) then getting bursaries in the last two years of school and a studentship with the State Department of Education to go to the University before training as a secondary school teacher, the only way it would have been affordable. *It also involved a very emotional tussle with my mother, who didn't want me to leave home, or to go to University because of her attitudes to class* ... I would have done a pure English course except that it was a requirement of the Education Department to have two teaching subjects. I was immersed in Shakespeare, English novelists and English and American poets, but I also loved history – partly from conversations with my parents about local and family history from an early age. These choices were also influenced by one young female English teacher and two older male left wing Irish Australian teachers of History, back from the war. Returned soldiers were also a great influence in the History department at university and the course was influential in my political development, including Marxist historical work, at a time of right wing backlash in the 1950s ... *I was already a proto-feminist at primary school.* I identified as a tom-boy, climbing trees – where I would sometimes sit doing embroidery after the example of the heroine of one of my mother's books which was loosely based on a combination of *Twelfth Night* and the *Taming of the Shrew* (Edwardian era girls' novels had some good stuff in them), *Ann of Green Gables* ... At university itself, being on the left wing and doing arts subjects we didn't rub up against overt personalized sexism all that much. That came after graduation. And of course that was before we had the reinforcement of *New Wave Feminism*, so had to fall back on our own personal resources – though Engels' *The Origins of the Family* helped. The first important new text was a translation of Simone de Beauvoir's *The Second Sex* which appeared in the early 60s. We did, though, have Communist women's groups. I and my friends were personally pretty fiercely independent in our attitudes. Having called myself a Christian Communist – a la Dean Hewlett Johnson while still at school, I had joined the communist party at eighteen, shortly after Khrushev's denunciation of Stalin ... There was a period in which I went back into school teaching, which was made exciting by the advent of the WLM. In trying to get to grips with what all this meant, I read across many disciplines, including anthropology as well as literature and history, and the burgeoning writings of the WLM itself ... .'

An Australian feminist, Lyn said, 'I went to Melbourne – the elite university in the state ... Like a lot of women I would say I have always been a feminist in the sense of assuming there should be equality and acting on that e.g. in my relationships when I was dating (e.g. paying) and in my expectations when I got married – though I did change my name (and the issue of not doing so was one that was enough on the agenda for me to have considered it). I can't remember when I read books like *The Second Sex* and *The Female Eunuch* and *The Women's Room* but I have the feeling that it was around the mid-70s when I was first working, doing a part-time MA, and later an M.Ed in England. The *influential period and associations* for me were not from my undergraduate time, but when I was working at La Trobe after coming back from UK, when I and many others across Melbourne formed a '*Feminism in Social Theory*' (FIST) reading group which was monthly for many years, and when I decided to do my PhD (part-time, began around 1981, finished 1986) on Curriculum Theory and Non-Sexist Education ... I have worked in the tertiary sector throughout, primarily in Education faculties but including a period at La Trobe as Director of Women's Studies ... *Feminism has been very influential*, both because a large part of my career has been spent working on and teaching and talking and writing about gender and education, but also in specific knowledge and agendas I bring to any of the work I do, and more generally in orientations to research and teaching – for example one of the reasons I got involved in FIST was that the centre I worked in which was basically Marxist in orientation and dominated by men, much of whose work I admired, were embodiments of those 70s arguments about feminism not being a real social theory with a capital T in the way Marxism was, and rated the personal and interpersonal as not as significant – and that is still a live part of my experience working in a senior role in a "top end of town" type of university. The interest in the micro and the personal also I think has been highly influential on approaches to research (and I particularly remember the collection *Doing Feminist Research* that Helen Roberts edited) ... .'

Several British feminists have similar stories about this process. For example, one married very young and was 'first-in-the-family': 'I became a feminist before I went to college. My family was pretty left wing so I got caught up in London feminism although I didn't belong to any key organisations. I read Germaine Greer, Kate Millett etc. and I helped form a local women's group made up of my friends. The thing I remember most was that we talked about sex, and it was so daring and exciting. We learned things about each other (and our respective husbands) that made it difficult for us to look them in the eye when we met them socially. So, when I went to Sidney Webb I took my feminism with me, and did all my projects on women. So, I was quite unusual as a feminist in teacher training in London at the end of the 60s. *And feminism has remained the abiding value that has shaped my life.* Fortunately it also enabled me to create and maintain an academic career and have a lot of fun. ... I have been interested in various theories over the years, from what I'd call the early liberal feminists such as Olive Banks, early radical feminists such as Germaine Greer, and Americans such as Betty Friedan ... to feminist action researchers such as Sandra Hollingsworth to socialist feminists influenced by Madeleine Arnot and you and US feminists such as Patti Lather and post-modernism and post-structuralism through Chris Weedon ... .'

Carol, from an upwardly socially mobile family but also 'first-in-the-family': 'I grew up in a very masculine household, having three younger brothers. I had a feeling of uneasiness about masculinity ... I read history for many reasons, some rather quirky. For example, at school I found most subjects fairly easy to get high marks in, but in the first year I got a lousy mark for history. This meant it became a challenge. I put some effort in and then got hooked. I liked the history teacher at school. She seemed sophisticated and reasonable. However, all through first degree studies I wondered whether I should have gone to Art School instead. I gradually got more committed to history *but the real turning point came* after graduating, when I started to investigate women's history. From then on it became *a passion.* I think I was always a feminist but didn't use the word until the late 1960s. *Feminism has probably been THE single most profound influence and driving force on my academic work ... .'*

Five women, three 'first-in-the-family', all went to LSE but had very different experiences. Jenny, from a working class background where she 'resented growing up in a block of flats and aspired to be middle class ... I was definitely politicized at LSE and I belonged to the Labour Club and being in the milieu of an international university. It was novel for me. I started but did not complete a Masters in sociology at LSE. There were many academic jobs available from after the Robbins Report in 1964 such as technical colleges doing external London degrees ... Those old technical colleges, which expanded their degree courses, gave opportunities for people like me to get a foot on the academic ladder and the sociology courses put on in them had the potential to radicalise faculty as well as students. I went to West Ham for seven years where I was further politicized by many of the staff at the college and being around them was very educational and I was involved in the "mayday manifesto" group ... and the troubles at LSE ... 1968 ... in the thick of it ... I didn't go to the 1970 conference at Ruskin but a series of feminist events in those years ... I became a feminist around that time but did not call it feminism until later ... .'

Another also said that she 'went to my first WLM meeting ... in September 1969 when my youngest child was a few weeks old. I had already decided to study at

LSE but postponed entry until the youngest was one. So I was already a feminist when I went to LSE and in fact discussed WLM at the interview. I was *passionately immersed in feminism* throughout the years I was a student and tried always to refocus academic subject matter onto women's issues etc. I didn't get a very good degree but I was deeply involved in the intellectual and political work. I lived in a collective household and also had to manage looking after three kids. So an intense time. With hindsight I don't really know how I managed ... The CR group grew very large and in 1970 approx divided up. I became part of another CR group for the following ten years.'

Linda thought that becoming a feminist was 'probably afterwards, though tellingly my undergraduate dissertation at LSE was on "Female roles and female magazines" so I think it was already influencing me then. It has been a big influence on my life. I've probably tried to influence disability politics around women's issues more than I've tried to influence feminism. I went to Bristol University in 1974 when I was 26 and started to do a PhD on birth control in the 1920s [you know that because you were my supervisor]. I was particularly interested in Eva Hubback and wrote a chapter on the new feminists ... Practical feminism was parallel to thesis research. I was involved in the women's centre rota ... and reading Sheila Rowbotham. Before Bristol I remember going to some kind of women's meeting or event in South London where Patricia Hewitt then of NCCL on Women's Rights and Anna Coote showing us how to do a vaginal self-exam ... and my feminism has mainly been just the women's movement rather than academic and teaching in adult ed ... not really done much teaching in uni ... mainly research ... but I've continued to be a feminist ... it has come and gone, a kind of *windy path* and patterns are around social justice or human rights or equal opportunities and a feeling of camaraderie ... .'

Mary from an educated middle-class family: 'did Politics because I thought Sociology was a "girls" subject ... I was an undergraduate at the point where the Labour government came in 1964 and the lecturers were publicly pro-Labour but said that the problem with the British electorate is that women vote conservative ... women are preventing social progress and so as a woman undergraduate I felt guilty ... so now I think about how much that has shifted ... The label feminist is too self-conscious for much of my life before about 1971 ... but I did know from about the age of ten that I valued my independence and anyway being "silly about boys" was frowned upon at home. "Real" feminism came later, when I got my first job (1971) at Kent, having started my DPhil at Sussex on the sociology of literature which was utterly unsupervised (with Helen Roberts and Michelle Barrett) ... My initial values (about independence/women being as important as men etc.) made me conscious of the problem of the ungendered person ... that evolved into a more developed reading of the world that can be equated with feminism. From 1971 on I became involved in three forms of academic feminism: 1. Transforming the curriculum; 2. Writing in feminist ways; 3. (and in some contexts) about the place of women in the academy ... .'

Mary from a middle class educated family where her 'Father was a head teacher principal of an adult education institution ... *I had always been taught to be a strong and independent woman; my mother was herself strong and independent.* She went out to work while we lived in on my father's job, so he cooked the lunch and he took me to school every day ... he stood at the school gate as they say! Was taught that it was my right to have a career – that what had happened to my mother (being made to stop teaching the day she married) was unacceptable in a fair society. I became more and more consciously feminist as I went through LSE, started teaching – and realized that what I had been taught at home didn't apply "out there". The constant refrain in my head was (and continues to be) "he wouldn't have treated me/spoken to me like that if I were a man" ... *I also read voraciously the copies of MS (the early US feminist magazine) which an American friend sent me ... and then started reading the literature – fiction and non-fiction ...* I suppose the fact that I was brought up a Quaker was also significant; women have always had a voice and a role and indeed equality in the Society of Friends (Quakers). We believe everyone is equal ... .'

Carol, a feminist sociologist, also 'first-in-the-family' said that she started to become a feminist at university (actually polytechnic at the time) when she was doing [an external London degree] in 'Sociology because it was different to my school subjects and it just looked interesting ... [*becoming a feminist*] with the publication of *The Female Eunuch* basically. At least that formulated *my nascent feminism* ... I don't like that binary distinction between activism and theory: it is meaningless as you can't act without ideas. But I have incorporated "both" in my time having campaigned as a student against women's imprisonment, then being involved in the Rights of Women and their campaigns and also briefly heading up The National Council for One Parent Families in the early 1990s. But I have also sought to be influential in my publications, especially around feminist jurisprudence and family matters ... .'

Marilyn, now in Canada, 'first-in-the-family' but upper middle class, said her feminist consciousness was slowly awakened: 'I went to Trinity College, Dublin in the early 1960s, doing Modern History and Political Theory. My choices were limited because of my inadequate schooling and Dublin seemed nicer than the large red bricks. Indeed, it was. I was well taught and I enjoyed myself, though I didn't work in any driven kind of way, and came out with a respectable degree and a husband. There was no feminism around, either in the literature or on the campus, and little radical activity. The Aldermaston marches were happening, but they were a long way away, and I was still too far under my conservative parents' thumb to make the trek. I remember picketing in support of Travellers' camps but not much else. I left university with a wedding weeks away and no idea of what I wanted to do, and with the words of the Dean of Women Students ringing in my ears: that as I was about to marry I should do something easy – like a Dip.Ed. So I did. I did history and then education – which was all pre-political awakening. What happened then was feminism, and subsequently a transitional diploma in sociology and a PhD in Sociology, which was one of the early explicitly feminist

PhDs in the UK ... *I first became aware of an overt feminist consciousness with an article in the Guardian weekly* while I was teaching in Botswana by Jill Tweedie or Mary Stott – I forget which – but it alerted me to the fact that women were meeting and discussing their problems with the way women were treated and located in the world as it was. As soon as I got back to the UK I tracked down a feminist group in Bristol. I think my early graduate teaching in feminism came in that group and at the feminist conferences and demonstrations of the early 1970s. I was moving rapidly towards a more radical view of the world – both socialist and feminist – and I wanted to root this new awareness in something more systematically intellectual ... .'

Being or Becoming a Feminist for '*Being or Not Being Like My Mother*'

Many mentioned their mothers as key influences either negatively or positively and this crossed class boundaries. The antipodean, Sue, echoed Sandra: 'I was born a feminist! I did NOT want to "end up like my mother" – frustrated by being bright and unable to complete her schooling; not "allowed to work" (married women "didn't"); not a city girl stuck in the country following a husband around; not having her own income; not having a driver's license – in other words I wanted to be INDEPENDENT ... *"Women's Lib" hit the air-waves during my teachers' college year (1969)* and along with my flatmates I read Friedan and Greer, who just confirmed what I believed already and always had done. Organized feminism wasn't around me where I lived and worked until my return to full-time study in 1975, when I met Phillida Bunkle who ran Victoria University's Women's Studies programme. We both had daughters in the crèche. We travelled together to the United Women's Convention in Hamilton in 1979 and here I heard Charlotte Bunch and other radical feminists. I discovered feminist theory and incorporated it into my Masters thesis: "A phenomenological perspective for the classroom teachers and its application to the education of women". My mission became one of developing a feminist educational theory. In 1980, when I moved to Hamilton as a lecturer at Waikato, I found myself the first and only woman in the Education Department. My office was outside the department and close to the Sociology department where I discovered a strong cohort of feminist scholars. I joined study circles and initiated my PhD, "Feminism and education in post-war New Zealand: A sociological analysis". At this point I also started courses in "women and education", wrote and published a great deal out of my thesis and found myself encouraged and accepted by Australian and British feminist educators.'

The Australian feminist Jane, from an educated middle class family, also said that she had always been a feminist, 'partly *because of my mother who was feisty and worked as a teacher* and I was the eldest with younger brothers ... I learnt therefore to question and not to be a good girl at school ... I was not sufficiently conformist but defiant at school but the process of claiming to be a feminist was much more gradual through Teachers College and then when I went to Murdoch to do another degree and teach teachers ... My feminist theories and practice have changed over time and I like to think that there are three strands to my feminism ... one is intellectual work, a second is my academic job especially the work that I did with Jill Blackmore at Deakin in developing courses on feminist teacher education, and thirdly how one lives one's life ... .'

Debbie saw her mother *and* grandmother as hugely important on her growing feminism in South Africa: 'My mother, aunt and maternal grandmother were all feminists. My grandmother Tybil was a suffragette in the South African context and a pacifist in the First World War, during which she continued to hand out pacifist leaflets as the police marched her away (so I'm told). *So not being a feminist was out of the question I think.* However, in the 1960s and early 70s, with my background in South Africa, my involvement in the politics of race/anti-racism was greater than my involvement in early second-wave feminist activism. I guess that increased when I joined a "women for peace" group around the time of Greenham and also a CR group. ... Very influential from early childhood onwards. I had strong feminist role models and education especially from my aunt Tikvah Alper, (who kept her maiden name throughout her life at a time when this was very unusual), my grandmother and my mother. I have tried to be both an activist in campaigns like NAC, Stop the Clause etc. and to influence theory, primarily through my writing on sexuality and gender ... . From reading my main influences have been Mary Wollstonecraft, Simone de Beauvoir's *The Second Sex* and *Memoirs* were so important. Barrett and Macintosh's *The AntiSocial Family*, Angela Davis for her work on race/gender, Valerie Walkerdine et al.; Fiction: Marge Piercy, Alice Walker (and her essays), Adrienne Rich on compulsory heterosexuality. Later Judith Butler, bell hooks – though I think her later work became self-indulgent. Through personal contact and also reading some of the black South African campaigners, mostly unknown outside SA, or only known as someone's wife, for example, Albertina Sisulu.'

Ruth wrote: 'both my parents did social sciences at university and they were politically active in the Labour Party so I felt at home with this type of discussion. *I have always thought of myself as a feminist, my mother did too so it was part of my upbringing.* Before university I was involved in Young Socialists and for a time I think I felt issues of class were more important than feminist issues. I remember "women's right to choose" marches in the 1970s as reintroducing a more overtly feminist slant. In the late 1970s feminist groups were established at university and I joined an academic one focusing on women "hidden from history". We self-published *Scottish Women: Uncharted Lives* because publishers regarded "Scottish" as too narrow which heightened nationalist issues at the time. It sold well. The women's group gave me confidence to develop the research-writing side of my career ... . My active participation in feminism has largely been part of an intellectual life, it has been an important influence on my career and central to sociology. I have not been a political activist beyond the odd demo and participation in women's groups, which have nonetheless been important to me ... My research interests were in sociology of housing and urban studies. Probably Doreen Massey was the single most influential feminist writer. A lot of my concerns were with empirical inequalities though I read Beauvoir, Firestone etc. ... .'

Pam, born during the war into a middle-class family, said: 'I can't think back to a time when I wasn't a feminist although it wasn't named as such until long after I had become concerned about discrimination. WL seemed a perspective which encapsulated the perceptions and resentments of continually coming up against examples of how boys and girls (putting the rubbish out) men and women were treated differently and unequally. *My mother said she had not wanted to have children when she did.* She would have preferred to have taken an active part in the war as a Wrac or Wren, as a cousin of similar age, on my father's side did!'

Helen, a psychologist like *Pam*, also said that she 'recall[ed] at the age of eight asserting girls' equality and often subsequently. We were brought up to believe in gender equality (mother always worked) ... Family was strong on gender equality and achievement however parents took traditional roles in the household ... I eventually joined WLM in 1971 *when I realized the need for action on a collective scale (my emphasis)* ... Key influences on me were Margaret Mead as a teenager. Simone de Beauvoir later; then Donna Haraway, Evelyn Fox Keller ... .'

Mothers' Advice: 'You Can't Rely on a Man' ... and We Need Collective Action

Mothers' advice and how important that was to their becoming feminists alongside their reading and political activity was also mentioned. Anna, with a Polish refugee mother said that: 'My mother always told us girls that you need an education then you will never have to rely on a man. This I knew early on, before uni. After I left uni I got involved in the women's movement, attended the first women's lib conference in Oxford in 1970, and was one of the four women who got together to produce a women's mag in the IS group (later SWP). *Women's Voice* had a circulation of 10k at its height and was produced monthly for some ten years until it was closed down by SWP leadership. I left soon after! ... At university in the 1960s I had read Simone de Beauvoir, and afterwards the SCUM manifesto and Sheila Rowbotham's *Hidden from History* ... Women in the Paris Commune ... later in the 90s when studying for an MA I read the work of French feminists ... .'

Another who is 'first-in-the-family' *and* working class: 'Probably when I was growing up – *talking with my mother and just seeing things around me* – I became a socialist feminist and I was always in primary schools – I started teaching in 1971 and lots was happening in ILEA – remember having the "right to wear jeans/trousers debate" in school etc. That old! Much of my activism has been within various unions – was Women's Officer at my previous institution etc. Feminism/socialism inter-related always – more about my actions in my life rather than scholarship though ... Don't know when I became a feminist but I was pissed off at all the middle class moaning I read about in the 1970s – so I very much identified with Black/socialist feminism – certainly not white middle class women ... some stuff like *The Women's Room* and stuff on primary schools like *Beyond the Wendy House* ... .'

Ruth also said her socialism and feminism were intertwined: 'I've always been a socialist first and foremost, which has always seemed to me to entail feminism. I went to a girls' school where there was an assumption we could do anything. My father left when I was fourteen – so I grew up with the assumption *men were not to be relied on* (and actually, no-one else could be either). Independence was necessary, even to the extent of being a necessary evil. I've never really oriented my work to feminism *per se*, although it pervades everything that I do. I'm principally a social theorist, and rarely write about feminism as such. But I've engaged with Charlotte Perkins Gilman, Marge Piercy and Ursula Le Guin in relation to utopias, and Angelika Bammer's wonderful book on feminism and utopia, *Partial Visions*. And I've spent a lot of time and energy fighting for gender equity in the academy ... .'

Being My Mother's Project Becoming a Feminist

The Australian feminist Jill Blackmore has the most poignant and powerful story of overcoming personal difficulties to being a passionate academic feminist through being *her "mother's project"* because of her polio. Her story echoes those who became feminists doing graduate work in the US, although a decade later. She was: 'born to parents who were both secondary teachers, who had won scholarships to go to uni in the depression, married and moved to Portland where I was born. Mum was 25–6 when she married and was 30 when I was born. She was always first in everything: as the first female graduate of a high school and the first female head teacher of a co-educational high school, first graduate of a distance Education Masters in Educational Administration, and first female deputy President of the Victoria Secondary Teachers' Association. She stopped teaching when pregnant. Both my brother and I got polio in the early 1950s when I was three. It was worse for me as it affected one leg while my brother recovered. I was in a special long flat pram for three years. Mum had wanted to be a Methodist lay preacher as she felt unfairly treated in her family compared to her younger brother because she was told that she could not be an architect or Methodist lay preacher. So *I became her project.* She fought with the doctors about my progress and whether I should use splints and bought me a bike to replace them. Mum cared for me and looked after me, working as a teacher because I only went to school half days – first at kindergarten, then primary and finally as a full-time science and maths teacher at high school. I had both my parents and brother at this country High School. She had such a battle with everyone to be treated equally and it was very difficult for my father and brother as she was seen to be different. This was in the 1950s. There had been early waves of feminism in 1920s – Australia got votes for women after New Zealand and before the UK and USA. Mum was a feminist as an individual not collectively as she preceded the women's movement. She never worked well with other individuals if she wasn't leading. You couldn't have a debate with her, she was always right. She was strong and determined to get her rights; in the teacher union movement, for me, and for other women as she later established as a lay minister and school principal and then she retired, child care facilities at a school, the church and she set up shared homes for single mothers. She joined the teacher union in 1960 after she won an appeal case when she got promotion. The Department said that she did not get funded for the cost of moving as was usual because my father owned the furniture. She was not an easy woman to live with; sometimes harsh on my father, brother. I went at an academic high school where dad taught and then to the elite uni in Melbourne … I didn't enjoy it … I met and married a guy who did teacher ed. at uni. I had won a teaching studentship which would have paid me a salary. It was taken away from me because I was told by the doctors that I was physically unable to teach. They ignored the fact that I played hockey, pennant squab, and had captained the swimming team. Mum put the union case to the government. So when I went into teaching in 1970 it was the first year there was equal pay for women teachers. Mum had just been made deputy principal. I was allocated at the secondary school where she had previously taught. When first married to Glen Blackmore aged 23, the bank and doctors would send the bills and credit cards to him. So I would not pay the doctors bill until addressed to me and I went down to the bank and chopped the credit card up and asked for two … one each in joint names. I was with him for five years but I married too young … he had done his Masters degree first … I was always typing his manuscripts … We spent a year overseas, me in Europe and him in the USA, but came back early and split up in 1975, the first year that the Whitlam government introduced no fault divorce! While I never used the term feminist until after reading Germaine Greer's *The Female Eunuch* (and we called our cat Germaine), I read a lot of women's literature, feminist politics and was active in the Labor party as President of a branch, running an election campaign. I tossed a coin with a friend as to whether to stand for Parliament or go to Stanford. My friend became Health Minister in the Labor government as did others, led by another branch member Joan Kirner, the first female Premier [in Victoria]. I had done a Masters where I did courses on feminist history and sociology. This was while I was teaching full time in a leadership position at a suburban secondary school where I was active in innovation e.g. General Studies as well as local branch president. Once at Stanford, I joined the feminist and lesbians grad network and did a history course with a wonderful historian, David Tyack, and Myra Strober a key founder of feminist economics. I wrote an Australian history thesis in which I focused on gender, but did not foreground feminist theory. After two years' contract at Monash University I developed a more coherent feminist perspective at Deakin in educational administration and policy … .'

Becoming Feminists After Marital Breakdown: Before or After University

Many, like Jill and Jean, became feminists after a marital breakdown. Alison, another 'first-in-the-family' participant: 'It took a few years for me to call myself a feminist. I was separated from my husband and doing clerical jobs for a living.

I was always different from the people I worked with and kept finding myself in the middle of office gossip – my skirts were too short (for which I was fired from one job), I was too mouthy, etc. When I started at Uni, I already called myself a feminist. There I met other women, students and faculty, who named themselves as feminists. I became involved in a CR group and took courses with a feminist point of view ... .'

Born during the war in Australia, Bronwyn said that she became a feminist after completing her BA and 'toward the end of my marriage and when I read Betty Friedan's *The Feminine Mystique*. I have waged war after war on behalf of women – including myself. I could not have done anything without it. I took my university to the anti-discrimination courts and won, I fought for university based child care, for anti-sexual harassment guidelines etc. But most of my contributions to feminism came through my writing and through my active sponsoring of other women and their work. I could not have imagined taking up high level leadership positions without feminism ... .'

Jay, from the British Older Feminist Network (OFN): 'Much later, after children, divorce, and four years social science evening classes, I went to LSE and took Sociology degree 1987. Life between 1960 and 1980 had shown me that social science was at least as important and interesting as natural science. *I had become a feminist, worked as a volunteer in Women's Aid, helped set up refuge, also worked as volunteer phone counsellor for parents under stress (Parents Anonymous) ... Feminism is integral to my thinking, whether at work or in the rest of my life.* It influences what I read and how I react and the questions I ask e.g. about what were gender relations like before patriarchy. I am more interested in changing policy and attitudes than in debates about theory; also in supporting activist groups such as the Women's Budget Group, Women Against the Cuts, Fawcett Society, Radical Statistics, Older Feminist Network and the National Pensioners Convention (NPC) (Pensions and Incomes Working Party). I have not consciously tried to influence feminism, having no wish to split theoretical hairs; but have crossed swords with some anti-feminist women who "blame the victim" ... .'

Susie, from a comfortable middle-class family, became a feminist after her marriage had ended and well 'after university where I had started reading for a science degree and transferred to psychology because I was interested in "people not dry bones". The marriage lasted five years – it ended six weeks after graduating with a PhD. In the years that followed, the analysis of this experience was core to my development as a feminist with the help of women friends. I became a feminist for two reasons: because of working on social identity theory and research work in Bristol, and teaching extra-mural studies about women's health in Bristol. *Feminism developed as a result of or as a key to the divorce* ... a trigger ... My women friends who were exceptionally important to me at that time and helped me develop my consciousness. *It was painful and also exciting* – it freed me up to become a university teacher ... important in consolidating an academic career. I came to Bath in 1976 and have stayed ever since ... [but left in February 2013 for a professorial post at the University of Manchester].'

Madeleine's story has resonances with others like Jill, about mother's influence and studying in the US, but for her the key was *encountering feminism in America and taking control of her life*. Madeleine is the youngest of cohort 1, on the cusp of cohort 2, born in London but spending the first 12 years of her life growing up in Cape Town, South Africa. She is from a university educated family background. Her story resonates with that of Anna as she also had a Polish Catholic mother who, 'pushed us to develop ourselves and go to university, whilst at the same time wanting us to marry and have a family'. She went to Edinburgh University having been schooled in a convent 'where there was no such thing as feminism. I married aged 23, and although I was very assertive, I was also very traditional – I cooked and left food cooked for my husband when I went away. I slotted into a Victorian styled marriage and, as we were both doing PhDs, I typed his. As a student of Basil Bernstein and having become a lecturer by the age of 25 at the Open University, I was familiar with theories of social inequality. However my writing was focused on social class not gender. It was only in 1978 when we went to the US that I first encountered feminist views. I lived in Oregon for a year since my husband had a postdoctoral fellowship there. I joined the editorial board of *Insurgent Sociologist*, met West Coast radical academics and started to think about myself and my marriage. By the time I came back to London my marriage had collapsed and I was now in control of my life. *I came back alone, a budding feminist*. The first thing I did was read Sheila Rowbotham, Juliet Mitchell and Simone de Beauvoir. I began to understand socialist-feminism and its concerns about the ways in which social class had been defined in male terms. I decided at that point to start writing about girls' education. This was an important decision for me and at the first conference on women's education at the LSE in 1979 I met Rosemary Deem who asked me to write a critique of Marxist sociological theory in education (mainly Bowles and Gintis). I subsequently wrote critical pieces on other male theorists – Bernstein and Bourdieu. Over the next 30 years I kept working on what I called the sociology of women's education. I was privileged to be part of the original team on the first Women's Studies course at the Open University working with the late Diana Leonard, Veronica Beechey and Sue Himmelweit, teaching with Gaby Weiner on the first Gender and Education Master's course at the OU and collaborating with such extraordinary innovators such as the late Carol Adams (Inspector of Equal Opportunities in ILEA), Kathleen Lynch at the Centre for Equality Studies in Dublin, Margherita Rendell and Elaine Unterhalter at the London Institute of Education amongst so many others in the UK and abroad. In many ways these early years of feminist work set me on a path that led in two directions, trying to engage critically with the dominant male paradigms in my own discipline and, at the same time, trying to keep up with the phenomenal growth of 'education feminism' and gender research in the UK, Europe, Africa and South Asia.

'A Frightening Blue stocking': Re-awakenings as a 'Red Stocking'?

Several became feminists after university, both for political and personal reasons. Fiona's story also resonates with Anna's in its socialist-feminism. She had gone to Bedford College, University of London and 'it had been a suffragettes' college so I was aware of feminism, though not particularly interested in that sort of blue stocking approach which seemed to me then to be a bit stuffy. However, while I might not have called it feminism, I was intuitively concerned with women's equality in a whole range of everyday practices, from the clothes I wore, to how I related to men, how I competed with my brothers and how I was seen by others. The physics master at school told the class I was a *'frightening blue stocking'*. I was also aware of being what I defined as bisexual from my teens. I was involved in anti-Vietnam protests in 1967, and 1968 but then went to Nigeria where I started a PhD on the effects of colonialism on Nigerian women after reading a pamphlet by a feminist anthropologist which I bought at the LSE bookshop which was a critique of Engels' *Origin of the family*. From 1970 became very active in revolutionary socialist politics, and moved into socialist feminist politics – *Women's Voice* etc. … By the mid-70s most of my political activism was centred on feminism and anti-racism. Central. Up until the mid-80s I was mainly a community activist (Well Women's Centre, pregnancy testing drop in, Reclaim the Night, WEA women's studies) though I was also involved in the OU women's studies courses as a tutor. After that, the balance tilted in favour of teaching and then, as activism dwindled, writing. Key feminists – To begin with the socialist feminist writers like Sheila Rowbotham, but also Adrienne Rich, feminist writers like Marge Piercy, Michelle Barrett, Mary MacIntosh, then I studied a lot of black feminists like Audrey Lorde, *Avtar Brah* … and more recently Iris Marion Young, Joan Tronto, Nancy Fraser and Judith Butler.'

Another Frightening Blue- or Red-stocking or More Personal Reasons?

For Jackie her feminism developed immediately after graduation: 'When I moved to Bristol for a lectureship, from 1971. At Exeter I was vaguely interested in student politics but, if anything, hostile to specifically women's issues. I even resisted options on women and children in history but since Margaret Hewitt taught so many other core and optional units (including religion, social history) I received an excellent education in it on which I drew from the outset when given the chance to teach gender at Bristol. But by the time I had completed my MA (in Criminology), I was (despite a dissertation on homicide) sufficiently interested in female deviance to consider that a possible doctoral topic. This came to nothing … but prostitution/sex work has been a strong feature of my recent work, although I have been critical of most feminist writing/activism on this. My own feminism in the 1970s developed organically with 'left staff' activities, Marxist reading groups, the Working Women's Charter and Consciousness Raising. *Having an abortion in 1974*, brought me actively into WACC, pregnancy testing and the defence of the 1967 Act, but it also created new links with my mother who then told me of her own abortion (arranged via a GP friend) which inspired renewed interest in inter-war history about birth control. I also became involved in education work in schools on abortion and this led me to an invitation to join the management committee of the Brook Advisory Centre in Bristol which led, some years later, to being vice chair ... *Feminism is crucial but I've always been a bit of a devil's advocate for critiques.* It has framed my intellectual career, even when arguing against it. I was raised as an undergraduate on theory for theory's sake and the philosophy of social science, though alongside a heavy dose of empirical research, but have increasingly found both feminist 'theory' and other theoretical paradigms (Marxist, post-structural or whatever) problematic. I was introduced to the Chicago school early on in my university education and its grounded approach to social analysis remains a key influence for me. So in my teaching of "sexual divisions" (as early as 1972), gender relations, the family and work, or, most recently, sexuality ... I have always emphasized critical thinking, including how much gender matters or even whether it does, and activism has also played a much less significant role. In my recent research I have come to know many sex work activists but my publications are theoretical! ... Influences ... first up Betty Friedan, then Sheila Rowbotham, Cynthia Cockburn, Julia O'Connell Davidson are top of my list of important challenging writers (who also importantly write beautiful prose) yet with whom I don't agree in key respects. Those who have inspired me are not the great theorists but those who have engaged in the minutiae of everyday life, including novelists – especially Alice Munro.'

Whilst Jackie's reasons for becoming a feminist are a mixture of personal and political, some proffer entirely cerebral or intellectual reasons. Hilary wrote a beautifully crafted piece about the readings that eventually led her to becoming a feminist, before taking political action. She, like several others, found the BSA feminist sociology conference a key moment: 'I read Margaret Mead and Simone de Beauvoir when I was an undergraduate. While preparing for pilot study of large families in 1965 I read Eleanor Rathbone *The Disinherited Family* (1924). She raised questions about how and why responsibilities for children are shared between parents and the state as well as how the state defined the marriage relationship. *She introduced me to feminism in theory and in practice, in particular as it can relate to social and economic policies and I've been working with her questions ever since.* Working with Roy Parker when I left the poverty survey in 1968 enabled me to write about the history of family allowances – published in *Change, Choice and Conflict in Social Policy.* This introduced me to various strands of "first-wave" feminism. In the late 1960s very few either in academe or policy circles were much interested in gender equality issues in the social security system; "the twiddly bits of equity" as a deputy secretary at the then DHSS called them at the time. In 1970 I joined Roy Parker in Bristol as a lecturer ... The first WLM Conference I attended was in 1973 in Bristol. 1974 was a critical year in my career. The BSA conference on Sexual Divisions in Society was an intellectual watershed for me and at that conference for example I met Christine Delphy, Lee Davidoff, Ceridwen Roberts, Mary Macintosh as well as Diana and Sheila … Mary Mac invited me to join a new group campaigning for financial and legal independence for women which later that year became the WLM's 5th Demand. The 1974 conference established the BSA women's network which was very supportive. The Southwest group was very active. Sharing research and publications was crucial for those of us introducing feminist issues, analyses, evidence of inequalities etc. into our teaching both inside and outside the university. (Ten years later there were still some senior members of the faculty who could not believe there was "a respectable literature" in gender studies!) Many of us were involved in WEA and extra-mural teaching as well as developing courses in the new Social Admin degrees in the Social Sciences faculty. Feminism was present in my teaching from the outset. It was an exciting time and working collectively with other feminists across the faculty was very supportive. It could not have been done on an individualistic basis. At the same time I was involved in producing the fifth demand group's discussion kit which was very popular. The group (about 14 of us) were also involved in giving evidence to various government policy committees as they affected women's legal and financial rights for in the mid-70s with the creation of the EOC Barbara Castle and Shirley Williams senior members of the Labour government these were beginning to be taken more seriously. My travel to meetings of the 5th demand group in London were subsidized in part by the Ministry of Defence (MOD) for during 1974–76 I was a member of the MOD's committee of inquiry on Army Welfare and had to attend meetings in London. (This experience also showed me patriarchy in the raw but it also gave me a chance to get data on the lives of Army wives in the public domain. (A source of much amusement to the MOD's chief statistician – how could wives give *reliable* evidence?) … .'

Gail, from an educated middle-class family went to Cambridge, and only later became a feminist through her work on her PhD: 'I have always found it easier to respect women than men. At an all girls' Scottish direct grant school our teachers were mostly single or lesbian and were very good. At university we were farmed out to long retired chauvinists and/or men who did not take us seriously. At that time I never intended to do a PhD or become an academic. I would say we were aware that women were not always respected, but being young and intellectually confident at school and university we took no notice … Later I interviewed 60 women and some of their partners for my PhD. Considering their situations and reading what literature there was on the allocation of family resources made it virtually impossible not to do so called "feminist research". I thought it was common sense as much as feminism. The nearest thing to a break through to feminism came when I found Bowles and Duelli-Klein's *Theories of Women's Studies*. Being in a desk next to Julia Brannen also helped. Once I … moved to being supervised by Diana Leonard it was full on exposure to feminism … .It seemed to me that teaching on most social policy courses at LSE was so male biased as to be seriously flawed but I was often more concerned with ageism and racism than feminism … .'

Enigmatic Women Teaching for a Change Across Cultures and Continents:
The Fragility of the Opportunity?

Finally I turn to women who first became teachers, like Kathleen and Frinde, before moving into academe and all 'first-in-the-family'. Judith, an Israeli feminist, told of how she: 'Started PhD straight after my MA but after discontinuing only returned to doctoral study after 11 years, when I was deeply involved in non-sexist education and felt that a doctorate would facilitate my activism. I then changed from literature to sociology. My MA is on *Sex and Violence in Jacobean drama*. My doctorate is on *Hidden Messages: gendered interactions in Israeli classrooms* I completed it aged 48. While doing it I founded a Rape Crisis Center. My feminist awareness caused me to change my academic field and hence my career ... I was a member of the board of the Israel Women's Network, and set up and headed the educational committee there, to ensure non-sexist education ... and a founding member of the Israeli Association of Women's Studies and feminist research ... .'

Diane is 'first-in-the-family' *and* working class: 'I went to Newcastle to read Politics and Economics because my father thought English, which was my first choice, led nowhere! And we were both very interested in Politics. Economics was by default. I then did a PGCE primary course at Newcastle College of Education ... I was a feminist in my teens but doing Economics with an all male teaching staff and an all-male student cohort apart from myself strengthened my feminism ... I was always a feminist and was involved ... in pacifism and CND in a very male university when I was a student. I was arrested because I invaded the Rugby pitch in Newcastle ... when South Africa was playing. I was in SWP and it was very macho and not at all feminist and I was disciplined for inappropriate dress ... saw that as part of my feminism ... very male and on economics course where I was the only woman ... very difficult and aware of feminist issues ... I got an economics essay back saying why was I writing about gender ... 1970s activism in a residents' group ... I have always tried to live a feminist life and work in feminist ways but more specifically I was involved in FAAB (Feminists Against Academic Bollocks)[with other participants from this and cohort 2 and others] for a number of years and intervened in academic debates through performance and parody. I have also always fought for improving the rights of women both in schools and universities. As a schoolteacher in the 1980s I was a member of the anti-sexist working party and we agitated to improve the situation of girls in schools and produced anti-sexist learning materials. We held girls only conferences and taught girls only groups in mixed sex schools. As an academic I was actively involved in improving the rights and conditions of researchers – nearly all women and am still trying to improve the conditions and status of researchers [in Cambridge] ... It is now a totally different world – I entered under Thatcherism. I think it has got worse ... .'

Maggie is also 'first-in-the family' *and* working class, her story resonating with Diane and Ellen's about having to persuade fathers to stay in education: 'my grandma was a TU activist and although she died when mother was 12 that is how she explains me to myself – I am a complete conundrum! *Lil was my gran's name – an enigma. Feminism came after socialism. Socialism is in my DNA, it is tribal* – us and them ... I didn't pass the 11 plus exam to go to grammar school so I went to technical college where I did O levels but the history teacher came to the house to see my dad, to support me doing A levels in Manchester and he was persuaded, God bless him! It still gets to me, that sense of the *fragility of the opportunity.* He loved his daughters, and his thwarted aspirations – he passed his exams for grammar school but couldn't afford to go. I loved the Manchester FE college ... fantastic place and very positive experience. Father applied for a charity grant for me £150 in 1962–3 to pay for my books and made a financial sacrifice (of my wages/keep) to support me in that way. I was somewhat careless about it. Surprised how I can still feel it ... I went to a Welsh University after Manchester and did a PGCE to teach secondary. I didn't seek alternative career advice: natural default position. Not a standard kind of student! It was a brilliant place to live but pretty third rate. I have no sense of feminism as a presence. I remember the 60s with the discourse of sit-ins and a Maoist bookshop in the city but no discourse of feminism and no feminist books there. Then we moved to a bucolic city ... 1972–73 it was quasi-feudal to be there, but I didn't have kids then ... formed a women's CR group in this rural market town; a non-metropolitan experience. I taught women and literature for the WEA ... my passionate love of George Eliot; I identified with thwarted women ... *Middle March* is still one of my favourite novels ... and absorbed from that – waking up from the world. *Feminist stuff is much harder ... it's about yourself.* Started in about 1977 when I became a teacher when I was on a mission to save the working class. I read *Spare Rib* ... plus emergent women's studies such as your *Half the Sky* ... *Liz Bird* and Mary Fuller these books taught me and I attended a women's convention convened nearby under the auspices of the WEA. In order to embed *ideas you need text and readings – process of self-education and about pedagogy.* Then I transferred to a college in the affluent south east after two to three years ... And then I went to do an MA in women's studies which was VITAL ... *My trajectory seems to me a miracle.* I have lived with the same man for 42 years. He is also from the north. I have two daughters with him now. Becoming a feminist has been a struggle including one with him. *The encounter was exciting and woke up and smelt the coffee – kind of uncomfortable ... .'*

Conclusions: The 'Second-wave' Turning into Academic Feminism?

All the women of cohort 1, across cultures, countries and continents, were influenced by the zeitgeist of the 1960s–1970s, especially through, not only the WLM as a *political* movement but also the literature and readings on feminism, as is abundantly evident from this wealth of stories. They were captured by the political mood and their own personal situations, which led them all into creating (academic) feminist knowledge and pedagogy with a passion, drawing on collective action and camaraderie. We turn now to cohort 2 to discover whether that, as the wave broke on the shores of academe, its ripple effects began to be felt more strongly, as seems to be the case with those who came into academia with some of cohort 2, such as those mature students, as we shall see.

Chapter 6
The Ripple Effects of Feminism Moving into Academe

Introduction: 'The Zeitgeist of the 1970s into the 1980s'

The women in cohort 2 are the centre of our attention, committed as they are to feminist values, including a notion of gender equality within HE, feminist knowledge and pedagogies. Their emphasis is as *academic feminists*: the ripple effects of 'second-wave' feminism moving into academe. Academic professional life, rather than wider political questions is paramount, although the personal question of how to live one's life is also raised. These are fine distinctions, and the senior women of cohort 2, are, like the baby-boomers of cohort 1, involved in international feminist networks. Many expressed views similar to Claire's about being '*radicalised at university*'. Unusually for this cohort, though, both her parents are university educated, and she went to: 'Bristol University to study social policy as I had wanted to be a social worker. I was "radicalised" at university although family was influential … subliminally! Mother was very independent and my current partner shares my values … *feminism has been very influential* – especially in my personal life and the early part of my professional life – mostly academic interest but some activism e.g. helping start a women's training workshop … It influenced my choice of PhD topic and subsequent research and teaching informed by feminism … my focus was on women and the labour market so I used Hartman on marrying socialism and feminism and *Hilary Land* on … analysing social policy from a feminist perspective … .'

Becoming a feminist was either before or during university although for several, being mature students, university was later in their lives. Many were mature students either married or divorced women returners to HE, significantly more than amongst cohort 1. Radically different from the older feminists, the materials influencing their learning and knowledge were, like Claire, academic feminists, illustrating networks of academic feminists. Some mentioned the importance of graduate school in their feminist formation, but not US graduate school, with only two Americans participating. Some are ambivalent about the term feminist, preferring gender equality and an overarching commitment to social equalities including class and race. One, a board member of *Gender and Education* and director of an Institute for Educational Research (IER) said: 'I am a feminist to the extent that I believe in women having equal access to education and careers as compared to men. However, I am ambivalent about calling myself a feminist as the term can have negative connotations.'

The Moving Women of Cohort 2

These women were born between 1950 and 1965, so many could be the daughters of the older of cohort 1: virtually all are 'full' professors with the exception of four,[1] only one does not have a PhD with two PhDs by publication. Almost all are now resident in the British Isles with only three outside, one each in Canada (Kari Dehli), India (Nirupama Prakash) and the USA (Wendy Luttrell). There are no women from Australia or New Zealand, despite my efforts as their lives were too busy and, sadly one Australian (Alison Lee) who volunteered was diagnosed with a rapidly growing cancer and died before we spoke (but I used her student – Kate Bowers' 2010 thesis as background).

Their birthplaces are more varied than the current countries of residence, illustrating the mobility of academics, significantly for their stories, like for cohort 1. The only American (Wendy) was born there, whilst Kari, now Canadian, was born in Norway, and several British residents are from other European countries – France and Germany – or former colonies, with one from South Africa. As we saw in Chapters 3 and 4, the majority of BME women are in this cohort, with one born in the Caribbean, one in India, one in Pakistan. Heidi was a child when she went to live in Trinidad, only returning for the end of her secondary education, whilst Ann came to England from St Vincent when she was just starting primary school. Some other geographic mobility is with one Scottish woman resident in England, one English woman resident in Wales and one in Scotland.

Religious background is significant in the life histories: one mentioned being the daughter of Oxford-educated C of E vicar father and mother, but 'mum had little paid employment, though she did have a background in rent collecting, and taught for a brief time, and then acted as a houseparent in a children's home, before ending up as a magistrate. They moved a lot with my dad's job. She always felt that she could have done more, though she was very active in the Church.' Many of those born into Catholic families found this influential like Wendy, and the four born into Jewish families. As with cohort 1, being the daughter of European refugees from the Second World War is also significant: Carrie's father came as a child refugee from Nazism: 'I was born in Oxford … my father was a teaching fellow at Wadham. When I was one, we moved to Nottingham when he got a job at the university there. He remained in the mathematics department there until he retired. He was a child refugee from Berlin and doesn't like change … .' Being a migrant is also significant for some such as Gabriele who has 'a strong sense of uprootedness' like the BME women, as is sexuality.

Graduate school in the US is not important, nor is being educated at elite British universities. Only five went to Oxbridge as an undergraduate, with four to Cambridge (Sally, Carrie, Corinne, Elaine) and one to Oxford (Gemma following in her parents' footsteps). Some did graduate work at Oxford (Alison) or at Cambridge (Tehmina, Gabrielle). What stands out as significant for this cohort is graduate work with

---

1　And to readapt at least one has become a professor since.

academic feminists as their advisors or supervisors either from cohort 1, or others, and being a mature woman student: the gradual maturing of academic feminism.

Becoming Feminists: Early Stirrings and Politicization

The four women (Alison, Lucy, Kari, Wendy) who are on the cusp of being in cohort 1, have similar early political stirrings as part of the WLM, becoming feminists during their undergraduate years, with earlier adolescent glimmerings because of parental aspirations or arguments. Two (Alison and Wendy) are 'first-in-the-family' *and* 'lower middle class', whilst the other two – Lucy and Kari – are from extremely well educated families. The literature that they refer to is the emerging work of academic feminists. Wendy told me that: 'I was born in Chicago Illinois USA, in 1953 ... Because of my mother's aspirations (for herself and her children) she raised us as Methodists and then Presbyterians as we became more and more comfortable. This is relevant in the sense that some of my earliest activism and interest in social theory came from my involvement with the church – my "confirmation" in 1966 included reading E.P. Thomson's *Making of the English Working Class* which was transforming, and being involved in the civil rights movement when living in Kansas City, Kansas. *My politicization was in conflict with my parents who were conservative republicans ...* I went to the University of Pennsylvania in Philadelphia in 1971, drawn to their new interdisciplinary "Urban Studies" program. I was in the first cohort of this program and I was in general fascinated by cities, immigration issues, ethnic/race relationships. I had a "work-study" fellowship that enabled me to attend, and was partially supported by my great aunt "Doll" who was excited by the possibility that *the first Luttrell would go to college. She sent a cow to slaughter and gave me the proceeds* (my emphasis). My work-study job was in the library where I shelved books 20 hours a week. I would say *I was first introduced to a collective sense of feminism in my first year in university* when I became involved in the anti-war movement and met older women activists who recruited me into their women's circle. I then became part of the "women's center" group who organized two things: a "university without walls" that would teach courses about women and women's contribution to society and demand various things of the university, including better lighting on campus (there had been many rapes on campus), a childcare center, and the first official "women's studies" course. I enrolled in this women's studies course on Virginia Woolf and admit I found it boring. English wasn't my subject, sociology was, and it hadn't yet any faculty offering women's studies. In my junior year I went to Boston Massachusetts to work in one of Jonathan Kozol's "free schools" and became involved in a socialist-feminist group that met at a women's bookstore in Cambridge Massachusetts. And after I graduated, I became involved in a women's community education center ... I was part of a larger community of women in Philly who were involved in women's health care, rape crisis centers, domestic abuse centers, women's legal services and women's educational access and learning centers ... I sang in a women's choir, and there was an underlying tension between gay and straight women, in all these various activities.

I co-founded the Women's College Program and after working there for two years, went off to University of California, Santa Cruz to study sociology. I didn't really envision myself becoming an "academic" … I more or less backed into becoming an "academic" – and would say that *my feminism has influenced every life and career choice that I have made along the way.* Mostly I would say my feminist "activism" has been more local than global, always finding myself involved in organisations dedicated to improving women's lives, and that my feminist academic contribution has been equally theoretical and practice-based … I have a PhD in sociology from University of California, Santa Cruz. My three areas were "family, community studies, gender". My committee consisted of Pamela Roby, Carole Joffe, Nancy Chodorow, Hardy Frye. When I arrived, I was part of a small cohort of ten students, one of whom was my ex-husband. I was called into the Department Chair's office and told that he was worried about letting a married couple into the program, warning me that I would not be taken seriously as a scholar if I were to get pregnant. While this was an explicit message, the implicit message among the women faculty was that they were all single or married without children – having a child in my second year of graduate school was very unusual at the time. I would say that my feminism was both strengthened and questioned by virtue of what I think was becoming aware of a certain kind of "careerism" within the academy that required women to forgo having children at earlier ages in order to succeed. Issues of family-work "balance" – a misnomer in my mind, have been central to me personally, professionally, and intellectually all my life … Juliet Mitchell, Nancy Chodorow, Dorothy Dinnerstein, Barbara Laslett, Heidi Hartmann, Sheila Rowbotham, Rayna Rapp, Carole Stack, Gayle Rubin – these were most influential in my graduate work – then your [Miriam David's] book became the foundational book for my dissertation interest in studying the relationships between women, family, education and the state – a lifelong pursuit. Later theorists and writers: Carol Gilligan, Jessica Benjamin, Ruth Behar, Naomi Quinn, Sherry Ortner, Lois Weis, Michelle Fine, Jean Anyon, Catherine Reissman, Madeleine Arnot, to name a few. I always use feminist work in my own teaching – starting with the very first adult literary classes I taught in 1977 – using Tillie Olsen, for example – and developing an adult literacy curriculum using women's own life stories … .'

Kari's story starts in the early 1950s similarly to Wendy's, in terms of university studies: 'I was born in Oslo to a father who was a physician in a small-town family practice, and mother was a nurse who worked with him in the practice. Father from middle-class family; mother working-class/small farmers. All of my three siblings went to university, and two are physicians and one teaches high school. I spent the first year as an undergraduate at the University of Tromso in northern Norway and it was probably then that *I began to get more conscious although it was a process over time, probably in secondary school with growing awareness of gender inequality in friendship groups, in the classroom and the curriculum.* I was more conscious of myself as a feminist in my first year at university, which coincided with the Norwegian referendum about membership of the EU. I was quite involved – on the No to EU side – and there were some very inspiring feminists on that campaign. I then spent another three years as an undergraduate at the University of Toronto (1973–76) and stayed on in Toronto working in community organizations. I worked as a community worker where I saw how women living poverty and poor housing were doubly oppressed. I also returned to Norway for a year in 1981 when I did the first year of the Social Pedagogy degree at the University of Oslo, and from there applied to OISE's MA program. My university education both helped and hindered me in that context because I thought I could understand gender relations, yet I was also distant from these women's lives because of my middle-class background and university education ... *feminism was formative in my political involvements*, though less so at university until I enrolled as a graduate student at OISE, in the early 1980s first for an MA and then PhD in the Sociology of Education. *Here feminism was front and centre* and became both a social and political home for me ... During this time I began attending academic conferences, presenting research papers and so on, often with and among more senior feminist researchers (including you). Dorothy Smith and Mary O'Brien who were both teaching at OISE were big influences, as well as feminist historians on the faculty, such as Allison Prentice. Valerie Walkerdine's work shaped my thinking, along with Black feminist scholars from the US, including Audre Lorde and bell hooks ... .'

Lucy: 'I come from London, and my father was a law lecturer at Kings: he had been to Oxford, my mother hadn't been to university. When I was born she wasn't working. Later she did some social work. Later still she ran an art gallery. I had two much older half-sisters. We had the same mother, who had me at 43 (my father was 29! Her third husband) ... I went to Manchester University to do a BA Sociology ... *I became a feminist during working on my MA in social anthropology also at Manchester* ... My PhD was in cultural history, in which I looked at campaigns and debates about sexuality and morality amongst feminists in the late nineteenth- early twentieth century. I taught women's studies for many years, but I have also been involved in activism ... *Feminism has been hugely influential to all aspects of my life. I became a feminist in early 1975 when I was 22. I read various things (my emphasis)* and it suddenly struck me that women's oppression was such an obvious truth. I wasn't part of anything at the time, but soon afterwards I joined a women's group, briefly got involved in rape crisis, and later was involved in various other campaigns (Women oppose the Nuclear Threat, Women against Racism and Fascism) ... Feminist historians such as Sheila Rowbotham, Joan Scott, Catherine Hall, Lee Davidoff ... .'

Alison, born on the cusp of 1950, in a London suburb said that: 'I went to Bristol University in 1968 and I attended *my first feminist group in Ellen Malos' house whilst I was in Bristol.* But I was more active as a Marxist and socialist. I studied Philosophy because I loved big questions and arguing! I realize now (after studying counselling!) that arguing with my father was formative for me and taught me to fight for causes ... I went on to do a B.Phil in Oxford in philosophy of language, logic and philosophy of science and a PhD in Sussex which was political – on Althusser. My PhD which came out as a book was on *Althusser and feminism* so I was using feminist theories then but mainly in an individualist way. I started off being interested in the student movement but mainly Marxist politics and *gradually saw the need for feminism* ... I was influenced by Simone de Beauvoir and many Marxist feminists, Sandra Harding (later), Sheila Rowbotham, but also by fellow students at Oxford e.g. Hilary Wainwright and then later many more ... I gradually incorporated feminism into my philosophical views. This was very difficult because the discipline did not then (and still in some ways does not) really recognize this. It is still a very male and masculine discipline ... *Feminism has been very influential both for me and how I have worked* ... in as many ways as possible – theories: politics and through taking on management roles in universities ... often being the only woman in the role and trying to carry it out in different ways, sometimes influenced, strangely, by the care ethic. Many men said that they had not felt valued before ... *but there were many negatives* ... I was active in feminist campaigns ... I was a founder member of Women in Philosophy but before that I was reading and thinking from a feminist perspective and trying to incorporate this into philosophy (which was and still is very difficult!) ... And I got involved in Radical Philosophy and also activist women's groups and more recently activism against Islamic fundamentalism (through my activities with Iranian women) ... .'

'On ne nait pas femme, on le devient' (Beauvoir): Becoming Feminists Before University

Several said that as far as they could remember they had always been feminist. Joelle, who being French, quotes Simone de Beauvoir and shows how her religious upbringing played a part in her growing feminist consciousness: 'I was not born in England ... I studied literature and linguistics at the local university ... [When did you become a feminist] *This is a very interesting question. "On ne nait pas femme, on le deviant"* (Beauvoir). All members of my family shared the burden of work equally; I went to an all girls' school, and an all girls' college. I don't think I was aware of gender inequalities in my childhood – *the regime (school-church-Sunday School) was the same for all*; the tasks were equally distributed between my sisters and brother; my mother and father seemed to both work equally hard and issues of inequality were not on the horizon as a child. At college, I was part of a quite rebellious group of girls – we labelled ourselves anarchists, but it never occurred to us to locate this within a gender struggle – we opposed power, bureaucracy and discipline without any sense of our own gender – a band of teenagers rebelling against the establishment with no sense of gender ... Later at university, I started to reflect on these issues as I was studying literature – gender stereotypes started to trouble me, and made me reflect on this – still however with no specific sense that this was connected to my real life. At university, I was part of a group of intellectual sharp friends of both genders. In the group, there was complete equality – my voice was as powerful as that of the boys. We talked of literature, theatre, revolutions and considered feminist issues through the analysis of literature texts more than through political engagement. I guess *I only became acutely aware of the power imbalance when I married and had children, and started to observe the roles of women with children, and the gender-bias structures,* and the relation to class (child-minders were being bought to ensure I could get some autonomy away from the family duties) ... I have tried to promote feminist behaviours in my children, and in all aspects of my own private life. I have also been observant of behaviours and structures that disadvantage or misguide women and sought to take this into account – both in practice and in the work that I have written (dependency on male supervisors, complex roles for women academics or women students) ... .'

Gabrielle: 'was born into a Catholic family in Wolverhampton ... Father's work took our family to France ... (aged 13–16), to Japan (aged 18–20) and to the US (aged 22–23). I went to ten different schools ... and several different universities for undergraduate and postgraduate work, completing my PhD in Cambridge as a mature student ... I sought out philosophers and found the department to be incredibly old-fashioned and very male. The only intellectual feminists I encountered were in the Education department (Madeleine Arnot) and in anthropology (Marilyn Strathern) ... *I was a feminist as far back as I can remember. My mother was a feminist, who battled long and hard against many church doctrines that excluded women.* She believed firmly that there should be women priests. As I was growing up there were priests from my father's time at the seminary in and out of the house all the time. My parents were intellectually engaged with theological issues all their lives and the visiting priests always stimulated debate. My father was quite a socialist catholic. My mother became more and more angry with the established church but has never left because it is part of the deep rooted cultural background and part of her daily practice. The conflicts between my feminism and my intellectual engagement as an academic feminist reached a peak when I returned to study as a mature student (after years teaching) ... Up to this point I had been an active Catholic and had married in a Catholic church to a person who converted to Catholicism. In the early 1990s, the tensions between being an active Catholic and a feminist started to break out ... I carried on and used the intellectual work to manage the crisis ... [Having divorced], I now live outside the established Catholic Church and am at ease with the intellectual resolution. I still go to church with my mother and she has stopped probing about whether or not I am a practicing Catholic. So, we avoid the problem ... . *Feminism has been absolutely central to my life.* It allowed me to gradually gain a perspective on Catholicism that eventually allowed me to leave the established church. For a long time I felt that the intellectual, theological knowledge was battling with my intellectual feminism. *I would say that through the twists and turns of my life the one intellectual endeavour that I have never doubted is my feminism. I passionately believe in a person's right to equality and especially to have freedom over their bodies.* I would say that I still teach from a feminist perspective even if my students would not always recognize this. Feminism informs my personal life profoundly. I have on and off been active in many feminist causes, big and small ... *I read Germaine Greer when I was an adolescent, this was a huge influence.* But I was reading Spare Rib as well. *I read de Beauvoir when I was an undergraduate*. But I found DH Laurence e.g. to be a feminist. I read much literature from a feminist perspective without necessarily having any theory to base it on. I think at that time of my life literature as my root into a deeper engagement with feminism, always tinged by theology. I found feminist scholars when I read outside my academic courses, and most when I was doing my MPhil. I now read Iris Marion Young, Karen Beard and other material feminists. I still love feminist philosophers ... .'

'Angry About the Unfair Treatment' So Feminism is Hugely Influential

Another British feminist: 'went to Manchester as an undergraduate; postgraduate Sussex; Kings College, London. I did a PhD on *The Politics of Women's Studies* (which was published) ... I was always good at literature plus I was interested in social justice issues ... Long before university [becoming a feminist] when I was about 7/8! *I was always angry about the unfair treatment that I received in relation to brothers, male cousins etc.* I started to theorise it when I was about 16/17 and through my gendered experiences in CR groups, through literature, with friends, going on marches, getting involved in campaigns e.g. abortion rights, Women against violence against women (WAVAW) etc. *Seeing so many thwarted women (and men) in my family was very influential.* My partner is a feminist and she is hugely supportive of my career and my politics. Feminism HUGELY influential. Too many to mention! When I was a young literature student, I loved Plath, Woolf etc. as I entered sociology ... *Feminism influences/is my whole life!'*

Similarly Elaine felt angry about how young women were treated in South Africa: 'I think at high school, although I didn't have the words or name for it. *I was incredibly angry in a very volatile and upset way about all the relationships around suburban dating*, who of my peers got family support to go to university, whose achievements were valued etc. In the middle of my time at university I had a trip to London and bought *The Female Eunuch* and read it in about one day, and then over and over again. *It felt as though it made sense of my life, when I couldn't.* Both my parents were very influential in different ways. My mother has been committed to herself and her daughters having as much HE as possible and taught sociology ... My father was also completely behind every aspect of our education, had a very strong commitment to racial equality, but sometimes found feminist concerns and demands perplexing ... I think it would have been more comfortable for them had my area of work been less challenging to aspects of the status quo, but they did not ever try to prevent me taking my ideas forward and actively supported my studies form many years and helped discuss many issues ... *Feminism has been incredibly influential in orienting a lot of my research on women* in the ANC, women's experience of forced removal, domestic workers in South Africa, and then later work on gender and education in Africa (Tanzania, Nigeria, Ghana, Kenya) and in international organizations, on gender and education policy etc. It has also been incredibly influential in all the courses I have worked on – both in designing forms of collaborative pedagogy and in trying to connect theory, practice and politics ... women's struggles were in different places ... I have been trying to get people to articulate what it is they do in their activism pedagogically ... Germaine Greer, Angela Davis, Olive Schreiner ... On a more academic level Susan Moller Okin, Nancy Fraser, Obi Nnaemeka because they all play with ideas ... .'

Strong Mother as a Key Influence

Gemma: 'I'd grown up a feminist, but became actively so at university ... My family – hugely influential. *Long line of strong women – a matriarchal lineage going back on my mum's side* that was also super posh versus my Dad's which wasn't. My mum always used to say that being married was second best to having a career. And became very interested in the women's movement too ... I'm not sure there was an active women's movement as such before I got there. I think one of the first conferences [at Ruskin] happened in my first year. I joined a women's group via JCR politics in college in my first year – how I made all my friends ... *at college I called myself an anarcho-feminist and lived in an anarcho-feminist household.* A lot of time was taken up talking with the broader left. And when I started teaching I got very active in the Union. I wrote about this in [my book] *Un/ Popular Fictions* ... I think it was very different in the early days when it was still possible to think that any group of women anywhere could change the way the world worked by sitting and talking about stuff – but out there in the bigger world life got a bit more complicated. I also changed my views about what feminism was for through contact with the working class girls I was teaching. Again this is all in *Un/Popular Fictions* ... I don't think I read much feminist theory. Greer I always found unreadable. I did read Spender, the *Tyranny of Tyranny* and the *Tyranny of Structurelessness*, which we discussed in CR and also *Sisterhood is Powerful* and *Our Bodies, Ourselves.* I think the latter was more important as it gave a way of re-describing and re-normalizing how women think about their own physicality. Put that alongside John Berger's stuff on women escaping the male gaze, those were key in helping me look in a different direction from the direction the social space expected me to face.'

I Was Encouraged Strongly (Pressured by Mum) to Be Successful Academically

Penny: 'Mum started paid work when I was eight, she went on to be a very successful saleswoman until her recent retirement. Dad had unskilled work until he trained as a domestic appliance engineer when I was around twelve. He then went on to establish his own business in repair work and later a pet shop ... both parents ... believed very strongly that girls should have a good education, and *I was encouraged strongly (pressured by mum) to be successful academically* ... although my parents were supportive of women's rights to a career and independence they found my [subsequent] choices (feminism and lesbianism) difficult to understand ... At secondary school I had a very clear sense that I was not going to be 'just' a housewife and mother. I wanted to have control over my own life as an adult, and didn't envisage having children. *My parents' passion for education no doubt influenced me here.* I can't be sure precisely *when I became a feminist but by the time I was at [Sussex] university I was very receptive to feminist ideas. I remember going to the campus bookshop and checking out books on women* – there was a very small section (about eighteen inches long on one shelf). I opted for a women's history course (the only one I can recall from my undergraduate days) *taught by Carol Dyhouse*, and that helped form and organize my ideas. In the early days of teaching (late 1980s and 1990s) *I made a very conscious effort to change how students thought by being out about my feminism and my lesbianism.* I also have drawn on feminism and contributed to it through my teaching and research, especially when teaching WS courses and directing the UG WS programme. The course I did with *Carol Dyhouse was very important* ... I applied for an ESRC-linked studentship with Penny Summerfield and did my PhD (supervised by her) at Lancaster. It was on girls' magazines 1920–50 (also topic of my undergraduate dissertation with Carol Dyhouse). One of the informal conditions of being selected for the funding by Penny S was to be involved in the WS centre at Lancaster, about which I was delighted. I was a very active member of the WS centre (attending reading groups, organising seminars etc.) ... coming out as a lesbian has been very important for my feminism. I've been lucky since meeting Carolyn to be able to share *my passionate commitment to feminist politics.*'

Not Wanting to Be a (Working Class) 'Housewife' Made Me a Feminist

Carole said: 'Dad was a Methodist lay preacher and wanted to be a Labour councillor ... soon after I was born Dad got a job with the union for agricultural workers so we then moved around a lot following his job ... ending up in Kent when dad got a TU organizer job for the National Union of Agricultural and Allied Workers; dad drove and visited farm workers; and in office. My new Maidstone girls' grammar school was a huge culture shock for a working-class northern lass and was horrendous so I left school at sixteen and went to Maidstone Tech to do A levels in Sociology, Law and "British Constitution" (now "Government and Politics"). I then decided on principle not to go to university but to a poly and went to Teesside Poly. So for me the main issue at this time was class ... . Recently I found my sociology notes and it had stuff on feminism and Simone de Beauvoir which I had forgotten about ... . I suppose one of the main influences for me in terms of feminism though, was seeing my Mum's life – as a "housewife" and bringing up children. Mum always seemed to be in the kitchen, making tea, putting on the chip pan for all the kids and doing housework. It seemed to me like household drudgery, in contrast to my Dad, whose work took him out of the house, meeting people, etc. – which seemed far more appealing and exciting. So I didn't want to be dependent on a man financially, didn't want to stay at home and didn't want children or marriage ... so at Teesside I was on the Student Union and its executive and a member of a women's action group which campaigned for a nursery ... But I didn't see discrimination against women/sexism as something that affected me – I thought at the time that I could compete with the men academically and hold my own, it was only for "less fortunate" women for example who had kids! I think my parents wanted me to go to university and they were so proud of me. They were committed to education and I was the first-in-the-family to go ... I came back down south and went to Canterbury Christchurch to do teacher training ... and during the summer before I worked in Kent county council offices which were completely sexist ... having calendars with naked women, fairly blatant sexual harassment ... two of us women met in a pub and worked out strategy to deal with the men. We came in early and ... used every technique they used we used against them. We said it's got to stop. We'll stop if you stop ... ! Real CR and completely turned it round ... the power of the look ... with cleaners' help we put up pictures of naked men. All hell broke out ... but we managed to stay the full eight weeks. Treated warily but no more sexual harassment! So this experience made me realise that sexism did affect me. This was just before my PGCE and during it a student brought in *Spare Rib* ... summer of 1977 I discovered feminism when I was living with a guy! I got totally excited by what London had to offer and got into feminist sc-fi. I read anything and everything. Novels and feminist novelists! ... went to loads of feminist theatre ... . Worked as a social worker ... then I went into FE teaching ... set up a girls' group and went to Grunwicks' strike ... Dale Spender was then a major influence too ... .'

I Had Feminist Friends at School ... Feminism on the Rise

Gabriele was born in Cologne, Germany into a large middle-class family, with five children (four girls and one boy). 'Mother was a housewife who bitterly resented not having a university education (which her brothers did) and father a human resources director. Both parents were clear that all their children would, as a matter of course, go to university. My parents were displaced from the Eastern Baltic, and ... I went to a British army school and so did not particularly want to stay in Germany ... my older sister went to Bristol and Lancaster ... I come from background where this was expected ... My father's paternal authoritarianism strongly influenced my dislike of certain men, my sense of men as irrational and emotional (rather than women being like that), my refusal of patriarchy etc. I also very much did not want to have the kind of relationship my parents had, so could never stand men who tried to tell me what to do ... So I did my BA in Leicester in Psychology, English, German – couldn't decide what I wanted to do, thought everything interesting (couldn't envisage doing a single subject degree) had no clear idea about career but thought of becoming a clinical psychologist (changed my mind following work on a closed psychiatric ward), started teaching in HE immediately after first degree and whilst doing various postgraduate qualifications in teaching and a PhD ... *I had feminist friends at school ... feminism on the rise* ... ideas from my mid-teens, lots of civil movement and groups in the town activism ... but extra-institutional and the woman I had a relationship with at the time was quite activist from a single parent family ... As an undergraduate I experienced institutions as highly patriarchal and hierarchical ... and a sense of disparagement of women and women being regarded as sex objects (a lot of sleeping around when I was an undergrad) so a generally sexist environment ... much later ... I had dinner with *Heidi* and we talked about sexual harassment and we were shocked about how we continued to be harassed - it was rampant ... men thought they were entitled and women didn't know how to question it ... my second PhD (I changed supervisors, institutions, and topics) was feminist on feminine philosophy ... I looked at Simone Weil and Iris Murdoch – women intellectuals in 1950s and their philosophies ... ideas about self-effacement, classic feminine positions rather than feminist ... but I never believed that suffering is good for you ... very secular background ... drew on eastern religions in the 1950s ... .'

Changing Cultures But Becoming a Feminist at 'University is Central'

Ann like Gabriele, abandoned her first PhD, and moved to do a more consciously feminist topic. Ann 'went to St Andrews University, for no good reason, and the Scottish system is to do three subjects, so philosophy, psychology and ancient history ... *University is central* ... I already thought of myself as a feminist at St Andrews ... then I went to Manchester to do psychology for an MA and followed by a PhD that I never finished although I had an ESRC grant. I gave it up after fourteen months having left my then husband when my baby six months old ... By this time I had been in several feminist CR groups, starting in Scotland and I was one of the founder members of Manchester Rape Crisis. Several things sparked an Ahha moment and Ann Oakley's *Becoming a mother* in 1981 was one as it was the year I became a mother ... it all adds up together and gives insights ... just wonderful ... and in psychology *Changing the Subject* ... Liz Heron's edited collection ... I was involved in black politics as well as feminist politics and the two were antithetical ... the split was occurring but I didn't feel myself split ... Both these groups became central to my political activity and to the friendships I formed ... it was lovely when things from black American feminists came out e.g. bel hooks' work ... and really exciting. Ronnie Frankenberg introduced me to bel hooks through his daughter who came over to a friend's house. People bringing together these intersectional elements ... Other people like Carolyn Steedman, Denise Riley, Val Walkerdine, ... it was just great ... I moved to London and started a second PhD at IOE on the effects of daycare on children and interviewed mothers, social workers and teachers. I observed bathtimes and mothers going back to work. *Young Mothers* was my book from my PhD and when I then worked with Peter Moss and then Julia Brannen ... .'

I Was Racialized Before I Was Feminized

Heidi comes from a similar background, also having a baby whilst a student but her politicization had a different trajectory: 'I went to an all girls' school in Trinidad, which was quite high achieving in a gendered way. High achieving girls didn't mean careers for girls, it meant good wives for husbands! The school was started up by my grandmother about thirty years before I had gone there. So *there was a tradition of education among the women in the family.* My aunts in Trinidad were all teachers – so *there were strong female "role models" in my early life* – but they lived very traditional lives in a very patriarchal culture. Growing up in Trinidad I was very influenced by the black power movement in the early 70s – I remember seeing Angela Davis on the TV – speaking confidently to crowds and raising her hand in a black power salute. I thought she was amazing. We had an attempted coup on the island – *black power was an empowering political vision and a crucible for my postcolonial/black feminist thinking.* When we came back to England in 1973 we lived in Brixton and I went to the local school. The racism there was incredible. I was determined to show the teachers and the girls in the school that I was as good as them, if not better. And that's what really drove me to do quite well in my O and A levels. I do think *I was racialized before I was feminized*! That came later at university when I got married. It was so important to get a place at university that was funded! I think if it weren't a free place at university I would never have gone! There was this whole expansion of education in the late 70s, there was a grant system. If I was growing up today I would not have that chance. *It was an opportunity that was there for everybody. HE was being opened out for the working classes, and for girls as well, and it was seen as a natural progression.* When I graduated ... it was very racist times in the UK with the National Front in its zenith. It was very hard to get a job and on top of that I had a young baby. I had got a first for my dissertation so I sent off to Goldsmiths College sociology department and I got an ESRC quota award in 1981. This amazing opportunity changed my life! My PhD thesis was a small-scale ethnography of young Caribbean girls like myself in a London school. Because of my experience I wanted to write about the interplay between career choices and educational structures. So in a way the thesis was about my own life, it was a process of exploring the practices of racism and exclusion which I saw around me. *Young Female and Black* became a best-selling book with Routledge. *It was a carthartic thing to see it in print.* I am amazed it did so well. At the time it was very exciting for me ... [but] there was a lot of sexual harassment of young women students by male lecturers in universities ... a group of women academics ... got together to speak out about their transgressions ... but ... no one would ... risk everything ... At least as women we felt some safety in numbers and found common ground and solace with each other. I began to learn about feminist theory from them. In 1985 I worked in Thomas Coram as a part-time researcher with amazing feminists like Ann Oakley and *Ann Phoenix ... My life chances shaped my feminism* which then spilled over into my academic development. My marriage was very pivotal for me as a black/postcolonial feminist. I got married in my first year of university when I was nineteen and I had my daughter as I was leaving in the third year. In fact I was very pregnant when I sat my finals! My husband was a very devout Muslim, and I wasn't! I converted to Islam during the time of the first Muslim uprisings in the 70s. There was a growing anti-imperialistic movement among the African and Middle Eastern students at university. For the first time I really felt I had a cause. I became personally politicized and wore a headscarf (*hijab*). Ironically for the first time in my life I understood about dignity and respect for women – that is not to be seen as a sexualized object, but to be myself. *So, ironically I became feminized through Islam ...* My degree built my confidence as a woman which I had not got at school ... there was a lot of passion and activism in what I was doing. Rayah Feldman was a part-time tutor ... who supervised my dissertation ... on women's issues ... we later worked together at South Bank – I was bowled over by the opportunity to be there! Stina Lyon took me under her wing and kindly shared her insider knowledge. Miriam you mentored me and gave me my first proper job as a lecturer ... .'

Becoming Mature Women Student Returners: *Early Eye-Opening Influences*

Many became young wives and mothers *before* going to university (like Gaby in cohort 1 but unlike Ann and Heidi), turning to feminism *after marriage and/or motherhood*, but with earlier parental influences. The stories of these five young wives and mothers are all quite similar: 'I had my children as a young woman, having failed A levels, and I returned to a further education college to re-take failed A levels. I fell in love with sociology, never knew about it before, but took Social and Economic History A level and thought they would complement each other. I became a feminist before university, *very strong grandmother and mother. Early socialization ...* I went on to do a BA and then PhD at Nottingham on the topic Women and Work: a case study of the civil service and have continued on from there at Nottingham. *All early eye-opening [feminist] influences.* Ann Oakley – one of the first I read at A level, *Sociology of Housework* – bringing women's issues into the discipline; Jane Millar – addition of poverty debates to feminism. Sheila Rowbotham – *Women's Consciousness: Man's World* – says it all – very political. Sylvia Walby – exposing patriarchy so effectively ... Feminism has informed learning and interpretation of teaching throughout. Very involved in women's groups of various sorts, especially around abortion rights and outworking. Teach Equal Opportunities and Diversity through a feminist lens ... .'

Ros was born in Brighton and moved to London, only to return to live in her paternal grandmother's house with her partner and five children: 'I went to Brighton Poly. I was thirty, with five children. My partner and I had moved down to Brighton from London about six years earlier. I did Soc Admin. I wanted to be a social worker at the time and that seemed to [be] most obvious route. Really wanted to do Sociology at Sussex University but going to a university rather than poly seemed rather intimidating at the time ... We are a middle-class Jewish family though not practicing very much ... . I had *a vague knowledge of feminism from my late teens,* but I think that *I only considered myself a feminist once I started studying with the Open University* prior to going to Brighton Poly [a new university]. I can remember challenging some of the lecturers at the OU summer school on the second level course I took because I thought that some of Barthes' (who we were studying) ideas were sexist ... I then went to LSE for a MA and to South Bank to do my PhD on "mature women student returners" (supervised by you, Miriam) ... *Feminism has been a part of my learning and life* – relationships within my family and my academic career ... I used to have debates with my own parents and actually fell out with my parents-in-law because they thought that I was turning their son into a wimp (he did washing up and childcare!). If my husband hadn't been supportive I think we would have split up. I brought my children up with knowledge of feminism ... I hope I've made some contribution to academic feminism. I've not been involved in much activism. I don't feel good about that last bit ... Lots of women influences – too numerous to mention them all. Your own work – which was why I wanted to come and do my PhD with you, Miriam. Liz Stanley's work. Socialist feminist ideas. They were influential because they spoke to me ... see my article with Natasha Mauthner on attempting to be a *feminist research manager* ... I've been part of a women's workshop since my PhD days. It's still going – now led by younger career researchers – and I'm still part of it ... .'

I Developed Through Study and the Associated Conscientization ...

Christina: 'I had just started a relationship when I started university at Warwick in 1982, so I was doing a lot of childcare right from the start of my studies. I chose sociology because I thought it was relevance to the lives of people like me. *I was first introduced to feminist thinking* via courses I took with Terry Lovell who was exceptionally inspiring ... I then went on to do a PhD on stepfamilies, supervised by Bob Burgess at Warwick ... and I have stayed there since ... my first permanent post was in the Continuing Education department where I did lots of work on women's studies and I regret the loss of women's studies departments ... moving to Sociology in the last five years ... [As to feminist theory versus activism in my sociological work], I don't believe in the activism/theory split. We all have theories (in use if not explicitly) and there are many kinds of activism (i.e. it's not just about marching and lobbying policymakers etc.) ... *I developed through study and the associated conscientization* ... My Birmingham family is not at all influential. They couldn't understand it and still can't!'

At University, Reading Literature on Girls and Schooling, Reinforced By My Father's Behaviour

Christina met Jane when they were both doing postgraduate work at Warwick, becoming firm friends and colleagues and *they share being mothers before going to university and becoming feminists together.* Jane's background is that her 'mother left school at fifteen and did secretarial work, whilst my father did national service followed by teacher training becoming a headteacher of a primary school. As a mother I studied at the OU, reading history and sociology, subjects I'd enjoyed at school ... *at university, reading literature on girls and schooling, reinforced by recollections of childhood insecurities and my parents' unhappy marriage* (in large part due, as I discovered in my 20s, to my father's infidelities and duplicitous behaviour) I did "learn" about women linked to the education courses that I took, some of the arts and social science courses also e.g. women and work, with Rosemary Deem, learning about housework as a form of work: Ann Oakley's work influential ... I did a full-time MA in Sociology of Education at Warwick, looking at the origins and development of gendered schooling with Margaret Archer; followed by a PhD at the OU on women members of the London School Board, supervised by Rosemary Deem and *Carol Dyhouse* ... her book *Girls Growing Up in Victorian and Edwardian England* Ann Oakley on housework: work on girls and science – all spoke to me, my experience at school *and as a young mother*; Miriam David *State Family and Education* blend of sociology and history; influenced by socialist feminism; also really enjoyed the work of Carolyn Steedman, like the way she writes, playing with form, ideas, use of biographical approaches, especially *Landscape for a Good Woman* influenced writing and how I try to behave, in work and out; limited activism, marches and petitions ... .'

The Degree Study Opened My Eyes to Gender Inequities...

Chris also studied at the OU as a mature married woman student: 'I went to the OU when I was twenty-six. I moved from teaching infant children to initial teacher training after my OU degree in Sociology and Education ... *The degree study opened my eyes to gender inequities* but I was, at that point, solely focused on the implications of this for me as a wife and teacher ... [Became a feminist] at university with my ever grateful thanks to people like Rosemary Deem, *Madeleine Arnot, Gaby Weiner, Pat Mahony, Miriam David* – whose work made me think completely differently. Up until that I was still labouring under *the delusion of many working class women who thought their husband's work more important than their own* and that men should be paid more than women. I shudder to think of this now! ... *Feminism has been absolutely fundamental to my life and career*. My activism has been somewhat muted in that I have focused on teacher education and undergraduate modules in education. However, I am committed to the practical aspects of feminism and worry that theory can swamp the importance of this ... *I started to adopt the 'feminist label' when I began my Masters degree (two years after completing my OU degree)*. At that time a fellow teacher had done an OU degree alongside me and had also applied to York but to do a Women's Studies degree whilst mine was in educational studies. Our shared interest in the area and the desire to bring about change through our work as primary school teachers resulted in numerous conversations as to whether we were feminists and "what kind?!" (i.e. radical, Marxist-socialist etc.) ... I took a year off work and studied at the University of York. My husband supported me for

this time. My topic was "Gender issues in initial teacher training programmes" ...
I then took nine years to do a doctorate part-time ... My parents and immediate
family referred to me as "Mrs Pankhurst" and thought I was "odd". My husband
left me for another woman when I was doing my MA at York (a classic "educating
Rita" situation). *Whilst not overtly supportive, it was my mother's hostility about me
getting "above myself" that made me want to help change this lack of acceptance
for other women in my position ...* '.

University 'Mothers' Turning to Feminism: Fathers' Influences?

Several became mothers as students, returning, having had their children, to academic
work: for one it was marital breakup with three young children whilst another's
story has echoes of Maggie's in cohort 1, needing to persuade one's *father* to stay
on at school! They had early feminist stirrings through their 'difficult' or 'unusual'
fathers but it was the influence of their studies that consolidated their feminism.
One was: 'born in Southampton to "adopted parents" ... going to Birmingham to
study Psychology – because I'd originally wanted to study biochemistry but had
taken a year out to be an exchange student in high school in California and got
rather waylaid ... I think [becoming a feminist] probably before – given my unusual
upbringing where my father did quite a lot of childcare and my mother spent more
time in one of the shops, I didn't have traditional role models and certainly found it
hard to see other men being let off doing home chores etc. ... I think it underpins how
I think and even now, I still rail against some of the ways in which mainly women
are expected to make hard choices around family and career ... .[I took some time to
raise my] children ... I had three children in three years so they grew up together but
by the time I started my masters, my first marriage broke up and they and I had to
adjust to a split life of being alone or a mum depending on when I had the children
and when they were with their father. My ex and I shared then but given my day
job involved evening work as an adult basic education organizer, they stayed in the
family home and I moved out – *so usual story of mature woman learner,* something
gives – the marriage, and then the struggle to manage everything. *I really began
to realize I was a feminist when I started teaching in a special school in Somerset
in 1977. I read Spare Rib* and was always questioning how the children at the school
were treated differently in relation to boys' and girls' subjects – especially given
there was no curriculum in special education at that time ... I then did a PhD at
UEL ... because it was easier for me to get there and my masters supervisor was so
inspiring I stayed on to work with him for my doctorate ... I have to say it was Dale
Spender who got me fully thinking ... .'

My Father Was Also Abusive and Violent to My Mother and All His Children

'I went to University to read languages – because I was good at school ... plus I
had an influential teacher, who persuaded my father not to make me leave school

at seventeen ... [I became a feminist] at girls' grammar school, partly as a result of reading *the Female Eunuch* – much discussed by my school friends and indeed teachers. But I was already well on the way because of the strong gendered power relations at home. *My mother always worked but my father never lifted a finger in the house, and this was replicated in division of labour between sons and daughters. My father was also abusive and violent to my mother and all his children* ... I learnt at an early age that women had a very poor deal in life and decided I would not put up with it. After various false starts in relationships, including a disastrous first marriage, my partner for the last twenty-five years has been entirely supportive of my feminism ... I dabbled with feminist groups at university but did not really engage in activism at that stage. *I was quite intimidated by the university women's groups – largely for reasons of class I think ... Feminism was extremely influential,* in that I became quite heavily involved in feminist activism as soon as I returned from voluntary work in Africa in 1981, despite (very unexpectedly) having a new baby within a few months of returning. Living in an African country gave me a sharp introduction to gender issues in developing countries and this kick-started me. I read a great deal on feminism in my 20s and 30s but this was not linked to any formal education programme. During this period I was very active – setting up and running a Women's Centre, involved in the women's peace movement, National Abortion Campaign etc. – but while my activism has influenced my academic work, I've never really been directly engaged as an academic in feminist theory, women's studies etc. ... [Influences are] *Sheila Rowbotham*, Michele Barrett, *Sandra Acker, Gaby Weiner* – socialist and educational end of the spectrum. I can't extricate gender from class and always found the wilder reaches of radical feminism and ... some strands of French feminism [are] rather alienating ... .'

Becoming Feminists After University

Several became feminists after university, through their work as teachers at different professional levels. Two women from Catholic backgrounds describe its influences with one seeing it as fairly positive, whereas another rails against it *and* her mother, although she, like another, became a feminist through *school teaching,* whilst two see feminism as important for their university work.

My Wish Not to Take a 'Typical Girl's Path'

Maria from an Irish Catholic family: 'I was an only (much loved) child with parents totally committed ... and supportive of my education – but never pushy ... my parents made the effort to send me to two convent schools which (as they were fee paying at the time in Ireland) were typically attended by middle class girls ... both were single sex girls' schools which gave me a very good education and a general environment which for me at least implied that girls could "do anything" ... like most students from Catholic backgrounds at that time I only applied to (and) went to

UCD ... Without any strong passion for a particular career (like medicine) I ended up taking a B.Comm – for three reasons. Firstly I did know I didn't want to be a school teacher (what 'most girls did') ... Secondly I was good at Maths ... thirdly, I had one hour's careers guidance and the BComm suggested to me ... Given *my wish not to take a 'typical girl's path'* although I did not read feminist material until after my first degree, I would say I was thinking as a feminist from an early time ... *Feminism has been enormously important in shaping my world view* – both in practice and theory. I was particularly active in women's groups (political) over the late 1970s and 1980s in Ireland and England ... . My topic [for my Masters by Research] was directly influenced by feminist theory – and this was the time of my fullest engagement with the literature and also activism. *Ireland at the time was just ablaze with debates about women's rights due to the extraordinary lingering effect of Catholicism and economic and social stagnation.* I undertook extensive interviews (*c.*100) with married women undertaking adult education – stratified to ensure working class representation. Fantastic learning experience for me ... De Beauvoir *The Second Sex* was a total revelation to me. I saw it as a comprehensive, integrating analysis. Then a mixture of the contemporary "classics" Millett, Greer, Rowbotham, Friedan. Oakley for *The Sociology of Housework* – influential for me. Then back to reading older classics J.S. Mill, Engels, Wollstonecraft; Wolf ... .'

Feminism Suddenly Made Sense and I Read Avidly

Sheila is from: 'a lower middle-class family (Dad a local authority clerk, mum didn't work from the point that she got married. She had previously worked as an untrained primary school teacher) ... Brought up as a Catholic. Rejected the religion at a very young age but kept a sense of social justice. Decided I was a communist and atheist round the age of eleven – didn't go down well *en famille* ... Was a bit wary of women's group at Sussex [university] I didn't particularly engage with student politics at university – the politicos were generally more middle class than me. I was terrified of failing and worked very hard. I met my boyfriend when I was nineteen and led quite a domestic existence. However, Sussex was infused with an air of questioning and liberalism ... *didn't really get into feminism until I was teaching and became pregnant* – everyone assumed I would leave my job – I wanted to carrying on working. *Feminism suddenly made sense and I read avidly.* Started a women's group in Puddletown where I lived (Dorset) and ran girls' groups in school. Went to Greenham Common and became an activist ... *My feminism developed in opposition to my Mum, who was an Irish Catholic Tory.* She scoffed at ideas she didn't understand and when I was a teenager tried to suggest that certain books, ideas etc. were not suitable. This made them all the more appealing. She insisted on referring to feminism as "wim lib" ... *Feminism is hugely influential.* PhD [at Bristol] with Sandra Acker as my supervisor was on gender and education. I learnt a lot more about feminist thinking and research from her. I attempted to place my experiences within school within a theoretical context. I have branched into other areas since (including disability studies and additional support needs) but always influenced by theories of social (in)equality ... . Ann Oakley when I was an undergraduate. Recently I particularly like the work of Anne Phillips and Carol Thomas who spans disability studies and feminism ... .'

Feminism Has Underpinned Most Things [Academic] ...

Carrie is from an interesting class background: 'My father's family was a fairly wealthy middle class German Jewish one and as a child refugee he was fostered by landed gentry. My mother's parents while originally working class themselves both had degrees and definitely joined the middle classes. So my family background is really middle class to the core by the time it came to my generation. My mother was a nursery teacher and for much of my childhood she ran a private nursery school from premises adjoining our house. Then she left my father for another woman and set up as a silversmith, which she still is ... both my parents were socialists (from longstanding socialist families) and my mother later became a peace activist ... *[I became a feminist after Cambridge] though not particularly long after. Feminism has underpinned most things*, though when I did my PhD I took a conscious decision not to do it about gender, despite having a gender and education specialist as a supervisor. Mainly I have been a theorist and researcher but in the early days I was an activist, working in my classroom and with the Gender and MatheMatics Association. I started teaching maths in a girls' school and so went to a GAMMA meeting because of this ... Actually the most important things for me have been radical constructivism (I stopped being a Marxist because the two were incompatible) and Foucault. Though people like Carol Gilligan, Susan Kessler, Judith Butler and Susan Heckman have been important too. *And when I was a teacher I was strongly influenced by Pat Mahony's Schools for Boys ... .'*

I Aligned Myself with Feminism When ... I Got into the Theory Through My University Teaching

Audrey: 'I was a socialist, social justice activist and a children's rights *activist before I aligned myself with feminism which didn't really happen until I got into the theory through my university teaching* and into considering the practice through my research. I was always strongly in favour of women's rights but not in any organized or coherent way ... Ever since I woke up to feminism I have been intensely conscious of whether I am reading a book – fiction or non-fiction – by a male or female author. I find their voices typically different. Of the three areas of research I am best known for, *one is all about feminist practice, being focused on domestic violence*, and has been used quite extensively in teaching I understand. I got a PhD by published work in 2002 and a DLitt demonstrating that a few people had taken notice of some of it by 2009. A feminist colleague supervised the PhD and gave me beautiful help with shaping the covering document ... *My mum was a feminist in her deepest self though not in her lifestyle* ... There was no concept of life without a man but of differential opportunities within marriage ...

My partners have been dragged around the country in the wake of my career, with no consultation. I have no children ... [Key influences] ... Ellen Pence, an American activist and writer on domestic violence, because she was one of the first and always the best ... .'

I Got Involved in Women's Studies When I Started (University) Teaching ...

Nirupama is from an Indian 'family of academicians ... I went to university in New Delhi to study botany and then post-graduation in sociology as I started to get interested in human relations ... [Becoming a feminist] after university. I have been influenced by feminism in course of my life and have tried to keep my head high balancing all relationships. I got involved in women's studies when I started teaching ... .'

I end with a narrative by Corinne Squire, head of a Centre for Narrative Research, about her 'cross-class' background and becoming a feminist through her passions and politics to illustrate how narrative writing has become vital to academic feminism. It leads us into cohort 3 in the next chapter:

Some Kind of Feminism Was a Given for Me: Given the 'Magnetic Women' in My Life

'I was born in 1958, to a woman in her 40s working then as a dance teacher. Our family did not fit an obvious class profile. My mother was the illegitimate child of a housekeeper (previously a maid) who had had her fostered for twelve years, before finding a much older and well-off man she could live with. She looked after this man, especially as he grew older and sicker. He would never marry my grandmother, possibly because he didn't want to divorce the wife from whom he was separated; this caused her continuing shame and dismay. However, he was willing to let her have her child with her, which drove her into and kept her in the relationship.

My mother's foster family ran a dairy. As prosperous tradespeople, they encouraged her to go to grammar school; she transferred to another grammar school when she went to live with her mother. But this transfer of care to the woman she had previously thought was her aunt was very difficult, and the man with whom my grandmother lived wouldn't support my mother going to university, something that strongly determined how she felt about my education. Eventually, she borrowed money to go to teacher training college from the parents of a much more wealthy friend at the grammar school. She trained as a PE teacher, but perhaps because of her rather unconventional background, she became deeply interested in modern art, music and dance ... I spent many weeks as a young child and later, during my holidays, accompanying her to and taking part in dance classes and festivals, especially when she didn't have childcare.

My mother was married for four years to my father, a B-movie actor with big alcohol and gambling problems, who could also be abusive. My mother, a sweet-natured woman, claimed he was very charming, but the couple of times I met him, I did not see this. She left him when I was born, returning to live by the seaside with my grandmother, who had by then buried her first "husband" and also a second, another man who again lived with this apparently very *magnetic woman* after his own marriage had split up. Once more, he would not marry her, but he left her their house. By this point, my grandmother was caring for another old, very forgetful woman, for which she may have received some small payment, running an extremely efficient household, cooking meals for us all, and producing a great deal of produce from her allotment-sized garden. My mother, the official breadwinner, went to London every day to work, returning in the late afternoon; I thought of this as normal family life. My mother taught "deportment" in a model agency for several years, until she had enough money for a house deposit. Then my grandmother moved back to the small country town where she had been born, and I and my mother moved to London, to a large and dilapidated house she bought specifically because it was near to a good school, a member of the Girls' Public Day School Trust group. The junior school was private, and she had to pay for it. At that point, she started to get substitute and then full teaching jobs, and continued dance teaching until retiring in her late 60s. At the same time, to make the school fees, she rented out rooms in the house to a diverse set of lodgers, with whom I grew up. This was a kind of *Tales of the City* life, with a man battling schizophrenia with the help of scientology in the middle bedroom, a couple of Thai students sharing the big downstairs room, a Harrods window dresser in the back bedroom and occasionally, people trying unsuccessfully to kick drug habits taking on one of the smaller rooms. All of them brought different food, books and music into the house, and talked about them. This cultural life, and the kind I accessed through music, gave me a really different understanding of literature and philosophy. *I didn't learn the stuff about Nietzsche, Plato and Heidegger I spouted callowly at my Cambridge interview from school, but from LPs, and from the book collection of the man who danced at the Talk of the Town and rented the front bedroom.*

These people were more inspiring for me than my rather staid school, aspirational but somewhat narrow in its expectations of girls. However, I loved the primary school, dominated by a group of lesbian teachers who lived (with occasional arguments) in the same house. Encouraged by them, I read forests of books from the school and public libraries. A woman teacher living nearby used to let me borrow hers, as despite my mother's efforts, we only had a couple of shelves-full. Later, I also briefly visited a retired woman who had been part of early ecological studies of the relations between predator and predated animal populations, and who now lived in bohemian splendour in an attic crowded with art and odd people off the Fulham Road. This made academic work look unexpectedly attractive. I began to realize how lucky I was not to live in my grandmother's cosy but stultifying little hometown. My mother never had a car, and I was used to walking down the Kings Road, up Piccadilly, across the park to Kensington, or hanging around Soho and the Charing Cross Road bookshops all weekend.

I was probably *much more aware of sexuality politics than gender politics* at this point as there were a lot of lesbians and gay men among the lodgers. *But some kind of feminism was a given for me. My mother and grandmother were both very independent women, and both were committed to my education. My grandmother helped my mother with my school fees before I got a scholarship for secondary school.* She was extremely proud when I did well, and in my mother's account at least, it was very important that she heard about my good O level results just before she died. She was, though, undone by the unconventionality of her own life. She was very reserved, she always called herself "Mrs" and she became tearful if she had to talk about her relationship history.

My mother spent vast amounts of her small income on my primary schooling, bought me encyclopedias and other books, took me to museums and libraries. Part of this was just for the fun of it; part was due to her longstanding fear of some social worker or perhaps my teachers thinking her an unfit mother. In addition, she was wholly determined that I should go to university. At the same time, she was incurably "romantic", as she saw it. She often told me that it was worth giving up everything for the "right man". However, we lived, ourselves, in considerable fear of the wrong man, my father, finding us and extracting money from us.

I often met friends of my mother in thrall to what seemed to be irritable and domineering husbands. When we spent time with my grandmother's family in rural Worcestershire, I saw my other female relations working entirely at home, as cleaners, as kitchen helps in cafes, or in Boots, while the men were farmers, postmen and car park attendants. The height of success was that one younger man was "in the council", and another trained as a teacher and emigrated to Australia. As I progressed through university and a PhD, what I was doing, vaguely referred to as my "studies", became more and more perplexing to my family. I spent a lot of time staying with some of these relations; I was very close to them. *But I felt that I had to get educated, get out, and keep away from serious relationships with men.*

Just as I got a scholarship for secondary school, the school stopped being a grammar school and became private. My mother repeatedly told me I would be among the poorest students at my school. I was acutely aware of her divorced status and our precarious class. The school encouraged me to apply to Cambridge, but I wanted to go to Sussex, which at that time seemed to offer a much more interesting curriculum. *I think my mother's distress at me losing what was for her a glittering opportunity played a part in my going to Cambridge in the end.* The *college I chose, Sidney Sussex, had only just started taking women;* I selected it because it was opposite Sainsbury's. This wasn't a facetious point. Throughout my childhood, my mother and I had shopped weekly at Sainsbury's on late Saturday afternoons to get the out-of-date reductions, braving the wire baskets of more determined older women to find what my mother thought was good but affordable food. While I was at university, I spent a lot of time getting food in Sainsbury's and eating it in my room, in preference to eating the food of an institution from which I came to feel quite alienated.

I'd spent the previous gap year working as a maid (a kind of family tradition) for an oil company family in Oklahoma, and then taking Greyhounds all across the US. I thought I was self-sufficient and in control. But in the first term, I discovered that my science education at a girls' school had not been as thorough as that of many of the male students. I had wanted to study zoology for many years; it turned out that the kind of ethological work I hoped to do was not considered real science and that ecological research, which also interested me, was being done by mathematical modelling – again, not what I wanted to do. In fact, there were people at Cambridge doing animal behavioural work of the kind that had interested me, but they weren't accessible to undergraduates unless you sought them out, something I was perhaps too passive if not too intimidated to envisage doing. Plus, to do zoology, you had to endure botany. I had a really excellent and encouraging biochemistry teacher, Sue Iverson, then a graduate student; that alone wasn't enough to keep me doing science, though quite possibly a few other women like her would have helped.

My mother was a Heathite Tory, though she later became an ardent Green Party supporter. I had joined the Labour Party, but later in my first university year, I moved to the Communist Party, then reinventing itself as a euro-communist organisation, and spent the summer at the Communist University of London, reading and discussing Foucault, Althusser and Lacan. *Gender was not yet a major focus in this work but it was more and more to be seen as integral to theoretical developments.* I read Lacan first through Juliet Mitchell; I read Ann Oakley's work; I even read popular books like Marilyn French's *The Women's Room.* I decided to major in psychology, taught as a natural science at Cambridge, but including some extraordinarily insightful lectures on Freud by Paul Whittle, and allowing me the possibility of also doing a philosophy of science course and of auditing the lectures on social psychology and on Lacan then taught within Social and Political Sciences by Colin Fraser and David Ingleby.

As my understanding of critical theoretical work became wider I started to think I should address *contemporary theories of subjectivity in dialogue with work on gender.* This was the project I got funded to do as a PhD straight afterwards, by a university fellowship at Exeter. My supervisor, Paul Kline, was intensely interested in psychoanalysis of all kinds and left me happily alone to write a long and almost unreadable thesis about Lacan, Althusser, Irigaray, and Derrida and his feminist critics. I was also greatly helped by second supervisor, the literary theorist Michael Wood. I had still had had no other formal teaching from female academics except Iverson and a couple of supervisions by Deborah Sahakian at the Applied Psychology Unit late in my degree. However, at this point, I spent a semester attending seminars on psychoanalysis and philosophy, including the seminars of Derrida and Rene Major, but also those of Sarah Kofman. I also attended a critical theory summer school at Northwestern, taught by Edward Said and, briefly, by Gayatri Spivak, both of whose work continues to be very important for me. Moreover, in the reading groups, the political meetings, and the campaigns I was involved with, there were always interesting, argumentative and very creative women around. Academically, this happened mostly for me in workshops, conferences and other discussions around the magazines *Ideology and Consciousness, m/f* and *Screen*, for which I wrote a piece on Chantal Akerman when I was supposed to be finishing my PhD. I remember meeting Mandy Merck, and her giving me some invaluable help with editing this piece and talking about what I might write later. But going to Greenham Common, writing about it for the *Leveller*, being involved with "Take back the Night" marches and working with women in the Communist Party in Exeter and London were much more relevant to my feminism. *The academic aspects of feminism were never considered by me and my friends as taking the place of activism. Nor of course was feminism on its own seen as a helpful frame for organisation or thought.*

I didn't really become an academic. I slid into academia, perhaps. I was half in and half out of it for a long time. I did a little teaching during my PhD, and towards the end of it, started to work part-time for the Workers' Educational Association, for the University of London Extramural Department, for a number of small colleges, including women's colleges, and for the then South Bank Polytechnic, near to where I lived, off the Walworth Road [When you Miriam were Head of Department]. Now I was meeting many women who were academics within social sciences and the humanities, often not working in a mainstream way, but doing the work that they wanted to. I was also trying to find out how to teach, inclusively and democratically, a very wide range of students with divergent skills and backgrounds. Feminism wasn't the only political frame I had to use to understand that. I also had to adopt some professional values about clarity and the conveyance of useful information that had quite little to do with feminism.

As a tutor for hire, I was teaching a really broad range of courses, from straightforward developmental psychology to women's autobiographical writing. Perhaps as a result, when I started to write more seriously for publication, I tried to bring together some of my theoretical and political understandings around gender with psychology, the discipline in which I had trained, which had so far been somewhat resistant to such understandings, in a book called *Significant differences: feminism in psychology.* I was encouraged to write this book by Valerie Walkerdine, who had co-developed a small critical psychology series for Methuen. Without her interventions in psychology and in my own academic life, I would probably have tried to publish in the much more mainstream journals around gender, psychology and sociology then established in the US. Walkerdine's and others' work at the time, particularly that of Sue Wilkinson, who had edited a collection on women and social psychology, led to the establishment of what is still a really innovative journal, *Feminism and Psychology*, with which I've been very happy to be associated, in a minor way, ever since.

While learning how to teach, I was also working half-time for a GLC-funded video collective, Masc Media, a group of part-time academics and filmmakers producing educational videos around masculinities, as well as occasional films for the new and at this point radical commissioning strands of Channel 4. We spent vast amounts of time theorising and a much shorter time making the films. It was an amazing experience to be applying complex theories of psychoanalysis and sexual difference to film making rather than film analysis, and to be working with film professionals who despite their theoretical interests knew how to edit, and when to stop. There were some professional values in play here ...

In the late 1980s I began a series of moves across the Atlantic with my partner, who I had, much to my mother's initial consternation, met at university, and who had job offers predominantly in North America. I spent a couple of years in New York and New Jersey in temporary posts; I returned to permanent UK posts at the University of Central England and then Brunel University in the early 1990s, and he accompanied me back to the UK at that point. We went back to the US a further time, and then settled in the UK in the mid-1990s. Initially, going to the US, where there was an established institutional tradition around gender studies, women's studies, women's psychology and gender psychology, was extraordinarily interesting. My work had hitherto been conducted in a much broader political frame that hardly existed in the US. There, by contrast, I was able to teach within a stand-alone Women's Studies undergraduate programme in New Jersey, and to be a visiting scholar in CUNY's Centre for the Study of Women and Society, a focus rarely so boldly, baldly or exclusively stated by UK institutions.

In the context of strong US academic interests in violence against women, and US feminist psychologists' severe doubts about psychoanalysis, I did some empirical work, the first I had tried, interviewing young women and men about their experiences of violence, and analysing the genres involved in their speech with the help of psychoanalytically-informed feminist literary theory, particularly that of Barbara Creed and Julia Kristeva. I was aided in this by a number of ambiguous factors. I was working in a US psychology department which, unlike the Cambridge psychology department and indeed many other UK psychology departments at the time, took social psychology seriously, albeit as 'science'. It also had an instrumentalist, credit-based approach to encourage students to take part in staff research.

Again *working slightly against the US feminist grain*, as I saw it, I tried to analyse the progressive possibilities of popular media often viewed as purely gender-oppressive, specifically, television talk shows. I was drawing again on feminist literary and cultural studies, at a time when US feminist social research was much less related to these disciplines than in the UK. Initially, *Ann Phoenix*, whom I had met at Brunel, asked me to write up a rather rough conference presentation on the topic, which would otherwise have mouldered and been forgotten. Some of this work, particularly on the *Oprah Winfrey Show*, became quite widely republished. I did not think of it as the most interesting work I was doing; like most people, perhaps, I can never judge what's most useful in my work. With a colleague, I then co-wrote a book about multiple discourses of morality in US popular culture, a between-disciplines text that was not clearly aligned politically either, though it was certainly conceptualised as feminist. I was only temporarily and marginally attached to academic institutions at this point, but I regularly attended gender and critical psychology and sociology seminars and conferences, and this was enough. Any deeper immersion in US academia, for instance through a tenure-track post, might have made it very difficult to do this work, rather insignificant in traditional tenure-track terms.

Since the mid-1980s, when friends had started to get ill and often die quickly from illnesses associated with HIV, I had been volunteering with HIV organisations in the UK and then the US. I worked with some HIV support groups in New Jersey; I was part of a number of ACT UP actions in New York, in particular some that campaigned for more specific care for women, and against trials of anti-retrovirals for pregnant women to reduce HIV transmission to their babies. This form of drug treatment was feared to be toxic at the time, though it turned out to be massively valued by women living with HIV and also medically highly successful and well tolerated ... I also spent nearly a year working in a New York City clinic where part of my duties were HIV antibody test counselling. None of these experiences were academic. There was rather little academic interest in HIV in the social sciences outside of behavioural risk reduction, and a wide divide separated that work from the cultural and feminist analyses of HIV significations made by for instance Paula Treichler and Cindy Patton, whose academic and activist writing has ever since strongly affected my own. Out of my largely non-academic experiences of HIV, I put together an edited book, spanning cultural analysis and social research, on *Women and AIDS: psychological perspectives*. This, the first edited book on the topic, turned out to have an unexpectedly wide readership. *Perhaps this has been the most important feminist work I've done. While it's an academically rigorous text, I hope, it came from an entirely non-academic context.*

In 1996, with a small child, I and my partner moved back to the UK where we both at last had jobs, though not in the same city. I've stayed at UEL ever since, in the social sciences, largely because I really love teaching the students there. They are always surprising and enlightening, and *many come to education later in their lives, via untraditional routes. The majority of them are women, and most have African, African Caribbean or Asian backgrounds.* This must be one of the only universities in the UK where I can teach a class on "HIV in the world" to a group of 50 students with personal experience of the epidemic from all over sub-Saharan Africa, Asia and the Caribbean, as well as Europe, and learn a vast amount in the process.

For the women students at UEL in particular, university education is often a really important part of their struggle to improve their lives and those of their children. The potential removal of such possibilities from these women, and our other students, heralded by the new economy of UK university education, is really troubling and led many of us to into campaigns against this restructuring. More locally, myself and my teaching colleagues became deeply admiring of our psychosocial studies students, almost all women, when in 2011 they over 30 of them attended what was supposed to be a small meeting of a couple of students with senior management, to make their case against some proposed internal structural changes. In the face of this kind of mobilisation and determination, we have a strong responsibility to act also.

Working at UEL brought me into contact with a group of politically active and aware colleagues, including many feminist colleagues with long histories of academic and political activism, something that one finds less frequently now in UK universities than before. One could certainly say that, in many schools and groupings, *this is a feminist and pro-feminist university*. This is a broad and continuing benefit that still makes UEL a really distinctive place. It has made it possible for many of us to work together in teaching and research, to take on administrative tasks and posts, and to feel that in the process we can do something useful and developmental, not purely regulatory.

Ten years ago, a group of us in sociology and psychosocial studies – myself, Shelley Sclater, Molly Andrews and later, Maria Tamboukou – put together a Centre for Narrative Research. This centre is not explicitly a focus of feminist scholarship, but it has enabled us to do feminist work and to support other colleagues doing such work, in the fields of qualitative narrative investigations of personal, public and media stories. Despite having few institutional resources, and even in a time of increasingly intense audit culture and managerialism, CNR has proved a resource in itself for us. It also seems to have taken on a life of its own through the graduate students that make it their own, through the visits CNR members make to colleagues all over the world to discuss their work, and through the visitors that in turn pass through CNR in London, and return again and again ... Our other collaborations, for instance with *Ann Phoenix* and others ... in an ESRC research methods node, NOVELLA, "Narratives of varied everyday lives and linked approaches", are also I think very strongly inflected by feminism – even down to the rather playful approach to fixing us by acronym. We are now in the position, too, of working with former CNR graduate students as colleagues and co-researchers, a kind of association that is really enlightening as these colleagues are very often from different national – and theoretical – backgrounds, and are going to take the work into entirely new areas ... *Mica Nava* and Lynne Segal have written about the integration of personal, political and academic collectivities in their lives. Possibly my lack of experience of that comes from being part of a slightly later generation, partly also from moving around a lot between countries ... Working in South Africa has been specially important because for a time we all stayed there; my partner – who is South African – became involved in projects to develop South African HE, and our daughter went to school there and attended a number of the research events with which I was involved. I have ongoing relations with and plans to work with some South African activist groups of women living with HIV, and we've also been able to make these relationships part of the work that students do on the HIV in the world module.

In the current rather precarious state of UK HE, particularly at a university such as UEL, I am involved in a number of pedagogical and research developments that are spurred by this situation and that address recession living, the Occupy movement, the nature of communities in straitened times. It's too early, really, to talk about the particular place of feminism within these developments. I think what's notable about them is that they are tending to re-ignite broader forms of activism, and that possibly gender issues are rather under-recognised within them. Transnationalism, however, is certainly integral to thinking in and about them ... .'

Chapter 7
The Crest of the Wave of Academic Feminism?

Introduction: 'The Zeitgeist of the 1990s'

Cohort 3, composed of only twelve participants, from the field of gender and education, is the focus of our attention: small but illustrative of women coming of academic age, during the expansionary period of global academia of the 1990s, in which gender issues and academic feminism had achieved a legitimate if not inclusive space and place. Is this the crest of the wave of academic feminism? These women benefit from entering academe when academic feminism had become legitimate, albeit with all the constraints, obstacles and limitations through its growth in neo-liberalism. These 'select' women were passionate and had a strong sense of the continuing importance of feminist education: of a vital task yet to be accomplished. Academic women's place remained subordinate and not assured, as we shall in the second part of this chapter.

I had originally not planned to speak with women of this age cohort, thinking that they were radically different from the previous cohorts, in the sense that they were indeed daughters of the previous generations of feminist passionate political engagement. I began to realize that, with the changing demography of global HE, around gender and education, linked with other diversities such as social class, family and BME, this was an opportunity to explore the changing character of feminist and other forms of academic engagement across education. What is particularly noticeable amongst this cohort of women *is* the transformation in feminist knowledge rather than feminist *values:* how these women build upon feminist wisdom, gleaned by previous generations, particularly as we move through from cohort 2 to 3. Like with some of the women of cohort 2, it is primarily feminist pedagogies around the now traditional feminist values that are central, alongside the augmentation of feminist knowledge, linked with other diversity issues. It is less about white metropolitan questions and more about interdisciplinarity and intersectionality creating a new feminist knowledge. Unfortunately, I did not interview many feminists, especially those based overseas, or several British women who were willing but given the timescale and the business/busyness of their professional and personal lives, could not participate.

An overarching commitment to gender equality within HE linked with or separately from feminist values is a feature of this generation, like many of cohort 2. Some, too, are ambivalent about using the term feminist, such as Delia, the Spanish sociologist of HE: 'I don't feel myself as a feminist. I am worried about equality in general, not specifically in gender equality ... .' Rajani, another sociologist of HE, said that: 'I never became a feminist. Growing up in apartheid South Africa I was very aware of race and class ... Feminism was not a focal point for me ... but Madeleine Arnot was my supervisor for my PhD in Cambridge and I learnt about some aspects of feminism from her ... .' When the others became feminists was either before or during university with specific influential women's studies courses or the gendered culture of academe, rarely after university.

The key texts relevant to their learning and developing knowledge or wisdom were other colleagues, and academic feminists, illustrating the spread of feminist networks now endemic in academe. Few mentioned the importance of graduate school and certainly not US graduate school, with only one – Jessica – of the three North Americans going to graduate school there: in Canada. What *is* significant, in addition to the landscape of academic feminism, just as in the previous two cohorts, is relationships with mothers. Do the women wish to extend their mothers' commitments, or to digress from them, especially working class families seeing their mothers' subordination? This small cohort is interestingly different from cohort 2, in that only one is a mature woman student returner to HE. The overall emphasis *is* as academics – feminists or women committed to concepts of social equality – in an increasingly competitive and difficult individualized environment of growing neo-liberalism in global HE.

In the second half of this chapter, I explore this cohort's feelings about the character of academe today, and its future in a changing world of global HE, as they are likely to be the pedagogues of the future. These are also in reply to my questions about the changing global university and the future and feminism's role within this. Interestingly these women were more expansive than the previous generations, given their continuing academic careers. For academic feminists in cohorts 1 and 2 who were still involved with work in academe, there was an overarching sense of *ennui* or melancholia, a feeling that the transformations in HE were contradictory, offering spaces for some feminist forms of pedagogical engagement whilst also limiting academic advancement, and career progression as specifically academic feminists. The kinds of ambivalent split lives, expressed so powerfully by Corinne at the end of the previous chapter will be augmented by these stories.

The Mobile Women of Cohort 3: *Equalities, Feminism, Gender and Education*

Small though this cohort is, it is also very diverse and varied, despite their participation in intertwined and professional academic networks: four of the women have been on the executive of the Gender and Education Association; two of the women on the editorial executive of the *British Journal of the Sociology of Education*, two on the executive council of the Society for Research in HE whilst four are colleagues through international feminist and social science networks associated with Keele University.

Whilst virtually all [at the time of the study] lived in the British Isles, with only one resident in the country of her birth, Delia from Spain, it is also true that half were not born in the UK. They are geographically mobile academics, illustrative of the changing global HE at the turn of the twenty-first century. Three come from North America, with two the USA, Penny-Jane and Kelly, and Jessica from Canada. Rajani is from South Africa, and Nafsika from Greece. Four were already 'full' professors (again in the US sense) with their explicitly feminist or gender perspectives (and three have become so since). This is a major transformation in the character of HE over the last two decades. Whilst all twelve have PhDs as we already seen, two came from overseas to undertake their PhD in the UK: Nafsika to do an MA followed by a PhD in Oxford in the Department of Educational Studies on changing forms of HE, and Rajani to do a PhD in Cambridge in the School of Education on the sociology of HE. This shows the global nature of HE, and, with these topics, how reflexive it is becoming. For this select group there is also the dramatic shift from cohort 1 where many undertook graduate studies in the USA, becoming feminists in the process: neither of these became feminists, although they learnt about the gendered nature of HE through their studies. Jessica came to the UK to undertake post-doctoral work with Valerie Walkerdine, having completed her PhD in Canada, moving from Victoria to York University, Toronto for her doctoral studies in *Sociology and Women's Studies*.

Only one other woman – Heather – went to Cambridge, as an undergraduate, to read mathematics, and trained to be a maths teacher. She then 'did an MA in Gender Studies at Newcastle where my dissertation was supervised by *Chris Skelton*. Immediately after this I did a PhD at Goldsmiths. My supervisors included *Debbie Epstein*, Dennis Atkinson and [the late] Leone Burton. I also met Rosalyn George there who's a huge influence. The topic was: why do girls choose not to study maths more than boys? I decided to do the MA because I'd done seven years as a teacher and didn't want promotion and needed a change. I didn't know what I wanted to do but was interested in sociology and literature (had done evening classes in these) and *my feminism had got stronger. I wanted to learn again.* The MA was difficult at first – I had to learn to use a library and to write. By the end I enjoyed it and wanted to carry on. I loved doing the PhD … .'

The two American women – Penny-Jane and Kelly – found themselves in England for personal reasons, settling here and conducting their PhDs, both at the London Institute of Education (IOE), under the auspices of the Centre for Research on Education and Gender (CREG). Five (Pam, Amanda, Davina, Fin, Carolyn) did PhDs that turned them into academic feminists through the specific topics. Kelly's was on the *History of Women's Studies in the UK HE System*, supervised by the late Diana Leonard, and examined by *Madeleine Arnot*. The one mature woman student Penny-Jane said: 'After my undergraduate degree, I was encouraged by my friend's partner (who was doing his PhD at the time) to carry on with my work at MA level – *I was passionate about women's access to HE* and he thought that I should look in to doing an MA at the IOE – I did – and discovered the women's studies course there – co-course leaders Diana Leonard and Debbie

Epstein – *Debbie* in particular encouraged me and suggested I pursue a PhD – I did under her supervision and got an ESRC studentship to do this (otherwise I don't think I could have managed it financially) … .'

Amanda went from undergraduate studies in Exeter to do a PCGE in Birmingham, then to do an: 'MSc Gender and Social Policy, Bristol ESRC award, supervised by *Sandra Acker* (gender and teacher training) PhD as a staff registration while a lecturer, at Cardiff, awarded 1993, professional and organisational socialization of graduate accountants, supervised by Paul Atkinson and *Sara* Delamont'. Davina did her undergraduate work in law at University College London followed by a PhD at Warwick, starting at LSE and then transferring to Warwick: 'I wanted to explore the potential of the local state to act against the status quo, what happens when public bodies try to promote a sexual politics that counters dominant forms of heterosexuality. It was very informed, at least at the beginning, by structuralist Marxism on the one hand; and social feminist work on the other – the idea that public bodies could only with difficulty, and only temporarily, work against dominant social relations. I had several supervisors including Terry Lovell, (the feminist sociologist).' Carolyn 'on graduating from my undergraduate degree I applied to do a Women's Studies MA at York and Women's Studies/Sociology MA at Lancaster but didn't get ESRC funding to do one. I got an eighteen-month job as a Research Assistant working in Educational Research at Lancaster) on an ESRC project on motivation. I registered to do a PhD part-time but didn't do much. At the end of the contract I trained as an ambulance person, and did that for about nine months. I left as I was offered an ESRC award to do a PhD, at Lancaster which I did … .'

Pam, similarly, undertook her PhD around the same time, also in psychology and supervised by Margaret O'Brien and Erica Burman, academic feminists, 'on parenting, family and feminism …' Fin again chose deliberately: 'after my undergraduate, I studied for a postgraduate qualification, a Masters in cultural studies, and then a doctorate in education. During my MA I *purposefully chose feminist and gender options*, and by the time I returned to study for my MA, I was keen to explore the gendered experiences of young women. *The academics I approached to consider supervising my work, were all active feminists, and my two supervisors were feminists with an interest in gender and education.* The PhD study came during a brief hiatus in my professional life. After completing my MA, I had tried to consolidate my professional work, and had taken work at a charity delivering drugs education in schools. This had not been a happy time for me personally or professionally, and I felt troubled by the direction and thrust of much of the policy and practice in the area. I decided I would quit and work the summer on playschemes. Luckily, I noted a scholarship and thought it might be a good idea to develop my proposal and see if I might have a chance. I did, and the scholarship enabled me to commit to my PhD studies, and resulting change in direction in my professional life … Delia chose to do her doctoral work on *Social Class and University* in Spain, supervised by … a professor in sociology of education … .'

There is only one from BME – Rajani – and hers was an unusual family in South Africa: 'Grandfather was a wealthy political activist. Father an investment banker and avid reader of philosophical books. Mother owner of a modelling agency. My family situation changed quite dramatically when I was a teenager and I became involved in the school level anti-apartheid movement.' Two participants mention their Jewish backgrounds – Davina and with Heather saying: 'we were a middle class Jewish family'. Kelly also mentioned her middle class, and, conservative family background from Ohio, USA. And two – Davina and Carolyn – are explicit about the importance of their sexuality to their feminism, with Davina saying 'the way my feminism developed in my late teens was completely caught up politically with identifying as a lesbian. Didi and I got together in 1989. Our politics haven't always been completely in step, but they've taken shape dialogically in relation to each other' and Carolyn said: 'Penny and I have been together as partners since 1996, and working with Penny in various ways has been influential and important ...'. Most became feminists whilst they were growing up, and through school and/or politics, although several were more influenced by their university education, seeing that as a major influence.

Becoming a Feminist Whilst Growing Up and/Or at School

Davina said that she became a feminist when: 'I was about seven and I became very conscious of the different ways my brother and I were treated, particularly at school but also in wider family circles. My first response was to try and pass as a boy. I got short hair, refused to wear dresses, was very stroppy, and people often thought I was the boy and my brother the girl, which I rather liked. My aim was to challenge people's common sense assumptions and different treatment by making it impossible for them to sensibly gender us. But after about a year, I realised that this strategy reinforced a kind of sexism – that I was only being treated "better" because I looked like a boy. I stayed looking "boyish" til my teens, but I reclaimed a girl identity on the premise that nothing could be read off or determined by it ... My twin sisters (who were 12 years older than me) were probably the biggest influence on my feminism growing up. And *Our Bodies Ourselves*. Their copy was in the house, and I devoured it in my last year of primary school, worrying over the merits of different contraceptions, home or hospital births in a kind of abstract, after-school leisure hours kind of way ... Feminism has always been an important part of my politics. As a kid my focus was the "fairness" of gender equality and freedom, but later I was very influenced by feminist organisational norms – the bottom up participatory politics of women's movement ways of doing things – the importance of culture and intimate relations as well as public and material ones. I've tried to bring both the form and substance of feminist approaches into how I work. I'm sure not always successfully, although it's been easier in environments where feminism had some legitimacy – on the council and in the research centre I was involved with (AHRC Research Centre for Law, Gender & Sexuality). Far harder being a feminist as a magistrate, where I was told my encouraging nods when defendants and witnesses were speaking, and even my shoes, were quite wrong!'

I Vividly Remember and Was Moved by ... Greenham Common ...

Amanda said: 'I think I was aware of feminism while at school – I went to Countesthorpe College and was taught by some relatively young feminist and activist teachers. I visited Greenham Common while on a geography A-level field trip ... *I vividly remember and was moved by this* ... I guess I was influenced by sociology and social policy ... and by wider feminist activism – reproductive rights, education and employment campaigns ... [But] Not sure when I became a feminist. I was taught by Anne Witz at Exeter and she was a big influence on my theoretical thinking. ... but [feminism has been] influential since I went to Countesthorpe at fourteen. It shaped my theoretical thinking during my degree, made me reflexive during my teacher training and led me to an MSc ... I have never been particularly active in feminist movements, though I have drawn on feminism in developing my theoretical and methodological work ... Marxist/socialist and radical; more recently post-structural ... Early influence was Christine Delphy; I have used Anne Witz' work. Also Stanley and Wise ... [when I started teaching women's studies at Cardiff]. My parents have not been influential directly on my feminism, though my mother experienced considerable domestic violence in a later relationship. So in that sense there were influences in terms of being able to locate gender and power within a personal frame ... my children are boys, and one has learning difficulties – I think they are influencing the ways in which I now value feminism as a way of articulating experience ... .'

My Early Dream of Feminist Journalism as a Teenager

One of the youngest participants, wrote, illuminatingly, of *the public feminists she read as a teenager* – Fin's story is powerful and moving: 'I was born in the 70s in Lancashire. The second of four kids, and the only girl, I grew up in police houses. My parents both worked night shifts (father a police officer/mother a nurse), so unlike my friends, our house was always silent as we had to tiptoe round as one or both of my parents would be sleeping during the day. This also meant that I from an early age had a larger role in child care and the domestic arrangements than many of my friends, and spent much of my holidays and weekends from the age of nine upwards looking after my younger brother. I was first-in- the-family to go to university. I saw university as an escape. I chose one as far as I could from the family home and saved all summer. After leaving home at eighteen, I never returned during holidays, and spent the vacations in the university city working as an office worker, a security guard and an usherette to fund my studies ... I became a *feminist probably from the age of ten or eleven*. By the age of twelve, I was writing to the editors of the now defunct *Shocking Pink* magazine asking to contribute. My father [a policeman] intercepted a missive from the radical feminist collective (based in a squat in Brixton) which somewhat *thwarted my early dream of feminist journalism.* By fifteen I was organizing a debating society at my school, on themes such as "Should page 3 be banned" and by eighteen I had read Valerie Solanas, Andrea Dworkin, *Germaine Greer, Kate Millett,* and happily introduced myself to a local feminist library ... The feminist library and community centre in the large city I moved to was a bit of a shock to me as a small-town teenage feminist. I met women there who described themselves as "political lesbians" and afraid that I might be found out for dating a boy, I promptly had my hair cropped short, wore dungarees and big boots. At times, I tried to "pass" as gay throughout my first few years at university, fearful that my heterosexual relationship might somewhat destabilise my "authenticity" as a "true" feminist. Of course, as my feminism developed it became more nuanced. I read more widely and peculiarly, it was my retreat from activism that gave me the space and air to deliberate and explore in a more thoughtful manner a broader range of issues from personal and sexual ethics, societies' attitudes toward sex and women's bodies, attitudes towards porn, to women's position in the labour market. Not that retreat into the academy saves me from such thoughts. After all, the academy can also be one of the more unsisterly of places. My professional background is very much tied up with the history of identity politics and an interplay between the theoretical, my practice and my activism is entirely possible. *My feminism for the most part has been largely self-sustaining. I grew up knowing few feminists in "real life". Those I knew were in books,* or by the time I reached my teens in the few feminist youth workers, and teachers I came across. My family have at various times been bemused, confused, irked, ashamed, surprised, and amused by my feminism. I think they saw it as a phase – a bit like dying your hair pink, when I was in my teens. *My mother is of the "second wave" generation, but the women's movement if it indeed ever indeed reached our town – didn't seem to have made much of a splash in our circle.* I do wonder what might have happened if my mum had attended a CR group rather than a Tupperware party in the lounge of a friend in the mid-70s ... I like to imagine a more content life, although I am not sure feminism makes any of us more "content" ... .'

At School Developed a Passionate Interest in Issues About In/Equality, Women's Roles, Employment

Carolyn is also very moving about when she first became aware of feminist issues: 'This is a tricky one to answer. Doing A level sociology I certainly became interested in feminist issues, and *developed a passionate interest in issues about in/equality, women's roles, employment etc. This was developed much further at university.* In the first year at Lancaster students studied (and still do for the most part) three subjects. I did psychology, education studies and sociology, so actually covered quite a bit about gender, inequalities and so on. I did a women's studies module in year two, and tended to take option modules that focused on gender/sexuality. So in a nutshell the answer is probably from A-level onwards, although I can't recall when I started thinking of, or labelling myself as a feminist. Very influential activism through protest marches ... and women-only events ... Women's studies (WS) was very strong at Lancaster when I was an undergrad. WS permeated my sociology and Ed Studies first year courses. Some psychology tutors were also involved in WS, and so adopted what might be called a critical approach to psychology. I did my third year dissertation on gender and language ... As an undergraduate Dale Spender stands out; PhD Jane Kenway and Sue Willis and then boys' panic and your work, Miriam, with Gaby and Madeleine ... plus many others e.g. Chris and Becky ... .'

This Was a Time of Profound Learning Which Was Precious

Kelly has a similar story of how *she learnt about feminism* through what she calls 'the nomadic existence ... [and] the nomad of time zones ... I first learned about feminism in North America when I was very young, whereas my journey through European feminist thought has developed as I have matured. For me, then, these 2 geographically-oriented distinctions are part of my own life history and I cannot disentangle the geographical locations from my experience of my journey through different times in my life ... (Davis and Evans, 2011, p. 79).' She went to Northwestern University, in Chicago to study liberal arts, and undertook some Women's Studies during her undergraduate degree, all of which she found 'a powerful experience'. Whilst there 'in the library, reading around some of the recommended texts for another module, I discovered *The Female Eunuch* (Greer, 1970) and *experienced a life-changing moment* ... My personal revolution, then, initially happened almost entirely in my head. I read books and selected as many feminist courses that I could squeeze into my programme ... This was a time of profound learning which was precious and now evokes nostalgia; the time to read, think, deeply explore new ideas, to have my ideas challenged and developed, and to enjoy learning how to employ feminist theories to most aspects of life ... (Davis and Evans, 2011, p. 81). She came to London on graduation originally for a brief trip, but found herself staying and undertaking various relatively short-term administrative jobs in universities, and later for the Feminist and Women's Studies Association (FWSA). During this time she decided to take an MA in gender and society at Middlesex University, and then moved 'to undertake a PhD in the history of women's studies at the IOE ... as I was finishing my PhD and looking for a starting point for an academic career, I fell more into doing mainstream HE research rather than feminist research. The funding for HE research often went to the men, and I was employed to work on a number of research projects with high-profile male academics. The environment was anti-feminist, really, and in some cases the contributions I tried to make in terms of highlighting gender within research were deleted. Now looking back on it and after reflecting on everything that has happened I think the male research teams I worked in were exceedingly patriarchal and anti-feminist. It wasn't just a chilly climate because it was more nuanced than that: there was patronage of a few women, exploitation of a few others, and hostility towards most other women. As it became increasingly difficult to bring a feminist perspective into collaborative work (the few bids I worked on with other feminists weren't funded) I had to find a way to remain being a feminist academic. I remember when one female colleague told me I needed to get out from under the men to find my own voice, and she was right. In the meantime I was very preoccupied with trying to support students with allegations of serious sexual harassment against one of these men and it was a very difficult time. [The late] Diana helped me a great deal but even now after about 6 years I am still angry about how effectively we were silenced and dissuaded from pursuing a formal allegation (I often think we should have just gone to the police). Some of the responses we got from the university when we tried to pursue formal allegations of sexual harassment were unbelievable ... .'

When I Was in a Women's Aid Refuge I first Explicitly Encountered Feminism: This Was a Life-saver

By contrast another young émigrée from the USA, Penny-Jane, was self-taught and expressing this poignantly, passionately and powerfully: 'I was born in New York City – raised and grew up in West Hollywood, California – parents professional artists, no university, father graphic designer, mother freelance illustrator ... *became a feminist during university* (as a mature student at Middlesex after an Access to HE course) mainly through my own reading ... good experiences taught me about inclusive pedagogies ... poor teaching practices taught me how not to teach!! ... Feminism has been crucial to my learning – indirectly and explicitly – e.g. *when I was in a women's aid refuge I first explicitly encountered feminism* and *this was a life saver* in terms of understanding and making sense of my traumatic experiences of domestic violence – and also learning about my rights and my position as a woman – this was strengthened at university when I started to read feminist theories for my coursework – theory has been more directly influential to me than activism which has not been a significant part of my history/experience (although I have participated in "activism" in more modest, localized ways) ... My parents never really understood what I was doing or why – always felt/feel I was a disappointment to them because I was not an artist – my husband comes from a working-class background and we married before I started the Access course – but he has always believed in me and supported my feminist perspectives and so his emotional support has always been important – I had three boys (when I started my degree I had a one year-old son, a four year-old son and an eight year-old step-son) – so I always felt I was moving across two completely different worlds – and trying to develop a way to be a feminist mother ... *developing an identity as a feminist was tied directly to developing an identity as an academic* – the two were completely intertwined – but I often felt "not good enough" – especially as I came to it so late and did not experience any of the activism of the 70s and 80s or of second wave feminism – the experience of escaping domestic violence was also key in my sense as a feminist and my passionate commitment to challenging assumptions about domestic violence and understanding it as tied in with patriarchy (and not 'battered woman's syndrome" ...) Initially Black feminist writers or feminist theorists of race – so Angela Davis and bell hooks really caught my imagination early on (this is partly because of their passion and the power of their writing but also because I have always felt "Other" myself, and have a lot of different ethnicities in my family background, and have been extremely committed to challenging racism since a young girl) – later on it was people like Patti Lather and Elizabeth Ellsworth because of their work on pedagogies and methodologies – and Bev Skeggs because of her work on gender and class – and Nancy Fraser because of her work on social justice – then later feminist poststructuralists like Judith Butler and those drawing on her work as well as feminist theories drawing on Foucault ... while I was doing my PhD I had a post at an FE college to develop and run a course called Return to Study – I created my own Women's Studies Level 2/3 course as part of that this was collaborative in the sense that I wanted to develop "collaborative pedagogies" with my students – but I didn't have the chance to work with anyone else ... then I worked with Diana Leonard and *Debbie* as a teaching assistant on the Women's Studies module at the IOE ... .'

In My College I Was the Only Girl of Fourteen Doing Maths in My Year

Penny-Jane contrasts socially with the feminist, *Heather*, who had an elite education: 'I became a feminist at university. I went to an all girls' school and moved into a mixed environment at Cambridge. *In my college I was the only girl of fourteen doing Maths in my year*. Some other students and tutors had sexist attitudes. I guess this is what provoked the move ... The influence has been huge – most obviously in my work but also in how I dress, what I eat, my friendships ... I do not do much in feminist activism ... more urgent is peace but feminism in daily life e.g. teaching ... women's studies came gradually ... .'

I Took a Minor in Women's Studies Which Changed My Life in the Second Year of University ...

Jessica also told me that she too became a feminist: 'at university though saw feminist trends in mum retrospectively. I come from a Canadian military family – father was an officer but my parents divorced when I was eleven, and so my main experiences are having a single mother with a meagre income. This meant that I first went to college as we couldn't afford university, failed that and so then went to university the following year, the University of Victoria, in my home town. I started in English literature because I was good at writing, hated it and then switched to sociology because I was brilliant at it and finally *I took a minor in women's studies which changed my life in the second year of university ... Feminism has been hugely critical to my learning since my undergraduate days* ... shaping every facet of life from decision to delay marriage and definitely shaped decision to delay child-rearing ... Mum has been very influential in supporting my education and not adopting the traditional mothering role of nurturer ... Women's Studies was central to my learning and development as an academic [but] Education Feminism is not a known term in North America ... Feminist theory from Wittig, Audre Lorde, Adrienne Rich, Susan Bordo, later poststructural and postcolonial feminists Mohanty, Weedon, then educationalists Luke and Gore, Britzman, Pitt, Klein and Benjamin (feminist Object Relations) and psychosocial Walkerdine, Hollway, Phoenix ... My PhD was on anti-racism in women's studies, defensiveness of white feminism, issues of intersectionality, problems of contradiction and wanting to relate as "feminine" and nurture: the relationality problems explored by Gilligan and Brown, manifesting and problematic learning dynamics for feminist pedagogies ... and so it continues to have a massive influence and is the reason for the continuing to live abroad for feminist, gender and education community in UK ... .'

At University and Afterwards: *A Profound Politicization Occurred ... Bedazzling Inspiration!*

Pam, researching gender-based violence and training or education for young people about it, said that she waivered about becoming a feminist: 'Part at uni, part afterwards. Perhaps because I didn't think to read about it! I was quite inspired by an essay question about why women suffered depression more than men and reading for it planted seeds of thought, then through volunteering on Nightline I got a lot more worldly wise and one of my best friends was (and is) a feminist so I was absorbing it and concerned about sexual abuse, volunteered to drive the women's minibus and had a keen though vague interest in the LGB society, but don't recall specifically talking about feminism, instead was arguing about No platform for Fascists whether ANL or ARA best for UK antiracism, boycotting South Africa and then Israeli goods and mostly working on green and animal rights campaigns. Straight after Uni I moved to London, into ex-student household of Uni psych graduates, one of whom would become my first girlfriend and who lent me feminist texts and feminist psychology textbooks. *A profound politicization occurred then [including an] evangelical enthusiasm about my newfound lesbianism was never quite radical feminist but had strands of/was influenced by.* Awareness of "the male in the head" and heterosexualisation of everyday life was profound. Simultaneous critique of liberal humanism and my "hippy" green politics – very unsettling but according to my consorts, a gentle version of what we called the "social constructionist breakdown". So seeds sown at uni but unfocused and untheorised. Actually *Erica Burman had a huge impact and was and is a bedazzling inspiration ... so feminism's woven through my personal journey* which is mirrored by feminist theory journey from liberal to lesbian feminism to socialist feminism to queer theory. Feminist frameworks and politics feel the most central to me although green and anarchist politics (well, activism) is important too. My journey across and between the various social sciences has been through feminist work that didn't respect the disciplinary boundaries and my finding that I could have sexuality as a legitimate research topic is down to this too. It was nice finding that the illicit reading on sexuality could be owned and legitimate. My later studies in teaching and learning (PgDip HE) looped back into feminist and queer pedagogies too. I don't think not to be "out" as a feminist in the academy in research or teaching. I tend to assume it is OK to be a feminist at work and have to be corrected sometimes. I have not shared my politics with my parents, and I am not sure how influential this is, neither simple opposition to them nor supported by. I think that my parents are heavily influenced by the ideas of their time but reject labels like feminist that I would put on discourses. My daughter seems to have great feminist instincts, is that possible? ... .'

I Never Thought of Feminism as an Identity, Until I Was Much Older

Nafsika, moving across the continent of Europe, wrote: 'On feminism, interestingly, *I never thought of feminism as an identity, until I was much older*. I was brought up in a very high aspirational middle class and highly educated family context (and that includes wider family) where women were all in ambitious careers, and gender was never an issue. My dad was a University lecturer (professor of law later) and my mum after her law training ended up working as a civil servant in the tele-communications sector (she retired as a head of economic services of a pretty large sub-division) ... Even though my father was the only one with a doctorate in the family, it was my mother (and to a certain extent my grandfather) who were pushing us both not just towards a university degree and *job* but towards a university degree and a *career* ... My first degree was in primary education, which at the time, I thought I wanted! My parents (my mother in particular) were very disappointed with this choice of mine ... so when I announced that I did not enjoy my degree and I was thinking of postgraduate studies, they were very happy, and more than willing to pay for a Masters study abroad ... It was unacceptable (inconceivable) to have low aspirations for either of us girls, or for any of my boy-cousins. We were a gender-blind family in that respect ... Of my fourteen cousins, only two women and one man did not study at university and ended up marrying early and having children before twenty (which was considered a scandal in the family circles). I did not come across feminism at university circles either, it was there of course but I never thought it was relevant to me. I became more fully aware of feminist debates once I was in the UK, but I still did not see it as particularly relevant to my life or career. I always saw it as a problem of others. If asked, I would have identified myself as a liberal feminist. This has changed now that I have a more sophisticated understanding of the forms of discrimination and prejudice that people and organizations can exercise, but I still consider myself very lucky and privileged to have had the kind of upbringing where family ambitions [and investment] were not limited at all by gender. I have never been particularly active in terms of promoting feminism as an ideology. In some ways I feel that I carry this through my life course and hopefully transmit it to my children as an embodied message! If asked, I would identify myself as a feminist now, but in the circles that I move socially and professionally I do not view it as a big issue ... .'

My Feminism is More An Attitude About Life

Delia similarly wrote that she came late to feminism and sees it more as part of her wider personal and political life than her professional activities: '*My feminism is more an attitude about life* than a theoretical bet. In this sense my partner and daughter have been an encouragement for trying to share in the real practicalities of the domestic tasks and specially the care of children ... My first contact with academic feminism was you, [Miriam]. Then when I started researching in care issues I knew some feminist academic women in Spain ... The main change in university is that now there are more women than men studying HE. I think this is in relation to a more egalitarian culture, and this is due to feminism. I don't think women need specific pedagogy or practices ... .'

Respect for An Older Generation of Feminists Many of Whom Are Now Professors

Rajani also sees feminism as part of the context for her life and academic work, rather than her educational project. Social changes have become embedded in the wider socio-political context, although not without the continuing challenges: 'My mother was keen for her daughters to have a career and avoid marriage ... Political activism in relation to race and class started as part of my membership of school social movements and continued at university ... Rosa Luxembourg ... was inspirational as a non-dogmatic socialist ... I have not fully engaged with feminist work but have ensured that students had access to lecturers who were engaged in feminism ... in later life and during my PhD I had some exposure to feminism and this has been incorporated into my curriculum development although I do not teach feminism myself ... I have a great deal of *respect for an older generation of feminists many of whom are now Professors who faced huge barriers when they first started in the academy, who worked together to influence structures, pedagogies and practices and who produced excellent and committed research.* Many of them have been incredibly supportive of me. They have made the position of women who came after them into the Academy much better ... However, I have also been disappointed by women in a particular Department who were older than me, who were disappointed in not gaining chairs and who attempted to exclude me and to put up barriers to my progress ... I think that European men of my generation including my partner who is a Professor of HE who lived much of his student life in a German commune with feminists has been influenced in his personal and professional life. Gender has become an important point of discussion in the School of Management where I work in relation to recruitment and promotion ... I think the unequal relations between countries, changing trade laws, multinational regulations and exploitation will give rise to new forms of feminism emerging from developing countries ... .'

What is clear from these women is that feminism has been vitally important in their learning and education across their lives. It has had at least an influence on the ways in which they now construct and conduct their lives, whether they learnt about it at school or university. Whilst preparing this manuscript I wrote in the *Times Higher Education* (31 January 2013) and had a range of passionate replies, including one on the website, which endorsed my cohort analysis and acknowledged that she too had an epiphany like Amanda's in going to Greenham. Catherine Harper wrote on 9 February, 2013 that: '*I'd fall into the third group of women. Background in rural N. Ireland during Troubles, politicised in the context, but "found" feminism via CND, Animal Rights and the NI peace movement. Went by boat and train to Greenham Common and had my "epiphany". Self-defined feminist ever since: it colours everything I do, and as I've become older I've realised just how vital that "awareness" is, both of the continued inequalities for women in academia and beyond, but also how tied to other inequalities – LGBTQI, race, ability, age – feminism is. It's the full flavour of my life, and recently I've adopted a "presence, voice, partnership, principle, persistence" mantra as a way of ensuring I (with a capital I!) maintain it proactively. I've always been very moved by other women's stories of their "personal political" struggles, and the piece above was very good to read.'*

An intriguing reversal of the role of HE in contributing to feminist engagement is Caitlin Moran, a young British journalist on *The Times* without any formal education, and certainly not any HE, starting off as a journalist aged sixteen and now of cohort 3's generation. She published a very feisty successful popular book *How to be a woman* (2011) paying homage to its feminist inspiration, Germaine Greer, recreating feminist political commitments, rather than a more measured academic feminism. This indicates the resurgence of forms of politically engaged feminism, amongst the generation of cohort 3 and younger women, part of the changing socio-cultural and socio-economic times to which we now turn.[1]

Part 2: Critiques of the Place of Academic Feminism in the Neo-liberal Global University

We have seen from the comments of three of this cohort – Delia, Rajani and Nafsika – the importance of the feminist critique of HE today, even if these three women prefer to distance themselves from active engagement with academic

---

1   In the last few years there has been a resurgence of popular feminism, which is sometimes now called the fourth wave, with writers such as Kat Banyard (2011) *The Equality Illusion* with which she founded UKFeminista, Laura Bates who founded *Everyday Sexism,* and the journalist and columnist Laurie Penny (2010) *Meat Market: Female Flesh under Capitalism.*

feminism, preferring to remain committed to research around diversities and other social inequalities, and especially in relation to HE. This is certainly where some of the feminist critiques have made considerable inroads into the emerging forms of the sociology of HE, and the wider research in this arena. Rajani's important comment is that: 'I think the unequal relations between countries, changing trade laws, multinational regulations and exploitation will give rise to new forms of feminism emerging from the developing countries' but this is countered by Delia who thinks that 'the most important challenge for feminism is to interconnect this form of inequality with others such as the relations between the global north and global south, class and ethnicity ... I hope that the underlining of difference between gender does not justify the regression of responsibilities in caring only to women (as a way of cutting costs) ... ' and Nafsika adds that: 'I suspect the contemporary form of university across Europe is to some extent a product of the feminist (and other battles) of the 1960s. Not sure if feminist debaters will continue to be of relevance, especially once the University faculties are predominantly female – then we shall see I suspect the reverse argument about the under-representation of men ... .'

Feminism clearly has had an enormous educational influence, as a learning experience par excellence. This is also the case for those such as Kelly, Pam, Penny and Carolyn who have had to struggle with the continuing patriarchal and/or sexist structures and lack of recognition of the forms of sexual harassment, for example, continuing to take place in the academy as elsewhere. They have tried to remain academic feminists, but see this task as immensely difficult. Kelly's comments about her struggles around this both personally and politically are courageous, telling me: 'one legacy I left behind is that there is now, in that university, a formal policy concerning harassment of students (there were only staff policies in place prior to our case) ... [nevertheless there remains] the distorting effects of research assessment or the research excellence framework: an academic can be accused of serious professional misconduct (and possibly criminal behaviour) but if his research record is considered important he will be kept on by any means possible ... I now see my role as a feminist academic to be mainly one of offering support to other women academics and trying to make universities less sexist places to work. My [then] ... university has the worst promotion rates of female academics in Europe ... and I've been involved in various initiatives around that. We are ... setting up a University Women's Network and a Gender Research Consortium. We probably need to revive the idea of a "Glass Ceiling" network because I know a number of women ... (myself included) who have hit it. I think I have a number of good women around me (in this institution and beyond) who will continue to offer amazing support and inspiration. But it is hard working in a patriarchal institution and continually feeling the disadvantages of being a woman. I honestly believe that there are male academics here who can't quite accept the idea that women can be scholars and leaders ... .'

Heather remains more positive and hopeful saying that: 'I want to change the views of my students about gender (and race, class, sexuality) – this is part of my feminism. My research is always informed by feminism ... I'm interested in pedagogies based on shifting power relations between students and tutors and that focus on students' lives and on shifts in consciousness. *I think of teaching as a political act.* I love being in HE because you get to create your own curriculum and assessment. Feminism strongly affects my work supporting students and other academics. I'm always offering to read stuff for people and really try to support early career academics. This is not self-sacrificing – it's great to see people develop and *I also learn a lot* and stay enthusiastic by working with "younger academics" and doctoral and MA students ... More women go to university now and many mature women ... Also since the curriculum has changed, this has changed the curriculum we produce. Feminism has changed the jobs available to men and women in complicated ways – the broadening of glamour modelling seems as much a result of second-wave feminism as rape counsellors ... [but] I feel uncertain [and a bit depressed] about the future of HE and the privatisation of HE in the UK ... .'

Feminism Has Entered into the 'Psyche' of the University ...

Penny-Jane has a less gloomy or melancholic take on these issues: 'Feminism has been highly successful and so there is no doubt that its influence remains even with increasing levels of global neo-liberalism shaping and reshaping the university – feminist influences remain as a resource for legitimate challenges to the assumptions of the "neoliberal university" and are often taken up (not always acknowledged though) by critical scholars – *feminism has entered into the "psyche" of the university* – I feel – in such a way as to make certain things unspeakable – keeping a check on issues of equality – but of course this is always under threat and it is also being overshadowed by the instrumentalism, "marketization" and neo-liberalism of the contemporary university – the university though is not a homogeneous unit – actually there are universities and differences between them – so that there are some spaces that are more influenced by feminism than others – it is crucial that younger feminists protect and develop those spaces ... I believe that feminists must be strategic and must be highly committed to influencing new spaces, new subjects, new students and new professions in and beyond the university – which is what drives me to do the research I do – feminist pedagogical practices have an important role to play in negotiating this process – in creating spaces of resistance and innovation – and in challenging new spaces which might erode the progressive, critical, transformative, subversive, empowering spaces that feminists have managed to create in and beyond education ... Feminists must be strategic about this – we live in an era where everything – even education – is being driven by "the market" – therefore feminists must create curricula that speaks but simultaneously subverts those markets – women's studies might not be as 'marketable' as it was a decade or two ago – so there need to be creative ways – and empathetic and responsive ways – to understand the perspectives of young people and their concerns but to demonstrate to them the relevance of feminist insights – this takes careful thought and lots of creativity ... there is an assumption that more women means more equality – but of course women can behave in oppressive, inequitable, competitive, individualist, self-serving and damaging ways just as men can – the importance is that feminist practices influence academia and wider society – however, at the same time, women must not be marginalised because they are women and/or because they do not perform in certain hegemonic masculine ways – I think there are continuities with young feminists shaped by second-wave feminists but inevitably reshaping the terrain in relation to the contexts in which they live and face challenge – as HE changes feminists will find ways to respond/subvert/challenge those changes that threaten agendas for equality and social justice ... with new technologies breaking down the constraints of communicating with feminists in other parts of the world, the focus on collaborating across different trans/national contexts will become increasingly important – however, this is not really different from contestations over time – feminist standpoint theory teaches us that our feminist perspectives are always shaped by our social contexts, influences, generation, ethnicity, class, sexuality etc. As new forms of feminism emerge they will do so in relation to the particular social issues, conflicts, contexts that are also emerging – younger feminists are as committed to this as ever, I believe. I have every optimism that new forms of feminism will continue to struggle against the emergent problems of the time and place – including for example issues about the increasing levels of poverty in certain parts of the world, new and environmental concerns, war and conflict and ways to promote peace, and many other ongoing and emergent issues ... Feminism has a key role to play in the struggle to defend public forms of higher education, struggles over access to HE as well as challenges ongoing and new inequalities in HE. This is an ongoing struggle – clearly we are facing new challenges – one of the key concerns is to find ways to work together and to undermine rampant individualism, which will always undermine activism and the struggle for change and transformation ... .'

The Neo-liberal University as a machine of Competitive Control

Jessica provides a nuanced approach to working in the neo-liberal university today, both agreeing with Penny-Jane about the ways that feminism is in the psyche of the university, and in our own psyches: 'For me academic feminism represents a set of painful conflicts and contradictions that are important to confront and face as part of a project of understanding where we are in the contemporary higher education institutions at this moment for those of us that make a living in this industry. The fundamental paradox we are faced with is age old. Feminism at its most basic purported to offer a shared understanding of the oppression of women and a political platform to fight against this. The idea of a shared vision is exclusionary and even violent in its imposition, however, if it does not address differences among women, as non-white, non-middle class women, non-Western have been pointing out to exclusionary liberal feminist reformers for a very long time.

Beyond these inherent problems with a singular feminism, being a "feminist" in academia or at various stages of one's schooling career contains the essential paradox that schooling and education equals competition. From the outset insertion into the schooling machine means you are competing for grades, status, reward, resources. Scholarships and studentships and later positions and grants and even the courses that you can teach about feminism or gender when you have a job are all competed for. When you are inserted into the academy you must compete to secure and maintain any position of power. That means that you are in completion with your "feminist" colleagues. It is a war zone, rather than some idyllic place of shared ideas and mutual respect in working towards the common goal of gender equality.

This is the basic scenario that we have to take as our starting point to forge genuine recognition of ourselves and others (Benjamin, 1998) with the thorny couplet of "academic feminism". We have to confront the deeply divisive nature of the power hierarchies, structures and discourses that mediate our relationships with our female (and obviously male) colleagues in academe. We need to work to manage this competitive conflict in ethical ways – through a feminist ethos – that would require somehow addressing how taking up positions of power means negotiating a phallic mantel of control that does not need a gendered body: confronting the displacement of male power from the male body – that women can wield their exclusionary power the same as men, and why would we expect differently? An unproblematised notion of "academic feminism" actually sets women up to fail if it does not teach us how to confront and manage these complexities of masculinist control, power and division through which the university and its constituents operate.

That being said, there are possibilities for forging ethical alliances in the university if the ethics of feminist academe are confronted in reflexive ways. There is also potential for engaging in research through feminist methodologies and theories and shining light on the vast web of gendered power relations connecting us. Feminist research trajectories are typically marginalized as 'political' however, particularly if they employ feminist methodologies that are qualitative, but more so if they are action oriented. In many ways we are still trapped in the science wars that have occupied my feminist post-structural thinkers in the USA since the 1990s (Lather, 1995), confronting over and over the 'god trick' claims of 'objective' research findings (Haraway, 1987). This marginalization of feminist politically oriented research is also a paradox in relation to desires for 'objective' science and social science. These types of deep divides in our theoretical investments and methodological approaches have to be continually acknowledged and worked through if we hope to forge out spaces of feminism within academe.'

Pam has an optimistic take tinged more with her radical critique, training people to work on gender-related violence saying: 'Neo-liberalism allows both third wave and new managerialist practices … performativity is the key word in both. This is a good example because it is good in places (making explicit what the criteria are for a good essay, a person spec, promotion) and also problematic (assumes a level playing field, assumes particular goals and values etc.). The danger is that women are left without feminism to find biographical solutions to structural problems e.g. me and current career promotions/applications ... My sense is that feminism has to fight its corner and will be a decreasing force but that some mainstreamed feminist things are in the mix ... That reflects a problem in designing curricula that appeal to globalised student markets ... do up-and-coming Indian academics look at my references and see the relevance of feminist texts or any other for that matter? This is also a problem for the commodification of HE so that I feel that my courses have to appeal to students in order to attract them in a competitive market. Yuk, yuk but I use the language in all sorts of ways these days ... .'

The Luxury of Doing Something I Enjoy Despite the Tough Balancing Act

Fin has a more pessimistic perspective although still having 'the luxury of doing something she enjoys': 'On a disciplinary level feminist thought has revolutionised many subject areas completely. However, I note how institutionally based the changes were and how like the tide some of the earlier won battles have slowly become eroded. For example, the demise of university based crèche and childcare facilities. Indeed I know of several UK campuses that have childfree policies, with no children allowed on site. A pain for many student and staff parents. There still remains a massive lack of parity in many institutions, in relation to promotion and career trajectory. Put simply, the impossibilities of combining a healthy work-life balance is an enduring issue ... [but] *the luxury of being able to do something I really enjoy*. It is a tough balancing act ... as a (fairly) young academic in the past I have often found myself making tea and cleaning up at Union and departmental meetings. It often appears patriarchy is still alive and well in many institutions ... I have a painful relationship with what passes as some continuation of the earlier radical activism. At feminist (activist) meetings I have been shouted down ... and realised that I am tired of orthodoxies. The thrust of much activism seems predicated around dogmatic certainties, that scholarship has supported me in questioning. I can't perhaps go back. Yet I like the energy and innovation of the activist space, in contrast to the sometimes-stultifying spaces of academia where the feminisms debated become increasingly abstract and reified. Hurrah! For our ability to theorise and contemplate, but we must not lose sight of the activist, policy and practice space too ... I am not sure where feminism can take us next. The move of a gendered analysis into the mainstream in many disciplines left women's studies, then gender studies programmes floundering, and maybe our success is also our loss. I think there was something very powerful about those women's studies programmes, but also, at the same time, the increased marketization of HE makes such spaces incredibly difficult ... Yet, the rise of neo-liberal forms of academic employment risks unpicking some of the battles partly won of prior decades. The modern university with its long hours, child free zones, and lack of crèche facilities, is for example, not a mother-friendly space. The notions of contrived collegiality in and across departments is unrecognizable from the mutuality present in feminist collaboration I have previously experienced. The pernicious individualizing thrust of HE settings remains incredibly masculinist, and often makes me consider my future within such a field. I note that I am sounding exceedingly gloomy. The marketization and potential privatisation of the rest of the sector means an increased proletarianisation of the HE workforce. I fear that this means many female academics will be pushed into evermore casualised, low paid, teaching only contracts in low status institutions. So what role has feminism to play? As always, a space to critically organise and think and teach against the grain, even if only to enable these newly casualised (or redundant) feminist academics space to consolidate and perhaps re-enter the academy when the HE reforms fail to "work" and there is a return to what the university is for beyond narrow market driven ideals ... . I think that new and existing forms of feminisms will come to the fore in dialogue with "Western" feminism – and problematize the kind of colonialist rhetoric used by some governments from the global North to make sense of their continued subjugation and dominance. At this juncture with the global economic crisis, I'm also not sure that the global power axis will remain in the US, and the shifting dynamics of economic and cultural dominance over the next decades may mean that contemporary taken-for-granted Civil Rights may need to be renegotiated and reclaimed in many cultural contexts ... The marketisation of HE makes me wonder what kinds of spaces there are for the myriad of feminisms that inhabit the academy. In my rather marginal area – the deprofessionalisation of youth work will leave the practice hollowed out. Indeed, the competency based route has little space for engaged epistemological debates around gender equity. Instead a light touch, "diversity-lite" based kind of paper exercise may take the place of engaged and thought through analysis of gender relations, heteronormativity, and feminist pedagogy. The current proposals for teacher education would point in a similar direction. This all sounds rather pessimistic, but the instrumentalist thrust of neoliberal education policy will push I believe feminist work to the margins, and/or concentrate it in elite institutions.'

Feminism Has and is Having An Influence on Power and Politics ...

Amanda is also relatively sanguine about academic feminism in the future although recognising the need for more work: 'Feminism has been influential in relation to widening access agendas, and in relation, I think, to what it is to be an academic. But that doesn't sit too comfortably with current drives towards performance management agendas. It was influential in relation to challenging the ways in which knowledge is packaged and presented, but I am less sure that is still the case ... I would like to think that there will be a return to women's studies and gender studies, as ways of making sense of and repositioning HE in new economies. We do need to think of new and alternative forms of education delivery in HE, and feminist pedagogies could be helpful and important here ... Gender is still on the agenda, but there needs to be better ways of articulating the value of contemporary feminisms for rethinking structures, processes and experiences ... I am not sure I would give that much significance in terms of current forms of HE ... I am not sure the feminist voice is very loud in contemporary discourse and debate in HE ... and I think there needs to be more work done in relation to this ... I would like to think that *feminism has and is having an influence on power and politics* ... .'

Carolyn and Penny wrote a joint response, bringing together views across generations of feminists. They are both heartened and depressed by the current changes both in academia and more widely: 'The rise and fall of Women's Studies (WS) is notable ... we seem to have come full circle from an attempt by individuals to inject WS into department provision, to a more coherent set of provision coordinated by centres, and now back to more disparate efforts of individuals in departments. Again (although there are clearly still some very important networks within institutions, especially relating to research), the argument that WS teaching is now 'mainstreamed' is not entirely convincing. Wider politics – there are questions about the ways in which university EO policies are/are not translated into practice – there appear to be large gaps between them. [Here] I (*Carolyn*) am committed to the anti-harassment network (which was set up by feminists) and have seen that it does some important work. However, I'm also aware (and have sympathy with) criticisms that university points to such networks as evidence of its commitment to tackling bullying and harassment, but the network is staffed by volunteers (mainly women) is largely unresourced, and arguably in some cases allows the institution to avoid tackling some deep-rooted issues ... both of us note with dismay how many UG students see no need for feminism as they believe girls and women are 'successful and can do anything. Most have usually shifted position by the end of our modules thankfully. However, it's a struggle getting them to see beyond their original notion that feminism is no longer needed. It was both heartening and depressing that there was a reclaim the night march in ... last month. Heartening in that it was organised, and reasonably well attended, by young women. Depressing that we still need them ... Our worries are that with the new fee regime students will choose traditional subjects (already evident from what we gather. Certainly applications in many social sciences are down, except in areas such as law and history) at the expense of sociology, gender and women's studies, education etc. Also, there will be an emphasis on STEM areas. This is likely to have a disproportionate impact on women academics. How do we fight this? Also there's a worry that increasing pressures in HE mean that feminists have less time and energy to keep fighting ... .'

Concluding Thoughts

The women of cohort 3 clearly have 'benefitted' from the expansion of global HE opportunities, just as the previous generation did, learning to become feminists through their participation in new forms of academic and feminist knowledge.

Feminism as an educational project has spread enormously through academe. Whilst these feminists were part of the crest of the wave of academic feminism, their current and future lives are clearly more heavily circumscribed by the strictures of new forms of global HE. This is exemplified in the complex accounts about both the nature of being and living in academe and the wider socio-political changes in the twenty-first century. The neo-liberal global university has become far more individualized and competitive, especially for the form of academic feminism that my participants would ideally like to espouse. It is not a comfortable place, and it raises serious questions of reflexive ethical practice, as Jessica has raised in relation to a feminist ethos. We turn now, in the concluding chapter, to the impact of academic feminism globally and its likely future within the globalizing universities worldwide, before concluding about the fundamentally educational project feminism is, has been and hopefully will continue to be. What is also striking in these accounts is the amount of social networking (through the internet) that has occurred within academic feminism both nationally and internationally, making for a wide-ranging diverse community of scholars and activists.

Chapter 8

Academic Feminism Today: Towards a Feminized Future in Global Academe

Introduction: The Zeitgeist of the twenty-first Century, especially the 2010s

Feminist values transcend specificities of generation, geography, time and place: they suffuse and shine through all three of my cohorts, despite the differences of age, location or changing educational, economic and social contexts. A commitment to social and gender justice is a passion for my participants, and they have held this dear, across the vicissitudes of their personal, political and professional lives. Nevertheless, there are clear differences in the struggles and achievements of these three cohorts to do with changing socio-political contexts, and the influences of academic feminisms on changing and more global neo-liberal universities. As we move through the cohorts, as women have entered and stayed within academe, academic feminism has changed the universities, although moves to the neo-liberal global university are now having contradictory, conflicting and paradoxical effects. Academic feminism itself has also changed, both in terms of who is now involved and how they are involved. As we have seen from this collective biography, feminist origins in working class and lower middle class as 'first-in-the-family' to go to university have increased as HE has expanded. And yet such women, despite this social (and geographic) mobility, are still constrained and constricted in their reach into the upper echelons of academe: there is still male domination.

It is clear how empowering feminism has been for these women's teaching and research, and how important it is for their own academic and personal lives. It has resulted in a huge array of publications and scholarship, too numerous to mention, ranging across inter-disciplinarity from multidisciplinary women's studies to critiques of the disciplines, from the arts, media, cultural studies to the social sciences including especially education, HE and educational research. Perhaps this also has something to do with the necessity of research and publishing in academe and the inevitable commercialization and marketization of literature, especially as books: a new avenue for intense capitalism? Yet it is the literature which has underpinned the development of academic feminism across the generations or cohorts, ensuring that this is a measure of the educational essence of feminism. What is also, from this particular perspective, most important is the role that feminism has played in creating a more reflexive and imaginative, cross-cutting interdisciplinary approach, especially to being in HE and conducting HE research, as we have seen in the voices of the cohort 3 feminists.

I now weave in comments about the influences of feminism in the transforming and global neo-liberal universities to think about futures, from my two older cohorts. I stitch together the reflections of my three cohorts, and review the usefulness of a cohort analysis for understanding how feminism has impacted upon academe. What are the paradoxes of the changes both in the global academy and in the wider globalizing world? There are clear downsides in the increasing and intense individualization and competition for place and space, as I myself have felt in the process of writing this narrative. Given past achievements, I review the successes of feminism as an educational project to think about the future of feminist pedagogies in the global academy and the wider world. Just how can new social networks and media be used to contribute to feminism as a movement for gender and social justice?

Many participants in cohort 1 struggled to enter and stay within academe, campaigning for feminist curricula, embedding feminist pedagogies, 'minds of our own' within and across subjects. Whilst the politics were often contentious these feminist activists remained passionate about the struggles, and as HE opportunities expanded felt the 'chilly climate', finding the recent struggles within academe, ever more difficult to contend with. Some express this as 'feminist melancholia', whilst others have developed professional and reflexive analyses of neo-liberal HE or educational policy analyses. These struggles were similar for the second cohort, who are mostly still in academe, reaching positions of influence and seniority, including managerial and administrative positions that they could barely dream of, when first involved, in an era of social democracy and the welfare state. They too provide reflexive analyses that engage feminist knowledge and pedagogy.

Together these two cohorts have contributed to the creation of the heyday of academic feminism – the period of the 1980s and 1990s. This was the time when the third cohort was entering academe and benefitting from feminist pedagogies and the creation of feminist knowledge. The complexities and the wider changing socio-economic contexts have meant that feminism is now multifaceted and contributes in a myriad of ways to women's lives – personal, political and professional. And, yet if anything, the struggles are greater now than they were in the past, when there was at least still some glimmer of social democracy, despite the fact that there are now as many women as men as undergraduate students in academe. *Gender equality in terms of numbers is indeed misogyny masquerading as metrics.* And the continuing and increasing forms of neo-liberalism in universities make for increasingly competitive and tense environments for the play of academic feminism. We have already seen how this plays for cohort 3's voices and values.

Feminism Has Been 'Seduced' by Corporate Models of Action, Belief, and Goals

I had asked my participants to ponder the question of the intertwined influences of feminist activism and academe for the future in the contexts of global socio-economic transformations. Jean argued that, as the renowned feminist Hester Eisenstein (2009) would put it, feminism has been 'seduced' by corporate models of action, belief, and goals. *Socialist feminism has lost out to this seduction.* Many participants, from cohorts 1 and 2, agreed that forms of academic feminism were constrained by neo-liberalism, especially socialist-feminism. Avtar also said: 'Feminism has had a huge influence on my colleagues and my teaching and research ... Apart from developing women's studies courses and lesbian studies, we also had an equal opportunities committee which for a while required all subject areas in the faculty to introduce equality perspectives in the curriculum in subject specific relevant ways. Our pedagogic practices were very student centred ... The university in an age of austerity is bound to emphasize the cost effectiveness of course programmes. If a subject is popular, it will survive. With the increase in fees, perhaps there will be a reduction in the intake of women. Neo-liberal feminisms will survive in a new world order. We have already seen the demise of socialist feminism, although the questions it raised remain hugely pertinent. As always, feminism will remain a contested space the world over.'

The Neo-liberal and Increasingly Illiberal University is Fundamentally Anti-pathetical to Feminism

Marilyn also argued that 'the neo-liberal and increasingly illiberal university is fundamentally anti-pathetical to feminism, and I think Women's Studies as an academic discipline is in an increasingly uncomfortable tension between the ideals of feminism (in so far as they continue to exist in Women's Studies) and the demands of a neo-liberal university ... OK – neo-liberalism got us into the mess, but their solutions certainly won't get us out of it ... My sense is that in the 1990s we were in some kind of ascendancy. We i.e. women, and certainly academic feminists, have made some concrete progress since then – in terms of hiring, postgraduate degrees, getting grants etc. but that there have been huge intellectual and political losses. I think in the 1990s we were still supported by a coherent, activist and theoretically challenging women's movement and I don't think that exists now – at least not in the economic north. Then there was a movement – now it's more disparate. Then the centre of gravity was towards the radical end of the spectrum; now it's definitely more conformist if not rightist. But the picture is so complex. I keep seeing and reading and hearing about really radical things happening and really radical positions being taken – but they never seem to quite come together as they used to ... .'

Several participants have given professional thought, as both education researchers and HE scholars, to the issues of changing forms of HE and educational policy analysis, making it a huge field of endeavour in the last two decades. Judith, who was very active in two American research associations in HE, serving on the board as chair of the publications committee of ASHE (American Society for HE) and chair of SAGE (Standing Committee on Gender Equity) of the American Educational Research Association (AERA) said: 'Faculty has lost a great deal of influence in the neo-neo university; today it's all about globalization with everything that implies. We are now beginning to outsource education in the same way we outsource call centers and manufacturing. Universities are siphoning off scarce resources to set up branch campuses in Asia where students and faculty will have to abide by local laws, rules, and regulations. In repressive regimes, this does not augur well for issues of gender, race, and social class ... it seems that technology drives a lot of our thinking about teaching and learning ... It would have to be cost effective and serve a broader purpose; people are vocationally focused now; and the cost-benefit ratio is high on the agenda. Look at what is happening now in the sexual harassment case at Penn State and how the "revered" 84-year old coach who probably makes more money than the president is being protected. There seems to be one case after another, e.g., Dominic Strauss Kahn (former head of the IMF) ... Berlusconi (former President of Italy) – what kind of balance can we expect when those in power behave so badly? ... I have concerns about the fact that women are in the majority of undergraduate students (but not beyond) in the US (and perhaps other nations) threaten women's progress ... The political economy of HE favors entrepreneurial actors who set up their own institutes and centers, often with external resources. Women have not been major players in establishing these new structures. Perhaps as more women take leadership roles at the head of major institutions like IBM, etc., this may change. But just look at who the major players were at the G20 – mostly men in suits except for Angela Merkel. I don't see the changes emerging from current feminist thinking ... I am not terribly optimistic right now about the future of feminism or the shape of a "new world order".'

'Maleness' Has Influenced the Neo-liberal University in Its Relentless Focus on Performance, Competition, Achievement ...

Sandra, another internationally renowned higher education researcher, said: 'The university seems to be changing without much input from feminists and it is interesting to see how little attention to gender HE research pays. I have seen umpteen co-edited books with chapters on different countries *vis-à-vis* some aspect of higher education such as accountability or governance. Gender is hardly ever featured. *Perhaps we could say that "maleness" has influenced the neo-liberal university in its relentless focus on performance, competition, achievement ...* Women's studies courses were both stand-alone and part of the curriculum of other disciplines, especially in the humanities and social sciences ... Women's studies departments are closing and there is little scope for experimentation.

Looking at the current situation, women academics and doctoral students are better represented than they were in the past; women are a high proportion of those in contingent positions (Canada does not collect national figures); differences between disciplines continue; women's responsibility for children still makes a big difference to their career chances especially combined with labour market changes that make certain jobs scarce and often part-time and short-term. Although there are some prominent women politicians, politics remains a male-dominated pursuit. Changes can be seen in the arts, in professions like law, medicine and pharmacy. In reflecting on my career some of the themes that stand out are changing technologies ... (huge differences in the last 40–50 years); the rise of the research culture; the changes in the academic job market; the changing university (neo-liberal, global); the increases in women's representation and feminist methods, theories and curriculum in certain fields; the rise of other aspects of equity and the concept of intersectionality. Another point is the changing relationship between students and faculty (staff), related to change in the student (and staff) body (more diversity), to student "consumerism" and perhaps to feminism. When I was a doctoral student we didn't even call our supervisors by their first names, let alone expect them to be endlessly available and inclined to mentor us. We did not get extensive comments on chapter drafts or instruction in how to publish ... I think our generation [of feminists] mentored each other and then went on to mentor new generations ... But probably more important was the "peer mentoring" and the simultaneous growth of many other women in the same stage of life with similar interests ... *Younger doctoral students and faculty now get much more help and advice. However, the academic world into which they try to go is less open, less forgiving, and expects constant, intensified productivity ... .'*

Women's Studies Might be Reframed as a 'Boutique' Subject?

Kari, her colleague, added: 'I've always worked with and through versions of feminist pedagogy, though not always explicitly so ... I tend to be open to students' ideas and interests; I invite their critiques and questions and so on. I do a lot of thesis supervision and the large majority of students I work with are women and feminists ... I tend to seek out women colleagues who are feminists to work with, make strategic alliances in the university. For example, during my three years as head of department I initiated an informal group of women heads who met informally to plan our responses and initiatives in relation to the university administration ... working with feminist colleagues within academic organizations; hosting feminist visiting scholars; working on conference organizing committees and so on ... I would say the generation of feminist faculty before mine had a major influence in my own institution ... many of the gains that were made in the 1980s and 1990s are now disappearing ... In Canada I think we're doing fairly well in these terms, such as recognizing same-sex partners, paid maternity and adoption leaves, etc. ... For me, anti-racist and intersectional perspectives, as well as post-structural feminism continue to be important ... I don't see this as post-feminism, rather an extension of it ... The austerity probably looks and feels differently in different places ... in Canada there is austerity, but I think notions of neo-liberalism, with HE viewed as a market and an individual consumable good, might have stronger influences. *Women's studies might be reframed as a "boutique" subject?* Interesting to think of gestures toward inter-disciplinarity in Canadian universities, where women's or gender studies can find a place ... *My hunch is that divisions among women will grow,* with an elite group of women securing access to a cosmopolitan and globalized world, while the world's majority of women are sinking further into poverty, living in conflict zones and so on. *I'm not sure whether or how feminism will or can influence this unless connections between social justice social movements in the North and South are strengthened substantially and strategically ... .'*

Indeed, the question that Kari raises of 'divisions between women' growing are within and outside academe, and a growing issue even for feminists within the neo-liberal university: the competitions for research grants, for scholarly publications and for support and mentoring intensify as the forms of metrics and control intensify. These are not comfortable times within academe or even academic feminism, despite the commitment to collective and collaborative values.

It is a Hard Time for the Academy, for Feminism, and for Academic Feminism

Frinde also argued that the neo-liberal university is not a comfortable space: 'As a college professor, I always taught and did research from a feminist perspective. My classroom was always discussion based and collaborative, as has been much of my writing. Both *The Feminist Classroom* and *Privilege and Diversity in the Academy*, our second book, were researched and written with Mary Kay Tetreault ... Feminist pedagogies have been at the base of my research and teaching for many years. Since the 1990's however I have been equally interested in the progress that women and people of color have made to become members of the professoriate. *Privilege and Diversity in the Academy* is based on research done at three American universities to find out on what terms, in what departments and disciplines, based on what kinds of policies, have these "newcomers" joined the faculties. We interviewed over 100 people at the University of Michigan, Stanford University, and the University of Rutgers in Newark. We found out that a "hidden curriculum" of racism, sexism and classism keeps people out of academic careers and that explicit hiring policies promoting diversity are necessary ... The publication of this book has led me to visit colleagues in South Africa for many years now, especially going to the University of the Western Cape, which is a formerly "colored" university outside of Cape Town. There my colleague Beverly Thaver is doing similar work on "deracializing" the formerly all-white professoriate at South African universities and we have collaborated on research and presentations on our results ... In the work for our second book we have found that there has been a lot of change at the policy and official level, differing by department and by institution. Day care centers, maternity leaves, more flexible tenure policies, and explicit policies to hire women and minorities are much more common now, although still few and far between nationwide. Some places, like the University of Michigan, are much more progressive in this regard than others ... Women's Studies and Gender Studies, to use the new turn of phrase, can influence the modern university by sticking to the feminist agenda of international equality and international rights, for women but for everyone. The new subjects seem to include the effects of globalization, which is very important, and the new students seem as far as I can tell to want to travel and do feminist organizing work in a number of places. I teach a graduate course in Feminist Theory sometimes, and have students from all over the world doing important feminist work in local settings. An example – the student who worked in a women's health center in Mongolia, whose official policies on abortion were much more progressive than anywhere in the United States right now ... I think that the future of the university depends on courses, curricula and subjects which are neither the liberal arts of the past nor the instrumental "career" based subjects of the current day. Right now in the USA universities are increasingly divided between elite schools, both private and a few public, for the few who can afford it, who are being trained in the liberal arts and "critical thinking" to run the society, and the rest of the public university system, which is being systematically starved of funds and increasingly made to focus on narrow training for careers in industry and technology. Feminists can call for and enact a new liberal arts curriculum, based on history, literature, psychology, sociology and the sciences, for and about the many and not the few, for and about working people in the US and Britain but also South Africa and Indonesia and Somalia and Yemen, to bring the concerns of women in each and all of these places together in conversation – a conversation in which Western privilege and exploitation, women's as well as men's, is fully acknowledged and dealt with. Academic feminism is fully up to this task, although as always it will take a social movement outside the walls of the academy which I am not sure is there right now. I think HE must be public and widespread, and that public funding should be its basis. The US should follow the *old* tuition policies in the UK rather than the other way around, and both countries should expand, of course, rather than constrict access as they are doing now. *It is a hard time for the academy, for feminism, and for academic feminism. Time for another Women's Movement!'*

The question of how younger generations of feminists are beginning to re-assert political practices, through a new women's movement is now on the agenda, by feminists critiquing the austerity policies for education, HE included, as well as challenging forms of public policy control. This raises public policy analysis too. Catherine as an American education policy analyst reflecting on the changes and future in the USA addresses the question of 'feminist melancholia': 'Right at the moment, I am pretty depressed about the future in the United States. I think that, as you know from things I've written, that the economy is being used as an excuse to cut out things that are seen as frills and, you know, things like elective courses, things like professors who are not teaching the things that are the required, from above, kinds of curricula. And that would include, I see, Women's Studies, if they're not under attack yet, they will be. Long before things like African-American studies will be. LONG before anything like football will be! *So, I'm, I'm very pessimistic about the future to tell you the truth.* I don't know how that can be recovered from because the people who could recover it are either, tired like me, or retiring or getting no funding or *learning that in order to be able to stay in their positions they better shut up about these issues* ... I think that's why I see something like a WLE – *Women Leading Education* Conference – could have a future. In my little three days of being part of that it was an incredibly empowering and fun and feminist kind of environment among scholars, international scholars. And I thought: wow! If my women grad students could experience that, they might really want a gender in education course, and they might clammer to have it be required. And they might say: You know what? When I become a school superintendent, I'm gonna do something with this! Or when I become a professor, I'm gonna do something with this! And that is the kind of environment that, I'm not saying that Radcliffe was ever like that, let's say, but, or Wellesley or anything, but now, today, there's enough, there's more, like there's Women's Studies, there's a few women scholars internationally who are caring about these things, where there wasn't back in when Hillary Clinton was going to Wellesley, I don't think. So, I think that that could be a future … Just realizing that it's invigorating to recognize that all of these questions are played out somewhat differently in other parts of the world. And that it's fun to know that, and for example to know at the *Women Leading Education* [meeting] I realized that some people are back in asking the question: Can women get mentors? Well we were asking that question back in the 60s and 70s here. So that's an old question for us in scholarship here. But, at the same time, in other countries, a question about women's activism in labor unions is HUGE and important and vibrant whereas it's not in the United States. It's there as a question, but it's a quiet question … I think that there's a real future of seeing things globally, and recognizing that, and I'm speaking kind from an intellectual point of view, but recognizing that too the issues for women in other countries are like [my former student] … was looking at mothers who can't get food and water for their children, never mind get to the school in Kenya … And that, that's not about scholarship but it's still a feminist question. It's a feminist in education question. And that too, that the recognition, looking globally but also looking within the United States, recognition that of the intersectionality of issues – gender intersecting with race and class and age … are exciting and important and coming to the forefront … And challenging earlier feminisms that were so intellectual and so much of the elite white Radcliffe types that you didn't even know there was a Rosa Parks out there being an activist and a woman. So that's my concluding remark. Is that glorious?'

A New Wave of Energy?

The question of women's leadership in education, global HE especially, combined with an intersectional analysis has clearly come onto the academic feminist agenda, but how it can be enacted in the future remains a troubling and paradoxical one, in the context where breaking the vicious cycle of male domination remains hard. First, the Australian feminist Lyn Yates who held a leadership position as PVC for research at the University of Melbourne, gives a measured comment upon the situation in Australia: 'I do think there are some generational issues and not sure what form is most appropriate … In many parts of the world feminism and specific women's institutions and opportunities are vital. In the west, the problem is more about the problem of the gap between the theoretical sophistication by those interested and the lack of even basic sensitivities by many who are not interested.' Her colleague, Bronwyn Davies (Petersen and Davies, 2010) addresses the forbidding climate of both neo-liberalism and austerity in her work: 'I see neoliberalism as having undone so much that was good, turning universities into alien and horrible places. In the early 90s I would have said feminism had changed everything – that nothing was untouched by it. I didn't see neo-liberalism rising up at the same time to oppose and squash it all. It took me completely by surprise and at the same time enticed many female academics to support it by promises of ensuring gender equity. Ha! What a massive con that was … Despite what I said, I have to admit that a lot has changed – so much so that young women often don't know what all the fuss is about and take their equal access to all things totally for granted. At the same time the evidence is now out that those same young women end up defeated and giving up on the workforce because they can't manage it all as they thought they could … Neoliberalism denies that gender is an issue which makes it very difficult for feminists to get any purchase on it. Feminists who take up the newly accessible management positions do so at a considerable price as they have to play the neoliberal game and in my observation become at best gender-blind, at worst brutal to any who do not support their eager take-up of neoliberal discourses and practices. Neoliberalism is based on one value, which is money, and in particular the flow of money toward the rich. It is rabidly individualistic and competitive and deeply destructive of anything to do with ethics, with human welfare, with values other than its own. The only way feminism survives in such a context is by going under the radar. It amuses me to publish highly critical papers that "score University productivity points" without the administrators realizing their potential impact … Perhaps I am wrong to be so pessimistic about the current state of things in universities, but for me the shutting down of critical thought (inimical to neoliberal managers) and the reduction of face-to-face encounters, and the imposition of measures of productivity that have zero to do with quality of thought or innovation – all this has led me to resign my position at university and to take up my life as an independent scholar where I can just talk to people who actually want to hear what I have to say. I have an honorary university position, thankfully, as some universities can only get their heads around paying me if I belong to another institution. I left the university in order to be free to get on with my work – my research and writing and my teaching. So you can see my pessimism runs quite deep. I hope you get some good answers to this question that can contribute to a *new wave of energy* … .'

Feminist Reflections as Feminist Melancholia?

An overriding impression from amongst all my participants is the feeling of melancholia or concerns for the future of both academic feminism and of universities across the globe: the increasing individualization, intensity and competition amongst scholars. The majority of my participants felt that there was a heyday of academic feminism in the 1980s and 1990s when social welfare and democracy was still in ascendance. With the advent of neo-liberalism and its impact upon universities in a globalizing world, its effects had been pernicious and a cause of the reversal of many of the gains achieved. Debbie expressed this clearly: 'A few years ago, I would have been much more optimistic, but the clock is being turned back and I fear for the future ... Well, it's the danger of the loss of focused politics for me. Also I fear that "post-feminism" feeds on and into the individualization inherent in neo-liberalism ... I think this is hard given the stress on economic profit for universities but hope that there will be room for this as women begin to see their advances rolled back and a new generation find the necessity of feminist politics ... I despair – everything is going backwards with this wretched government – the purpose in the UK is to privatize everything – and the world crisis in capitalism ... it's really time to take on the questions Raewyn Connell raises about *Southern Theory* ... .'

The changes have also led to heightened competitiveness between and amongst academic feminists and especially across the generations. This raises the issue of whether academic feminism is now taking a different form with the rise of new forms of social media. Not all my participants felt depressed and pessimistic about the future: what the indefatigable education feminist Gaby called 'left melancholia'. She, and Sue, for example, dismissed such pessimism, arguing that it is necessary for subsequent generations of feminists to develop their own strategies for the future, as the first cohort are ageing and bowing out of academe. However, whilst this is indeed an enormous transformation in HE, and in the work of academic feminists, many of them also feel constrained by neo-liberal universities, just as cohort 3 did. Gaby said: 'I think that the university is changing dramatically, but also that feminist academics are coming through who will be able to succeed and do well nevertheless. Feminists have always been pragmatic ... there is a huge chasm now between academic feminism and what is going on in schools, and that needs to be addressed. Certainly the massification of HE has meant a change in students attending the university, but in the main, my HE experience has been with these newer kinds of students. So I have been aware of the opportunities available as well as of emergent problems ... I dislike what has been termed "left melancholia" and discourses of pessimism, and have detected in newer, less-academic feminisms, an energy and hope that has been missing in the recent history of academic feminism ... I am less confident as globalization and privatization of HE seems to be creating rather than reducing gender inequalities ... I am more hopeful of national feminisms than global feminisms as women are rarely powerful enough to protect their own and other women's interests at an international level ... .'

The Twitter/Facebook Phenomenon Reshapes and Possibly Renames Feminism

Sue argues that: 'I don't think today's young women are any better off than we were. They have their own issues to deal with e.g. sexualisation of little girls; new forms of alcoholism; compulsive consumption (consumer throwaway culture) ... . This generation's politics are quite different – their "organization" is via Twitter and Facebook and their activist "groups" are "virtual". The decline of the "public" and the protection of "education for democracy" are my major concerns. *The Twitter/Facebook phenomenon reshapes and possibly renames feminism* ... Their activism is online. They belong to green/socialist rather than explicitly feminist networks. Feminism always accommodates to new conditions and "our" feminism won't work for "their" contexts ... The emerging feminisms will be based in the Arab/Islamic world, in India and POSSIBLY (but not necessarily) China as the consequences of its one-child policy come to the fore. Western young women seem to have inherited a terrible situation – required to have careers to pay basic bills and not being able to choose to spend time with children. Young girls seem to see equality as "getting as drunk as the boys" and having indiscriminate sex. This isn't what "we" /I fought for. The West has lost its way ... .'

The Hideous and 'Hideously White' Place of Academe Today

The question of the differences between the generations of academic feminists through experiences of neo-liberalism and academe, networks and communication, is one that needs to be addressed. Whilst my collective biography using cohort analysis showed a commitment to overarching feminist values, it also revealed clear differences between the generations in terms of experience, especially of the increasingly forbidding nature of the global university, with its now endemic forms of competition and measurement. Many participants from cohorts 2 and 3 expressed this as being both stressful and more – hideous, unable even to reach out to colleagues and friends in this forbidding climate. Even my uses of naming particular individuals' comments, so as not to be seen to be claiming authorship of ideas, becomes itself problematic, as it may have far-reaching consequences for careers and positions within and across global academe. The question of feminist ethical practice becomes far more difficult in forbidding times, going far beyond the traditional notions of 'informed consent'. Indeed, the notion of informing, or being informed take on contradictory and paradoxical meanings. What now constitutes civil liberties in a cyber-world is also difficult.[1] Whilst the beginnings of academic feminism were felt as stressful even at a time of social welfare, this is much more the case for the younger generations in academe today.

Heidi expressed the dilemmas of being in and out of academe and its deformed nature extremely appositely: 'As a feminist professor I find the academy a very stressful space now. The individualism of the neo-liberal culture means there isn't a lot of sharing or camaraderie in universities any more. To stay on top of the food chain – which you are as a highly visible black woman professor – you have

---

1 I was writing this before the news of Edward Snowden, the US so-called whistle-blower, and his evidence about the official and secret uses and abuses of the internet were made public.

to keep producing. There are high expectations and it is exhausting. There's a sense in which you never feel complete and you always feel that the knowledge you are chasing is illusive. Especially now, with the internet where there is so much new information. I've talked to other senior female academics and there is a feeling among them of being a fraud or an interloper in the academic space – which they often attribute to their class or gender – and in my case, ethnicity ... In the specialist field that I work in, which is about the intersectionality of race and gender in education, my peers are small in number and getting smaller in the age of austerity where there are so few new appointments and promotions. Many minority ethnic women are choosing to leave HE as racism is as entrenched as ever. Despite the raft of equality policies and legislation they see no future there. HE in Britain remains a "hideously white" place, (like the BBC!) – there are still only 1.3 per cent BME staff in HE. In the context of policies on widening participation in HE, and the continued lack of equity in access, particularly for working class black and white young people, "diversity" has become an all-consuming discourse. However black women's experience at the institutional level is still very much shaped by the power of whiteness in such places of privilege. Being a body "out of place" in white institutions has emotional and psychological costs to the bearer of that difference. Many just leave ... Feminism is as important today as it has always been. Global gendered and raced inequalities are as entrenched as ever. Patriarchy and religious fundamentalism still dominates the majority of women's lives globally. Violence against women is endemic and trafficking of women and children is on the increase. Global capitalism depends on the exploitation and sweatshop labour of women from the global south. It is important to continue to develop our theoretical and activist thinking about the universal interconnections between race and gender inequality and its integral relationship to educational opportunities in HE. Ultimately it is feminism that is still – after all these years – at the vanguard of these outrageous justices against women.'

Rampant Misogyny Has Partly Retreated into Direct Violence

How to deal with both the hideousness of academe today, and remain within it, clearly is a dilemma for many, making it a very uncomfortable place, although there are also benefits of being able to be a creative, if individual scholar, within academe. These are complex questions, because as feminism has become embedded in academe, inevitably feminist knowledge, theories and perspectives have developed in untold ways, so that there are differences of approach, albeit that the overarching commitments may stay the same. Certainly the critique of patriarchy has become stronger, with the overt naming it as misogyny nowadays, rather than the previously less contested notion of patriarchy and male power: this also has unintended consequences. Gemma's involvement in a specialist HE institution means that she focuses on research rather than teaching: 'My own academic work has developed along its own trajectory, and become more sociological rather than specifically feminist, though I see these two as blurred. I think the ways I think about social difference are very profoundly influenced by my feminism – but my own writing isn't mainstream women's studies ... I don't know how others position my work on gender – I am committed to gender equality and exploring social difference, but I don't do identity work, which I think makes my stuff slightly odd to place, given where the discourse has gone to now ... I do identify very much as a feminist within the left and trade union politics, though my most active period was as a teacher. On coming into the academy I've mostly been active on contract research issues, so redefining feminism to encompass issues that aren't specific to women, but speak to a politic of the dispossessed ... I've also done very little teaching, mostly research ... Feminism has changed loads of things, and other things have changed loads of things too ... There are loads more women in the academy these days, but maybe that's because all the men have gone to banking ... Often now as a woman academic I find myself sitting in a room with mostly other women – is that because the men have all cleared off to better paid jobs? ... I think a lot of issues that were women's issues or only women raised have become mainstream – like child care. *Rampant misogyny has partly retreated into direct violence,* or turned into a discourse around sex (who's doing it, how much) which objectifies men and women both, not sexuality (straight or gay), in a way it wasn't before. Overt sexual harassment it strikes me is far less acceptable or likely, or maybe I've just grown too old. It means new ways of worrying about old things ... I do think professional *third wave feminism has turned feminism into a private language you more or less have to have a doctorate to speak.* If feminism means something then it means something in the real world, not as a theoretical object in the knowledge-making factory of the academy. This doesn't mean not holding on to basic principles – but I think something odd has happened to knowledge-making too. So it's a question of sorting out what has really shifted, what stays the same ... .'

The Potential for Feminist Research and Activism

Drawing together the voices of my participants across the generations appears to sound rather melancholic despite the pleasures of being an academic feminist that some have voiced. Life in the second decade of the twenty-first century – whether in academe or outside – is clearly a very different place and space from fifty years ago, when this story began. Dramatic change has taken place, especially in forging new ideas about the place of women in society, their rights and their education. This is increasingly recognised in more popular and mainstream publications, a really important one being Melissa Benn's *What Should We Tell Our Daughters? The pleasures and pressures of growing up female.* She reviews a huge amount of second-wave feminist evidence about being a woman in today's society. Feminism has been a major force for change, and for good, especially in being able to take a place at the academic table, if still not the academic high table. Changing the rules of the patriarchal game in academe (to use Louise Morley's 2013 idea) has eluded us so far, although it is far more on the agenda nowadays than even ten years ago, despite shifts towards a more global neo-liberal academy. And feminism is on the public agenda in a myriad of ways, through new media and print media, as well as in books, films, videos.[2]

Jessica argues: 'Spaces outside academe may prove the most freeing and thought-provoking for feminists working inside the academy. Social media has made networked online feminism a growing source of information and support, although as well another space for competitive hierarchies that must be managed by academics engaging with or "plugging into" this wider feminist assemblage (Ringrose and Renold, 2012a and b). The UK Gender and Education Association is one such academic forum, run through the voluntary actions of its members and executives rather than officially supported through university funding, for instance. Thus feminisms' most radical potential may be connected to the thinking of academic feminism but takes flight outside the institutional walls. This is evident in the range of amazing feminist action and protest happening around the world in various sometimes controversial ways from the internationally viral *SlutWalks* to the protest group *Femen*, who bare their breasts in a bid to get exposure from a media apparatus consumed by commodifying the female form and parts (breasts especially). There is a wide range of inspiring young feminists who are organizing on Facebook, Twitter and via other networks to raise awareness of the issues related to sexism and girls and women's rights, but also issues related to masculinity, heterosexism and LGBTQ and queer activism and thinking. The USA blogger Feminist Teacher has over 5,000 Twitter followers and there are other groups like Youth Twitter Feminist Army who are actually using tweets to challenge sexism at school. There are highly committed teachers in the UK who are organizing to fight repressive educational tactics, including the curriculum revisions that have removed a concern for social well-being including sexual and relationship education from school. These groups spring up and mobilize partly through social media, with Feminist Fight Back's S-word event geared at challenging the problems with current UK Sex Education an example in point. The challenge for academic feminism is to watch learn and listen from these important ripples of activity, action and challenge to power from outside the academic pulpit. When older feminists reproduce a generational melancholic and typically Oedipal and maternal narrative of suggesting girls and young women are simply succumbing to sexism, or failing to live up to the opportunities paved through earlier feminist struggle they are missing the point entirely. They are failing to recognize the different forms of engagement and feminist life-forms that are becoming in the world – even *gasp* if they do not call themselves feminist!!! Indeed the biggest challenge for us academic feminists is to use the magnificent powers of critical analysis that we have generated through our time in academia

---

2   Popular blogs, books and articles written by feminists abound with examples such as *The Guardian* and other columnists – Laura Bates, Kat Banyard, Bidisha, Hadley Freeman, Tanya Gold, Laurie Penny to name but a few.

to try to see and possibly connect with the feminist waves that are continually churning up in the world. And this is not just in some first, second and third wave analogy but rather in the repeated rhythms of everyday discussions, negotiations and actions through which gender and sexual power relations are unfolding and sometimes being contested and transformed.'

Feminism is Now in the Air-waves: The Popular State of Feminism Today – Fifty Years On

When I was drawing the threads together, there were several celebratory online and 'real' events in the UK around international women's week which was inaugurated in the media. It culminated with a weekend festival of arts called *Women of the World* organized by Jude Kelly, indomitable director of the Southbank Centre in London, starting on international women's day: to consider the popular state of feminism today, not only in the UK but worldwide. What has been achieved and what has changed over the last fifty years? Some were media discussions, others public debates, and yet others, written commentaries: a veritable melange, as Jessica has already mentioned, feminism is now everywhere and yet still nowhere important. Examples include the launch of the British Library's oral history archive: *Sisterhood and After* together with the Women's Library and the University of Sussex. Another was the opening of the Women's Library in its new venue of the London School of Economics (LSE), moving from its feminist architect-designed space at the London Metropolitan University, based in the East End of London. Intriguingly, this library is now-based in the Lionel Robbins building at LSE, named after the chair of the UK government committee to inaugurate the expansion of HE, fifty years ago (and as we have already seen). Yet others were to celebrate the fifty years since Betty Friedan's *The Feminine Mystique* was published in the USA, arguably, the publication that led to the launch of second-wave feminism initially in the USA (as we have also seen).

The Guardian newspaper and online was at the forefront of publicizing International Women's Day (IWD) with articles and letters galore, including pages headed simply feminism. Their lead letter (8 March 2013, p. 45) was entitled '*Men and women must unite for change' and was from singers and artists, perhaps led by Eve Ensler, one of the signatories, who had inaugurated 'a billion women rising'* around Valentine's Day.[3] The letter covered issues of gender and sexual violence across the world, including issues of female genital mutilation that had been raised earlier in the week, but started with Malala Yousafzai, the Pakistani schoolgirl shot for demanding girls' education: This led to their byline 'WE MUST ECHO MALALA YOUSAFZAI'S WORDS AND ALL COMMIT TO ENDING VIOLENCE AGAINST WOMEN' ... *UKFeminista* has also begun a very welcome campaign, based upon American protest, to get women and young

---

3 And this was repeated in 2014 on V.day and IWD Valentine's Day.

girls to say why they need feminism, and most of the young women, as reported by *The Guardian* (8 March 2013, pp. 18–19) for IWD talk about issues of gender and sexual abuse, or harassment and domestic violence. And they have learnt to talk about these matters through school, and feminist teachers. Jane Martinson's analysis article is headlined *"School is equality's new frontline"*. The new social media such as Twitter (#twitteryouthfeministarmy) are aiming to spread the word of feminism to girls as young as nine, she argues and mentions several more outlets for spreading feminism to very young girls, in ways unheard of before.

Whilst it might be expected that *The Guardian* would produce copy for IWD it is far more unexpected that the free paper *The London Evening Standard* would. And yet on IWD (8 March 2013) their lead editorial was entitled amazingly 'Why we still fight for women's rights' and was yet again dedicated to arguing for EDUCATION as the key: 'So it is that we have to fight for women and girls' basic rights, such as education ... the cause for which Malala Yousafzai almost died' and it also mentioned female genital mutilation [FGM] and 'meanwhile, other British women face violence elsewhere in their daily lives – or else are degraded in ways such as those highlighted ... by [UK] Home Secretary Theresa May, who announces a drive to stop girls being pressured into sending males explicit photos of themselves ...' Whilst May may have a simplistic view of sexting, compared with Jessica Ringrose's (2012) more feminist analysis, it is now hitting the headlines in a more welcome way. Quite a dramatic week for feminists, and one that those of us setting out in the 1960s could not have dreamt of ... We have been amazing, despite all the vicissitudes and the violence and girls having to endure shooting is perhaps why this has now reached the top of the agenda, but we are especially now celebrating the power of education ... .

What I take from all these events, discussion and debates is the focus on feminist writing, the ongoing influence of books or the written word on how feminist values are spread but in myriad new forms such as online and via global publishing: another nod towards neoliberalism's new tentacles. *The Guardian* now frequently has a commitment to publicising feminism and in its Review (2 March 2013) had an article with a picture entitled MY HERO BETTY FRIEDAN by Lionel Shriver, the writer, in which she mentioned that '50 years on ... it is worth touching base with *The Feminine Mystique* which reminds us not to idolize that bygone life of lie-ins ... such leisure came at a heavy price: a marriage that was in no way an equal partnership ... [it] goads me to gratitude that, thanks to forerunners like Betty Friedan, I've had the opportunity to pursue a career ... [but] we have come full circle', as Lionel Shriver argued, 'actually being at home when a delivery arrives from Amazon ... there remains dissatisfaction.'

At the now annual British event – *Jewish Book Week* – there was also a panel to discuss *The Feminine Mystique* – *50 years on* in which the chair and panellists commented on their 'personal and political' readings of the book, followed by a discussion about the state of feminism today. What was fascinating about the discussion was the fact that, as the poet Leah Thorn put it, she was very pleased to be there as she got to think and *talk about feminism for a whole hour uninterrupted*!

She also mentioned that she was in New York in September 2012 for the memorial for Shulamith Firestone, who had died in the summer. Her book *The Dialectic of Sex: The Case for Feminist Revolution* was published seven years later than Friedan's and was altogether more radical and revolutionary in tone, although Friedan's book had launched consciousness-raising (CR) groups which quickly spread across the Atlantic, and the National Organisation of Women (NOW). Yet Leah argued that she had not been politicized through a book, but more through immersion in political activities as a young woman.

It is quite clear to me from my cohort analysis that books and writing were clearly very influential on creating feminist values and pedagogies. As we have seen many participants from cohort 1 cited *The Feminine Mystique* and many of the other books published in the 1960s and 1970s, so that academic feminism became above all a passion as well as politics and pedagogy. Cohorts 2 and 3 also referred to feminist scholarship, but as feminism was gradually embedded in academe it was academic feminists' work that gradually created the 'feminist cannon' (Davis and Evans, 2011).

The global academy now has a multitude of academic feminists or feminist academics, still feeling passionate about their work, but nevertheless, feminism is still an ongoing struggle. Whilst there are more women than men as students in universities, the problems of male violence and sexual abuse or harassment have not gone away. Indeed, as Carolyn Jackson an Alison Phipps (2014), amongst others, have argued the culture of laddism in HE has been developing rapidly amongst undergraduate students. Questions about this are raised almost daily in Facebook campaigns or causes and other digital media.

Betty Friedan for the Digital Age

As we have already argued, though, whilst we can indeed celebrate the array of new cultural forms for the expression of feminism, not just confined to the sidelines anymore, there are also downsides to this multiplicity of media and networks which are also being celebrated as new forms of feminism. The week after major celebrations for IWD, we were invited to learn about these new forms from Sheryl Sandberg, chief operating officer of Facebook, whose new book was published in the UK with great fanfare. Entitled *Lean In: Women, Work, and the Will to Lead* the book develops an argument, ostensibly supported by the older liberal American feminist Gloria Steinem, to help women stop sabotaging and limiting themselves in work places. Sandberg is a Harvard-educated economist, who went on to work with the former President of Harvard University Larry Summers (who resigned in 2008 over his comments about women's brains being smaller than men's). She has had a meteoric business career, becoming the most senior woman at Facebook at a relatively young age and itself a young organisation for the digital media age.

Sandberg has thus imbibed the spirit of capitalism and liberal feminism with a vengeance and now writes to advise women on how to take a leaf out of her book. What is clear is the paradox of hyper capitalism, with such a woman at one of its helms and the attempts still to use new social media as a platform for feminism of the most liberal kind. *The Guardian* and its sister Sunday paper *The Observer* devoted several pages and column inches to interviews, reviews and comments on this phenomenon. It is the same as in academic feminism: the contradiction between working for collective values and at the same time having to compete in an intensely individual and competitive environment, and wanting to come out on top. The journalist Maureen Dowd (*The Observer*, 17 March 2013, The New Review, p. 15) wrote: 'She has a grandiose plan to become the PowerPoint Pied Piper in Prada ankle boots reigniting the women's revolution – *Betty Friedan for the digital age*. She wants women to stop limiting and sabotaging themselves. Sandberg may mean well ... but she doesn't understand the difference between a social movement and a social networking marketing campaign. People come to a social movement from the bottom up, not the top down. She has co-opted the vocabulary and romance of a social movement not to sell a cause, but herself ... .'

The problem for feminism, and academic feminism especially, is the intensity of competitiveness combined with the increasingly rivalrous culture of the world around us with all its contradictory consequences but a feminist future is still possible ... *Feminism is now in the air-waves*, quite unimaginable fifty years ago. Feminism has been an unbelievably successful educational project, creating knowledge and wisdom, and pedagogical approaches around gender and social justice, within and beyond the university. It can indeed be seen and felt everywhere, and yet the struggle continues: whilst gender equality is on the global public agenda, gender-related violence continues across the globe. How can we embed a stronger commitment to change, ensuring a way to stop both symbolic and real violence against women? What are the necessary educational projects to combat continuing forms of misogyny?

Feminist Pedagogues and Pedagogies for the Future

Given the contradictory changes, it is not just a numbers game, because if it were we would now have achieved all the goals of academic feminism; it is also important to think about how resistant to progressive change the structures of capitalism and of universities within the global north are. How can real changes towards social and sexual justice be achieved? It does mean changing the rules of the game, and thinking about alternative forms of management and leadership, as well as changing the wider cultures of sexual relations. So this work of the generations of feminist scholars and academic activists is still vital, invidious though it is to name particular scholars and perspectives. Nevertheless, '*women leading education*' to use Catherine Marshall's term or that on leadership and pedagogies in higher education by Bagilhole and White (2013), Hey and Morley (2013) is vital if we are to forge new ways of being in HE, less susceptible to capture by global university elites, and ones in which we do not feel deformed or constantly stressed out.

Equally the work of many of my cohort 3 feminists around education and young people will surely make a difference to future generations creatively critiquing the new socio-cultural forms of education in a hyper-capitalised society? Malala Yousafzai's story (2013) is a bitter-sweet illustration of the importance of narratives in educational settings and the ongoing work on addressing gender-based violence. Jessica Ringrose is working with Emma Renold (2012 a and b) on sexualisation, sexting and new cultural forms in and out of school, and the various impacts and consequences of these new social media on children's learning. Pam Alldred and Fin Cullen are working on a new EU-funded Daphne project – the Gap Work Project (GAP): Improving Gender-Related Violence Intervention and Referral Through 'Youth Practitioner' Training – to develop the tools and skills to train teachers and youth workers and others to help young people, young women especially, to learn about gender-related violence and anti-homophobia/anti-transphobia within an array of new contexts, not only school, but community and youth settings within the new networked world. This international project [funded by the EU and through the Daphne programme which is specifically about dealing with violence against women and children] is using a third-wave feminist concern with gender norms and heteronormativity to do both feminist anti-violence work and broader gender-violence work such as against homo/transphobia. The GAP project is coordinated by Brunel University and has partners based in universities in Ireland (the National University of Ireland at Maynouth), Italy (University of Turin), and Spain (University Rovira and Virgili, Tarragona, Catalunya) and associate partners in Hungary and Serbia (http://sites.brunel.ac.uk/gap). There is clearly the need for a continuing struggle over politics and pedagogies, which is more than just about education. This struggle is now to deal with how neo-liberalism and globalisation are deforming global academe and the wider society, including relations between men and women, rich, privileged and poor, cultures and ethnicities. But without the passion and politics of academic feminism we would not have made these gains and changes in women's lives, making sure that women's right to education and to live a life free of violence are continually on the public agenda.

Appendix 1

Questions for Discussion and Possible Online Replies

1. Start with some contextual material:
   a. Where and when you were born, and into what kind of family – class, siblings, parents to university and their employment?
   b. When and where did you go to university?
   c. What did you study and why?
   d. When did you become a feminist – at university, before or after?
   e. How have you used your university education since graduating?
   f. How influential has feminism been on your own learning across the lifecourse, and how have you tried to influence feminism – activism versus theories?
2. Now some specific questions about changes in education, including HE, society, and work/employment and gender from when became involved in HE and linked to civil/civic and equal rights:
   a. What was university education about when you went – role and mission (as liberal arts?) and for women versus men?
   b. Did you 'learn' about women as an undergraduate student and linked to subjects – what about women's studies?
   c. Did you do a higher degree/doctorate – when and how? What topic and who was supervisor?
   d. How influential was your family – parents, partners and children on your feminism and its continuance?
3. When did you become a feminist and when did you become an 'academic'?
   a. Was becoming a feminist part of either student movement (with socialism) and/or feminist activism – campaigns within society-politics (EPA/SDA/Civil and human rights), university e.g. nursery/crèche, maternity leave etc.?
   b. What about feminist theories and research and question of 'evidence' plus women's studies?
   c. How involved in research and what kinds? (Education feminism and research/social sciences e.g. social policies or sociology or literature/history)?
   d. Which feminist theories and writers were key influences and why?
   e. When did you start using feminist 'work' in your own teaching and research and how collaborative/individualistic?

4. What influences has feminism(s) had on your
    a. Own continuing research and teaching, locally, nationally, internationally
    b. Curriculum or not of teaching and specific pedagogies as well as practices e.g. changing forms of women's studies
    c. Your wider activities as well as academic work within universities e.g. TU
    d. Activism i.e. wider 'world' of policies and politics and setting up feminist networks and groups e.g. FWSA, GEA etc.
5. What influences has feminism had on the changing university?
    a. How has your or other feminisms influenced the changing university – structures, pedagogies and practices?
    b. The wider politics of equal opportunities or equity questions around childcare, work and employment/TUs, maternity etc., or abortion/FP, sexualities etc.
    c. Specific influences of 'second wave' versus 'third' or post-feminism and practices?
6. How has the global university been changing with successive 'waves' or generations of feminists and how different are they/how transformative?
    a. Do you now consider yourself a second-wave feminist?
    b. How does this differ theoretically/methodologically or substantively from subsequent generations?
    c. What about its influences on the changing modern or neo-liberal university?
    d. What about the development of new subjects, new students, new professions within and beyond the university?
7. What influences do you think feminism can/may have on the future of the university in an age of austerity?
    a. Development of new curricula around e.g. women's or gender studies?
    b. Development of new subjects, levels of education e.g. new EdDs
    c. Future practices and balances between men and women in academia and in wider society
    d. HE in a global world – universities for women (single sex vs co-ed) and private versus public etc. …
8. Concluding comments about gender, feminisms and changing forms of HE in a globalizing world.
    a. What significance would you give to changing forms of feminism and impacts/influences on changing forms of HE?
    b. How significant will new forms of feminism be in a new world order? Balances between global north and global south? The BRIC countries versus USA/UK/France/Germany etc. and China, India, Russia and Brazil or others e.g. Japan, South-East Asia etc.
    c. Types of HE – public versus private etc. …

Appendix 2

International Participants in
the Three Generation Cohorts

Cohort 1: (Born between 1935 and 1950)

AUSTRALIA Jill Blackmore, Bronwyn Davies, Jane Kenway, Lyn Yates. **CANADA** Sandra Acker, Margrit Eichler, Jane Gaskell, Alison Griffith, Meg Luxton, Marilyn Porter **ISRAEL** Judith Abrahami. **NEW ZEALAND** Sue Middleton. **UK** Madeleine Arnot, Jackie Barron, Liz Bird, Avtar Brah, Pam Calder, Barbara Cole, Vaneeta D'Andrea, Sara Delamont, Carol Dyhouse, Debbie Epstein, Mary Evans, Jay Ginn, Dulcie Groves, Helen Haste, Val Hey, Sue Himmelweit, Maggie Humm, Heather Joshi, Hilary Land, Annette Lawson, Ruth Levitas, Ruth Madigan, Meg Maguire, Pat Mahony, Ellen Malos, Merilyn Moos, Mica Nava, Caroline New, Anna Paczuska, Jocey Quinn, Diane Reay, Terri Rees, Jenny Shaw, Suzie Skevington, Carol Smart, Mary Stiasny, Helen Taylor, Clare Ungerson, Linda Ward, Gaby Weiner, Jackie West, Fiona Williams, Elizabeth Wilson, Gail Wilson, Nira Yuval-Davis. **USA** Jean Anyon, Michelle Fine, Harriet Freidenreich, Frinde Maher, Catherine Marshall, Judy Glazer Raymo, Maxine Seller, Kathleen Weiler, Lois Weis.

Cohort 2: (Born between 1950 and 1965)

CANADA Kari Dehli **INDIA** Nirupama Prakash **IRELAND** Maria Slowey **UK** Alison Assiter, Barbara Bagilhole, Tehmina Basit, Lucy Bland, Claire Callender, Ros Edwards, Joelle Fanghanel, Sally Findlow, Gabrielle Griffin, Gabrielle Ivinson, Yvonne Hillier, Chris Hockings, Christina Hughes, Carole Leathwood, Janice Malcolm, Jane Martin, Heidi Mirza, Louise Morley, Gemma Moss, Audrey Mullender, Carrie Paechter, Ann Phoenix, Jocey Quinn, Sheila Riddell, Chris Skelton, Corinne Squire, Penny Tinkler, Elaine Unterhalter; **USA** Wendy Luttrell.

Cohort 3: (Born between 1965 and 1980)

SPAIN Delia Langa Rosado **UK** Nafsika Alexiadou, Pam Alldred, Penny-Jane Burke, Kelly Coate, Amanda Coffey, Davina Cooper, Fin Cullen, Carolyn Jackson, Heather Mendick, Rajani Naidoo, Jessica Ringrose.

References and Select Bibliography

Acker, S. 1999. *The Realities of Teachers' Work: Never a dull moment*. London: Cassell & Continuum.

Acker, S., Smyth, E., Bourne, P. and Prentice, A. 1999. *Challenging Professions: Historical and contemporary perspectives on women's professional work*. Toronto, Canada: University of Toronto Press.

Acker, S., Wagner, A. and Mayuzumi, K., eds., 2008. *Whose University Is It, Anyway? Power and privilege on gendered terrain*. Toronto, Canada: Sumach Press.

Aga Khan University, Institute for Educational Development East Africa. 2012. *Inclusion and Equity in Education: Focus on gender current issues for research and practice* Annual Research Institute 2012 14–16 November, Dar es Salaam, Tanzania.

Ali, S., and Coate, K., 2013. Impeccable advice: Supporting women academics through supervision and mentoring *Gender and Education* 25 (1) pp. 23–37.

Alldred, P., and David, M.E. 2007. *Get Real About Sex: The politics and practice of sex education*. London: McGraw Hill and The Open University Press.

Altbach, P., 2010. Trouble with Numbers *Times Higher Education* 23 pp. 48–50.

Andrews, M., Squires, C. and Tamboukou, M., eds. 2008. *Doing Narrative Research*. London: Sage.

Appignanesi, L., 2013. How we got the F-word out of the shade *The Observer* March 17, *The New Review*, p.38.

Appignanesi, L., Holmes, R., and Orbach, S., eds. 2013. *Fifty Shades of Feminism*, London: Virago.

Arnot, M., and Weiner, G., eds. 1989. *Gender under Scrutiny: New enquiries in education* Maidenhead, Berkshire: Open University Press.

Arnot, M., David, M.E., and Weiner, G., 1999. *Closing the Gender Gap: Postwar education and social change*. Cambridge: Polity Press.

Assiter, A., 1987. *Althusser and Feminism*. London: Pluto Press.

Association of Commonwealth Universities (ACU) website https://www.acu.ac.uk/

Bagilhole, B., and White, K., eds. 2011. *Gender, Power and Management: A cross-cultural analysis of higher education*. London: Palgrave Macmillan.

Bagilhole, B., and White, K., eds. 2013. *Gender and Generation in Academia*. Basingstoke: Palgrave Macmillan.

Banks, O., 1985. *The Biographical Dictionary of British Feminists. Volume One: 1800–1930* New York: New York University Press.

Banks, O., 1986. *Becoming A Feminist. The Social Origins of 'First Wave' Feminism*. Athens: The University of Georgia University Press.

Banyard, K., 2011. *The Equality Illusion. The Truth About Women and Men Today.* London: Faber and Faber.

Barker, D.L., and Allen, S., eds., 1976a. *Sexual Divisions and Society: Process and change.* London: Tavistock.

Barker, D.L., and Allen, S., eds., 1976b. *Sexual Exploitation in Work and Marriage.* London: Longman.

Barrett, M., and Macintosh M., 1982. *The Anti-Social Family.* London: New Left Books.

Beauvoir, de S., 1953. *The Second Sex.* Translated from the French by H.M. Parsley. London: Penguin.

Bekhradnia, B., 2009. *Male and Female Participation and Progression in Higher Education.* Oxford: Higher Education Policy Institute.

Benjamin, J., 1988. *The Bonds of Love: Psychoanalysis, feminism and the problem of domination.* New York: Pantheon Books.

Benn, M., 2013. *What Should We Tell Our Daughters? The pleasures and pressures of growing up female.* London: John Murray.

Biklen, S., Marshall, C., and Pollard, D., 2008. Experiencing second-wave feminism in the USA. *Discourse: Studies in the cultural politics of education* 29 (4) pp. 451–71.

Blackmore, J., 1999. *Troubling Women: Feminism, leadership and educational change.* Maidenhead, Berkshire: Open University Press.

Blackmore, J., and Sachs, J., 2007. *Performing and Reforming Leaders: Gender, educational restructuring, and organizational change.* Albany, NY: SUNY Press.

Blackmore, J., Brennan, M., and Zipin, L., eds., 2010. *Re-Positioning University Governance and Academic Work.* Rotterdam: Sense Publishers.

Blackmore, J., 2013. Forever troubling: Feminist theoretical work in education. In M.B. Weaver-Hightower and C. Skelton, eds., *Leaders in Gender and Education. Intellectual self-portraits.* Rotterdam: Sense Publishers.

Boserup, E., 1970. *Women's Role in Economic Development.* London: Earthscan.

Boden, R., Epstein, D., and Kenway, J., 2006. *The Academic's Support Kit.* London: Sage.

Boursicot, K., and Roberts, T., 2009. Widening participation in medical education. *Higher Education Policy* 22 (1) pp. 19–37.

Bowers, K., 2010. *Rethinking the possibilities of feminist scholarship in the contemporary university.* University of Technology Sydney (UTS), Sydney, Australia. (unpublished thesis).

Brah, A., and Coombes, A., eds., 2000. *Hybridity and Its Discontents: Politics, science, culture.* London: Routledge.

Brah, A., and Phoenix, A., 2004. Ain't I a woman? Revisiting intersectionality. *Journal of International Women's Studies* 5 (3) pp.75–86.

Bristol Women's Studies Group (BWSG), 1979. *Half the Sky: An introduction to women's studies.* London: Virago.

Brooks, R., and Waters, J., 2011. *Student Mobilities, Migration and the Internationalization of Higher Education.* Basingstoke: Palgrave Macmillan.

Brown, L.M., and Gilligan, C., 1990. *Meeting at the Crossroads: Women's psychology and girls' development.* Cambridge, MA: Harvard University Press.

Brown, P., Lauder, H., and Ashton, D., 2011. *The Global Auction: The broken promise of education, jobs and incomes.* New York and London: Oxford University Press.

Burke, P.J., 2012. *The Right to Higher Education: Beyond widening participation.* London: Routledge.

Burke, P.J., 2009. Men accessing higher education: Theorizing continuity and change in relation to masculine subjectivities. *Higher Education Policy.* 22 (1) pp. 81–101.

Burke, P.J., and Crozier, G., 2013. *Teaching Inclusively: Changing pedagogical spaces* resource pack from the *Formations of Gender and Higher Education Pedagogies (GaP)* research project. London: University of Roehampton and The Higher Education Academy.

Burman, E., ed., 1990. *Feminists and Psychological Practice.* London: Sage.

Burman, E.,1994. *Deconstructing Developmental Psychology.* London: Routledge.

Butler, J., 1990. *Gender Trouble: Feminism and the subversion of identity.* New York and London: Routledge.

Butler, J., 2004. *Undoing Gender.* New York and London: Routledge.

Callanan, R., ed., 2012. North London University of the Third Age (NLU3A), *Newsletter* June 6 email communication.

Chodorow, N., 1978. *The Reproduction of Mothering: Psychoanalysis and the sociology of gender.* Berkeley: University of California Press.

Chodorow, N., 1989. *Feminism and Psychoanalytic Theory.* Berkeley: University of California Press.

The Chronicle of Higher Education, 2012. *Diversity in Academe The Gender Issue* section B November 2, USA.

Clegg, S., 2011. Academic identities re-formed? Contesting technological determinism in accounts of the digital age. *Contemporary Social Science* 6 (2) pp. 175–91.

Clegg, S., and David, M.E., 2006. Passion, pedagogies and the project of the personal in higher education. *21st Century Society: Journal of the Academy of Social Sciences* 1 (2) pp. 149–67.

Coate, K., 2011. Writing in the dark: Reflections on becoming a feminist. In K. Davis and M. Evans, eds., *Transatlantic Conversations: Feminism as travelling theory.* Farnham: Ashgate.

Cockburn, C., 1993. *Brothers: Male dominance and technological change.* London: Pluto.

Cole, B., 2010. 'Good' Vibrations: Good girls, good wives, good mothers and ... good heavens – a PhD. In B. Cole and H. Gunter, eds., *Changing Lives: Women, inclusion and the PhD.* Stoke-on-Trent: Trentham Books.

Connell, R., 2007. *Southern Theory: The global dynamics of knowledge in social science.* London: Allen and Unwin.

Daniels, L., 2011. *Pulling the Punches: Defeating domestic violence.* London: Bogle-l'Ouverture Press Limited.

David, M.E., 1980. *The State, The Family and Education.* London: Routledge.

David, M.E., 2003. *Personal and Political: Feminisms, sociology and family lives.* Stoke-on-Trent: Trentham Books.

David, M.E., ed., 2009a. *Improving Learning by Widening Participation in Higher Education.* London: Routledge.

David, M.E., 2009b. *Transforming Global Higher Education: A feminist perspective.* An inaugural professorial lecture. London: Institute of Education, University of London.

David, M.E., 2011. Overview of researching global higher education: Challenge, change or crisis? *Contemporary Social Science.* special issue. *Challenge, Change or Crisis in Global Higher Education.* 6 (2) pp. 147–65.

David, M.E., 2012. Feminism, gender and global higher education: Women's learning lives *Higher Education Research and Development (HERDSA)* 31 (5) pp. 679–89.

David, M.E., 2013a. Still personal, still political. *Times Higher Education.* 31 January pp. 40–43.

David, M.E., 2013b. A "Mother" of Feminist Sociology of Education? In Weaver-Hightower, M.B., and Skelton, C., eds., *Leaders in Gender and Education. Intellectual Self-Portraits.* Rotterdam: Sense Publishers.

David, M.E., and Clegg, S., 2008. Power, pedagogy and personalization in global higher education. *Discourse: Studies in the Cultural Politics of Education* special issue on *Second-Wave Feminism and educational research.* 29 (4) pp. 483–499.

David, M.E., and Epstein, D., eds. 2013. Introduction: Thinking education feminisms: engagement with the work of Diana Leonard. *Gender and Education* 25 (1) pp. 1–6.

David, M.E., and Naidoo, R., eds. 2013. *The Sociology of Higher Education: Reproduction, transformation and change in a global era.* London: Routledge.

David, M.E., Hey, V., and Morley, L., eds., 2011. *Contemporary Social Science:* Special Issue *Challenge, Change or Crisis in Global Higher Education* 6 (2) June.

Davidoff, L., and Hall, C., 1987. *Family Fortunes: Men and women of the English middle class, 1780–1850.* London: Taylor and Francis.

Davidson, J.O'C., 2001. *Children in the Sex Trade in China,* Stockholm: Save the Children Sweden, available at http://shop.rb.se/Product/Product.aspx?ItemId=2967801

Davies, B., 1989. *Frogs and Snails and Feminist Tales. Preschool children and gender.* London: Routledge and Australia http://bronwyndavies.com.au

Davis, A., 1971. *If They Come in the Morning: Voices of resistance.* New York: Third Press.

Davis, A., 1974. *Angela Davis: An autobiography.* New York: Random House.

Davis, A., 1983. *Women, Race, & Class.* New York: Vintage.

Davis, A., 1990. *Women, Culture & Politics.* New York: Vintage.

Davis, K., Evans, M., and Lorber, J., eds., 2006. *Handbook of Gender & Women's Studies.* London: Sage.

Davis, K., and Evans, M., eds., 2011. *Transatlantic Conversations: Feminism as travelling theory.* Farnham: Ashgate.

Deem, R., 2009. Leading and managing contemporary UK universities: Do excellence and meritocracy still prevail over diversity? *Higher Education Policy* 22 (1) pp. 3–19.

Dehli, K., 2010. Toward a new survivalism? Neo-liberal government of graduate education in Ontario. In J. Blackmore, M. Brennan and L. Zipin, eds., *Re-Positioning University Governance and Academic Work.* Rotterdam: Sense Publishers pp. 85–100

Delamont, S., 1989. *Knowledgeable Women.* London: Routledge.

Delamont, S., 2003. *Feminist Sociology.* London: Sage.

Delamont, S., 2008 No such thing as a consensus: Olive Banks and the sociology of education. *British Journal of Sociology of Education.* 29 (4) pp. 391–403.

Delphy, C., and Leonard D.L., 1992. *Familiar Exploitation: A new analysis of marriage in contemporary Western societies.* Cambridge: Polity Press.

Dinnerstein, D., 1987. *The Rocking of the Cradle and the Ruling of the World.* London: Women's Press.

Dubai International conference on gender equality in HE leadership. 2013. *The Guardian,* March 6.

Dyhouse, C., 1981. *Girls Growing Up in Victorian and Edwardian England.* London: Routledge.

Dyhouse, C., 1989. *Feminism and the Family in England, 1890–1939.* Oxford: Blackwell.

Dyhouse, C., 1995. *No Distinction of Sex? Women in British Universities, 1870–1939.* London: UCL Press.

Dyhouse, C., 2006. *Students: A Gendered History.* London: Routledge.

Dyhouse, C., 2010. *Glamour: Women, History, Feminism.* London: Zed Books.

Edwards, R., and Mauthner, M., 2012. Ethics and feminist research: Theory and practice. In, T. Miller, M. Birch, M. Mauthner, and J. Jessop, eds., *Ethics in Qualitative Research* Second edition. London: Sage. pp 14–28.

Eichler, M., 1991. *Nonsexist Research Methods: A practical guide.* New York and London: Routledge.

Eichler, M., 2008. To challenge the world. In W. Robbins, M. Luxton, M. Eichler, and F. Descarries, eds., 2008. *Minds of our Own: Inventing feminist scholarship and women's studies in Canada and Quebec 1966–76.* Waterloo, Ontario, Canada: Wilfrid Laurier University Press.

Eisenstein, H., 2009. *Feminism Seduced: How global elites use women's labor and ideas to exploit the world.* New York: Paradigm.

Ellsworth, E., 1997. *Teaching Positions: Difference, pedagogy and the power of address*. New York: Teachers College Press.

Engels, F., 1884. *The Origins of the Family, Private Property, and the State* Second edition 1980. London: Pluto Press.

Epstein, D., 2013. A feminist DNA: Exploring a political/intellectual history. In M.B. Weaver-Hightower and C. Skelton, eds., *Leaders in Gender and Education. Intellectual self-portraits.* Rotterdam: Sense Publishers.

Epstein, D., Elwood, J., Hey, V., and Maw, J., eds., 1998. *Failing Boys? Issues in gender and education.* Buckingham: Open University Press.

Equality Challenge Unit, 2011. *Equality in Higher Education: Statistical report 2011 part 1 staff* and *part 2 students* December.

Evans, M., 2004. *Killing Thinking: The death of the universities.* London: Continuum.

Evans, M., 2011. Mary Evans' Narrative. In K. Davis, K. and M. Evans, eds., *Transatlantic Conversations.* Farnham: Ashgate.

Figes, E., 1970. *Patriarchal Attitudes: Women in society.* London: Stein and Day.

Fine, M., 1992. *Disruptive Voices: The possibilities of feminist research.* Ann Arbor: The University of Michigan Press.

Fine, M., 2004. The power of the Brown v. Board of Education decision: Theorizing threats to sustainability. *American Psychologist*, 59, pp. 502–10.

Fine, M., and Weis, L., 1998. *The Unknown City: Lives of poor and working class young adults.* Boston, MA: Beacon Press.

Fine, M., and McClelland, S., 2007. The politics of teen women's sexuality: Public policy and the adolescent female body, *Emory Law Review*, 56 (4) pp. 993–1038.

Fine, M., Weis, L., Powell, L., and Burns, A., eds., 2004. *Off-white: Readings on power, privilege, and resistance.* Second edition. New York: Routledge.

Firestone, S., 1970. *The Dialectic of Sex: The case for feminist revolution.* New York: Morrow.

Fraser, N., 1989. *Unruly Practices: Power, discourse, and gender in contemporary social theory.* Minneapolis: University of Minnesota Press.

Fraser, N., 1997. *Justice Interruptus: Critical reflections on the "Postsocialist" condition.* New York and London: Routledge.

Fraser, N., 2013. *Fortunes of Feminism. From state-managed capitalism to neoliberal crisis.* New York and London: Verso.

Freeman, J., 1972. The tyranny of structurelessness. *The Second Wave* 2 (1) p.20.

French, M., 1977. *The Women's Room.* New York: Jove Books.

Friedan, B., 1963. *The Feminine Mystique.* Harmondsworth: Penguin.

Gaskell, J., 2008. Learning from the women's movement about educational change *Discourse: Studies in the Cultural Politics of Education* Special Issue. 29 (4) December. pp. 437–51

Gavron, H., 1966. *The Captive Wife: Conflicts of housebound mothers.* London: Routledge.

Gilligan, C., 1982. *In a Different Voice.* Cambridge MA: Harvard University Press.

Gilligan, C., 2011. *Joining the Resistance.* Cambridge: Polity Press.

Gilman, C.P., 1892. *The Yellow Wallpaper*. New England Magazine 5: 647–56; Boston: Small, Maynard & Co., 1899; Second Edition. 1973 New York: Feminist Press.

Gilman, C.P., 1915. *Herland*. New York: Forerunner.

Glasgow Women's Studies Group. 1983. *Uncharted Lives: Extracts from Scottish women's experiences, 1850–1982* (see Ruth Madigan's essay) Glasgow, Scotland: Pressgang.

Glazer-Raymo J., 1999. *Shattering the Myths: Women in academe*. Baltimore, MD: Johns Hopkins University Press.

Glazer-Raymo, J., ed., 2008. *Unfinished Agendas: New and continuing gender challenges in higher education*. Baltimore, MD: Johns Hopkins University Press.

Glazer-Raymo, J., Townsend, B.K., and Ropers-Huilman, B., eds., 2000. *Women in Higher Education: A feminist perspective*. Needham Heights, MA: Pearson Publishing.

Glendinning, C., and Millar, J., eds., 1992. *Women and Poverty in Britain* Brighton: Harvester-Wheatsheaf.

Government Equalities Office. 2013a. *Review of the Public Sector Equality Duty: Report of the Independent Steering Group* https://www.gov.uk/government/uploads/system/uploads/attachment_data/file/237194/Review_of_the_Public_Sector_Equality_Duty_by_the_Independent_Steering_Group.pdf

Government Equalities Office. 2013b. *Review of the Public Sector Equality Duty (PSED). Presentation by Rachel Clark Director of the Government Equalities Office 4 November 2013* https://www.local.gov.uk/documents/10180/5635376/Rachel+Clark+slides.pdf/bfa219cb-bbc0-4cf5-8b2d-64cf1ea8036d

Greer, G., 1970. *The Female Eunuch*. London: Picador.

Griffin, G., 2011. On not engaging with What's Right in Front of Us: Or race, ethnicity and gender in reading women's writing. In K. Davis and M. Evans, eds., *Transatlantic Conversations*. Farnham: Ashgate. pp 157–67

Griffith, A., and Smith, D.E., 1987. Constructing cultural knowledge: Mothering as discourse. In Gaskell, J., and McLaren, A., eds., *Women and Education: A Canadian perspective*. Reprinted 1990. Calgary, Canada: Detselig Press. pp. 87–104

Griffith, A., and Smith, D.E., 2005. *Mothering for Schooling*. New York: Routledge.

The Guardian Education Section, 2013. The professor is almost always white. Main feature article in 29 January p.30

Hall, P., Land, H., Parker, R., and Webb, A., 1975. *Change, Choice and Conflict in Social Policy*. London: Heinemann.

Haraway, D., 1988. Situated knowledges: The Science question in feminism and the privilege of partial perspective. *Feminist Studies*, 14 (3) pp. 575–99.

Harding, S., 1987. *Feminism and Methodology*. Bloomington: Indiana University Press.

Hartman, H., 1981. The unhappy marriage of Marxism and Feminism. In L. Sergent, ed., *The Unhappy Marriage of Marxism and Feminism: A debate on class and patriarchy*. London: Pluto Press.

Hemmings, C., 2006. The life and times of academic feminism. In K. Davis, M. Evans, and J. Lorber, eds., *Handbook of Gender & Women's Studies*. London: Sage.

Heron, L., ed., 1985. *Truth, Dare or Promise: Girls growing up in the 1950s*. London: Virago.

Hewitt, M., 1958. *Wives and Mothers in Victorian Industry*. London: Barrie and Rockcliffe.

Hewitt, N., ed., 2010. *No Permanent Waves: Recasting histories of US feminism*. Rutgers, NJ: The State University Press.

Hey, V., 2011. Affective Asymmetries: Academics, austerity and the mis/recognition of emotion. *Contemporary Social Science: Challenge, Change or Crisis in Global Higher Education*. 6 (2) pp. 207–23.

Hey, V., and Leathwood, C., 2009. Passionate attachments: Higher education, policy, knowledge, emotion and social justice. *Higher Education Policy* 22 (1) pp. 101–18.

Hey, V., and Morley, L., 2011. Imagining the university of the future: Eyes wide open? Expanding the imaginary through critical and feminist ruminations in and on the university. *Contemporary Social Science: Challenge, Change or Crisis in Global Higher Education*. 6 (2) pp. 165–175.

Hollingsworth, S., 1994. *Teacher Research and Urban Literacy Education*. New York: Teachers College Press.

Hollingsworth, S., 2002. *Personal, Community and School Literacies: Challenging a single standard*. New York: Teachers College Press.

hooks, b., 1981. *Ain't I a Woman: Black women and feminism* Boston, MA: South End Press.

Hoskins, K., 2012. *Women and Success: Professors in the academy*. Stoke-on-Trent: Trentham Books.

Hughes, C., 2002. *Key Concepts in Feminist Theory and Research*. London: Sage.

Jackson, C., 2014. Laddism and the culture of higher education. Seminar presentation at CHEER, University of Sussex, January 27.

James, E.L., 2012. *Fifty Shades of Grey*, London: Arrow books.

Joffe, C., 1971. Sex role socialization and the nursery school: As the twig is bent. *Journal of Marriage and the Family*, 33 (3) pp. 467–75.

Keller, E.F., 1985. *Reflections on Gender and Science*. New Haven, CT: Yale University Press.

Kenway, J., 2013. A defiant research imagination. In Weaver-Hightower, M.B., and Skelton, C., eds., *Leaders in Gender and Education. Intellectual Self-Portraits*. Rotterdam: Sense Publishers.

Kenway, J., and Willis, S., with Blackmore, J., and Rennie, L., 1998. *Answering Back: Girls, boys and feminism in schools*. London: Routledge.

Kenway, J., and Bullen, E., 2001. *Consuming Children: Education–entertainment–advertising*. Maidenhead: McGraw Hill/Open University Press.

Kenway, J., and Fahey, J., eds., 2008. *Globalizing the Research Imagination*. London: Routledge.

Kerry, J., 2013. Malala's vital lesson for US foreign policy *Evening Standard,* March 8 p. 14

Kim, T., 2010. Transnational academic mobility, knowledge and identity capital. In *Discourse: Studies in the Cultural Politics of Education. Special Issue on International Academic Mobility.* 31 (5) pp. 577–92, October.

Kim, T., and Brooks, R., 2013. *Internationalisation, Mobile Academics and Knowledge Creation in Universities: A comparative analysis.* Final report. London: Society for Research into Higher Education. (http://www.srhe.ac.uk/downloads/TerriKimReport.pdf).

King, R., Marginson, S., and Naidoo, R., eds., 2011. *Handbook on Globalization and Higher Education.* Cheltenham Gloucestershire: Edward Elgar.

Land, H., 1976. Women supporters or supported? In D.L. Barker and S. Allen, eds., *Sexual Divisions and Society: Process and change.* London: Tavistock.

Langa-Rosado, D., and David, M.E., 2006. 'A massive university or a university for the masses?' Continuity and change in higher education in Spain and England. *Journal of Education Policy* 21 (3) pp. 343–65.

Laslett, B., Brenner, J., and Yarat, Y., eds., 1995. *Rethinking the Political: Gender, resistance and the state.* Chicago, IL: University of Chicago Press.

Lather, P., 1991. *Getting Smart: Feminist research and pedagogy with/in the postmodern.* New York and London: Routledge.

Lather, P., 2013. An intellectual autobiography: The return of the (feminist) subject? In M.B. Weaver-Hightower and C. Skelton, eds., *Leaders in Gender and Education. Intellectual self-portraits.* Rotterdam: Sense Publishers.

Lawson, A., 1966. *The Recognition of Mental Illness in London: A study of the social processes determining compulsory admission to an observation unit in a London hospital.* Oxford: Oxford University Press.

Lawson, A., 1990. *Adultery: An analysis of love and betrayal.* New York: Basic Books.

Le Guin, U., 1974. *The Dispossessed: An ambiguous utopia.* New York: Harper Row.

Leathwood, C., and Read, B., 2008. *Gender and the Changing Place of Higher Education.* London: Society for Research in Higher Education and The Open University Press.

Luxton, M., 2008. Women's studies: Oppression and liberation in the university. In W. Robbins, M. Luxton, M. Eichler, and F. Descarries, eds., *Minds of our Own: Inventing feminist scholarship and women's studies in Canada and Quebec 1966–76.* Waterloo, Ontario, Canada: Wilfrid Laurier University Press.

Maher, F., and Tetreault, M.K.,2001. *The Feminist Classroom: Dynamics of gender, race and privilege.* New York: Rowman and Littlefield.

Maher, F., and Tetreault, M.K., 2007. *Privilege and Diversity in the American Academy.* New York and London: Routledge.

Mahony, P., 1985. *Schools for the Boys? Co-education reassessed.* New York and London: Routledge.

Malos, E., ed., 1995. *The Politics of Housework.* London: New Clarion Press.

Marshall, C., ed., 1997a. *Feminist Critical Policy Analysis I. A perspective from primary and secondary schooling.* London: The Falmer Press.

Marshall, C., ed., 1997b. *Feminist Critical Policy Analysis II. A perspective from Post-secondary education.* London: The Falmer Press.

Marsden, L., 2008. Second wave breaks on the shores of U of T. In W. Robbins, M. Luxton, M. Eichler, and F. Descarries, eds., *Minds of our Own: Inventing feminist scholarship and women's studies in Canada and Quebec 1966–76.* Waterloo, Ontario, Canada: Wilfrid Laurier University Press. pp 210–17.

Martin, J., 2008. Beyond suffrage: Feminism, education and the politics of class in the inter-war years. *British Journal of Sociology of Education: Special Issue: Olive Banks (1923–2006).* 29 (4).pp. 411–23.

Martin, J., 2013. Gender, education and social change: A study of feminist politics and practice in London 1870–1990. *Gender and Education.* 25 (1) pp. 56–75.

Massey, D., 1994. *Space, Place and Gender.* Cambridge: Polity Press.

Mauthner, N., and Edwards, R., 2010. Feminist research management in higher education in Britain: Possibilities and practices. *Gender, Work and Organization.* 17 (5) pp. 481–502.

McLean, M., 2006. *Pedagogy and the University: Critical theory and practice.* New York and London: Continuum.

McLeod, J., and Yates, L., 2006. *Making Modern Lives: Subjectivity, schooling and social change.* New York: State University of New York Press.

Mead, M., 1928. *Coming of Age in Samoa.* New York: Blue Ribbon Books. Republished Harmondsworth: Penguin.

Mead, M., 1930. *Growing Up in New Guinea.* New York: W. Morrow & company, (republished) Harmondsworth: Penguin.

Middleton, S., 1993. *Educating Feminists: Life histories and pedagogies.* New York: Teachers College Press.

Middleton, S., 1998. *Disciplining Sexuality: Foucault, life histories and education.* New York: Teachers College Press.

Millett, K., 1970. *Sexual Politics.* New York: Doubleday.

Mirza, H., 1992. *Young Female and Black.* London: Routledge.

Mirza, H., ed., 1997. *Black British Feminism: A reader.* London: Routledge.

Mirza, H., 2009. *Race, Gender and Educational Desire: Why black women succeed and fail.* London: Routledge.

Mitchell, J., 1966. Women: The longest revolution. *New Left Review.* Republished In J. Mitchell, ed. 1984. *Women: The Longest Revolution: Essays on feminism, literature and psychoanalysis.* London: Virago Press.

Mitchell, J., 1973. *Women's Estate.* Harmondsworth: Penguin.

Mooney, C., ed., 2012. *The Chronicle of Higher Education.* The magazine for academe, in a special issue on 'Diversity in Academe: The Gender Issue' special sections, B3, November 2.

Moran, C., 2011. *How to be a Woman.* London: Ebury Press.

Morley, L., 1999. *Organising Feminisms: The micropolitics of the academy.* London: Palgrave Macmillan.

Morley, L., 2011. Misogyny posing as measurement: Disrupting the feminisation crisis discourse. *Contemporary Social Science*. Special Issue: *Challenge, Change or Crisis in Global Higher Education*. 6 (2) pp. 223–37.

Morley, L., 2012. Cycles of domination of top roles by men must be broken. *Times Higher Education*. 6 December p. 29.

Morley, L., 2013. The rules of the game: Women and the leaderist turn in higher education. *Gender and Education* 25 (1) pp. 116–31.

Morley, L., and David, M.E., eds., 2009. Celebrations and challenges: Gender in higher education. *Higher Education Policy* 22 (1) pp. 1–2.

Morley, L., and Lugg, R., 2009. Mapping meritocracy: Intersecting gender, poverty and higher education opportunity structures. *Higher Education Policy* 22 (1) pp. 37–61.

Moss, G., 1989. *Un/Popular Fictions*. London: Virago.

Mullender, A., Hague, G., Imam, I., Kelly, L., Malos, E., and Regan, L., 2002. *Children's Perspectives on Domestic Violence*. London: Sage Publications.

Myrdal, A., and Klein, V., 1956. *Women's Two Roles: Home and work*. London: Routledge and Kegan Paul.

Nava, M., 1992. *Changing Cultures: Feminism, youth and consumerism*. London: Sage.

Nava, M., 2007 *Visceral Cosmopolitanism: Gender, culture and the normalisation of difference*. Oxford: Berg.

New, C., 1996. *Agency, Health & Social Survival*. London: Taylor & Francis.

New, C., and David, M.E., 1985. *For the Children's Sake: making child care more than women's business* Harmondsworth: Penguin.

Newman, J., 2012. *Working the Spaces of Power: Activism, neoliberalism and gendered labour*. London: Bloomsbury.

Nnaemeka, O., ed., 1998. *Sisters, Feminism and Power*. Trenton NJ: Africa World Press.

Oakley, A., 1974. *The Sociology of Housework*. London: Martin Robertson.

Oakley, A., 1976. *Housewife*. Harmondsworth: Penguin.

Oakley, A., 1979. *Becoming a mother*. London: Martin Robertson.

Oakley, A., ed., 2005. *The Ann Oakley Reader: Gender, women, and social science*. Bristol: Policy Press.

Okin, S.M., 1979. *Women in Western Political Thought*. Princeton, NJ: Princeton University Press.

Okin, S.M., 1989. *Justice, Gender, and the Family*. Princeton, NJ: Princeton University Press.

Pence, E., and Paymar, M., 1993. *Education Groups for Men Who Batter: The Duluth model* Amsterdam: Springer.

Penny, L., 2010. *Meat Market. Female flesh under capitalism*. London: Zero Books.

Petersen, E.B. and Davies, B., 2010. In/Difference in the neoliberalised university. *Learning and Teaching in the Social Sciences*. 3(2) pp. 93–109.

Piercy, M., 1976. *Woman on the Edge of Time*. New York: Alfred A. Knopf.

Phillips, A., 1991. *Engendering Democracy*. Cambridge: Polity Press.

Phipps, A., 2014. 'That's what she said': women students' experience of 'lad culture' in higher education. Report for the National Union of Students (NUS).

Phoenix, A., 1991. *Young Mothers?* Cambridge: Polity Press.

Phoenix, A., 2011. Re-narrating feminist stories: Black British women and transatlantic feminisms. In K. Davis and M. Evans, eds., *Transatlantic Conversations: Feminism as travelling theory.* Farnham: Ashgate. pp. 55–69.

Plummer, K., 2013. An influential sociologist known for her work on gender and sociology: Obituary of Mary McIntosh (13.3.1936 – 5.1.2013), *The Guardian* 11 February p.28.

Porter M., 2012. Review of Sylvia Walby *The Future of Feminism*. In *Atlantis: A Women's Studies Journal*, 35 (1) pp. 50–52.

Prentice, A., Bourne, P., Brandt, G., Cuthbert, Light, B., 1988. *Canadian Women: A history*. Toronto: Harcourt Brace Jovanovich.

Quinn, J., 2003. *Powerful Subjects: Are women really taking over the university?* Stoke on Trent: Trentham Books.

Rapp, R., 2000. *Testing Women, Testing the Fetus: The social impact of amniocentesis in America.* New York: Routledge.

Rathbone E., 1986. *The Disinherited Family* Second edition (with an introduction by Suzie Fleming). Bristol: Falling Wall Press.

Report of the Committee on Higher Education. 1963. *Higher Education. The Robbins Report.* Cmnd 2154, London: Her Majesty's Stationery Office (HMSO).

Research Council UK (RCUK) 2009. *Sustainability of the UK Research Workforce: Annual Report to the UK Research Base Funders Forum 2009* London: Research Councils UK.

Rich, A., 1977. *Of Woman Born: Motherhood as experience and institution.* New York and London: W.W. Norton.

Riley, D., 1983. *War in the Nursery: Theories of the child and mother,* London: Virago.

Riley, D., 1988. *Am I that name? Feminism and the category of "women" in history,* London: Macmillan.

Ringrose, J., 2012. *Post-feminist Education? Girls and the sexual politics of schooling.* London: Routledge.

Ringrose, J., and Renold, E., 2012a. Teen girls, working class femininity and resistance: Re-theorizing fantasy and desire in educational contexts of heterosexualized violence *International Journal of Inclusive Education* 16(4), pp 461–77.

Ringrose, J., and Renold, E., 2012b. 'Slut-shaming, girl power and 'sexualisation': Thinking through the politics of the international SlutWalks with teen girls', *Gender and Education* 24 (3), 333–43.

Ringrose, J., Gill, R., Livingstone, S., Harvey, L., 2012. *A Qualitative Study of Children, Young People and 'Sexting'.* London: NSPCC .

Robbins, W., Luxton, M., Eichler, M., and Descarries, F., eds., 2008. *Minds of our Own: Inventing feminist scholarship and women's studies in Canada and Quebec 1966–76.* Waterloo, Ontario, Canada: Wilfrid Laurier University Press.

Roberts H., ed., 1981. *Doing Feminist Research*. London: Routledge.

Roby, P., 1973. *Child Care -- Who Cares? Infant and early childhood development policies*. New York: Basic Books.

Roby, P., 1981. *Women in the Workplace*. Cambridge, MA: Schenkman Publishing Company.

Rowbotham, S., 1972. *Women, Resistance and Revolution*. Harmondsworth: Penguin.

Rowbotham, S., 1973a. *Hidden from History*. London: Pluto Press.

Rowbotham, S., 1973b. *Women's Consciousness, Man's World*. Harmondsworth: Penguin.

Rowbotham, S., 2012. *Discovering the Other America*. Public lecture as writer-in-residence in the Eccles Centre at the British Library, October 22.

Rubin, G., 2012. *Deviations: A Gayle Rubin reader*. Durham, NC: Duke University Press.

Ruebain, D., 2012. *Diversity and Equality – The Equality Challenge Unit*. Seminar presentation in the CHEER lecture series University of Sussex April 16.

Sandberg, S., 2013. *Lean In: Women, work, and the will to lead*. New York and London: W.H. Allen.

Scott, J., and Tilly, L., 1978 *Women, Work and Family*. New York: Holt, Rinehart and Winston.

Scott, J., and Butler, J., eds., 1992. *Feminists Theorize the Political*. New York: Routledge.

Sen, A., 2005. *The Argumentative Indian. Writings on Indian Culture, History and Identity*. London: Penguin Books. (Chapter 11 Women and Men pp. 220–385)

She Figures, 2009. *Statistics and Indicators on gender equality in science*. Brussels: European Commission Directorate-General for Research http://ec.europa.eu/research/research-eu

Shuller, T., and Watson, D., 2010. *Learning Through Life: Inquiry into the future for lifelong learning*. London: National Institute for Adult and Continuing Education.

Skeggs, B., 1997. *Formations of Class and Gender: Becoming respectable*. London: Sage.

Skelton, C., 2013. Feminism and social class. In M.B. Weaver-Hightower and C. Skelton, eds., *Leaders in Gender and Education: Intellectual Self-Portraits*. Rotterdam: Sense Publishers.

Skelton, C., and Francis B., 2009. *Feminism and 'The Schooling Scandal'*. London: Routledge.

Skevington, S., 1995. *Psychology of Pain*. New York and London: Wiley.

Slaughter, S., and Leslie, L., 1997. *Academic Capitalism: Politics, policies and the entrepreneurial university*. Baltimore and London: The Johns Hopkins University Press.

Slaughter, S., and Rhoades, G., 2004. *Academic Capitalism and the New Economy Markets, State and Higher Education*. Baltimore and London: The Johns Hopkins University Press.

Smart, C., 1976. *Women, Crime, and Criminology: A feminist critique.* London: Routledge.

Smart, C., 1990. Feminist approaches to criminology or postmodern woman meets atavistic man. In A. Morris and L. Gelsthorpe, eds., *Feminist Perspectives in Criminology.* Milton Keynes: Open University Press.

Smith, D.E., 1987. The Everyday World as Problematic: A feminist sociology. London: Routledge.

Smith, D.E., 2008. Women's studies: A personal story. In W. Robbins, M. Luxton, M. Eichler, and F. Descarries, eds., *Minds of our Own: Inventing feminist scholarship and women's studies in Canada and Quebec 1966–76.* Waterloo, Ontario, Canada: Wilfrid Laurier University Press.

Smits, R-J., 2012. European Commission (EC) Director General for Research and Innovation.

Spender, D., 1980. *Manmade Language.* London: Routledge.

Spender, D., 1982. *Women of Ideas and what Men Have Done to Them: From Aphra Behn to Adrienne Rich.* London: Routledge.

Spender, D., 1983. *There's Always been a Women's Movement this Century.* London: Pandora Press.

Squire, C., ed., 1993. *Women and AIDS: Psychological perspectives.* London: Sage.

Stacey, M., and Price, M., 1981. *Women, Power and Politics.* London: Tavistock.

Stambach, A., and David, M.E., 2005. Feminist theory and educational policy: How gender has been "involved" in family-school choice debates. *Signs: Journal of Women in Culture and Society* 30 (2) pp. 1633–58.

Stanley, L., and Wise, S., 1983. *Breaking Out: Feminist consciousness and feminist research.* London: Routledge.

Steedman, C., 1986. *Landscape for a Good Woman.* London: Virago Press.

Steedman, C., Urwin, C., and Walkerdine, V., eds., 1985. *Language, Gender and Childhood.* London: Routledge and Kegan Paul.

Strathern, M., ed., 2000. *Audit Cultures. Anthropological studies in accountability, ethics and the academy.* London: Routledge.

Szreter, S., 2006. Obituary of Olive Banks *The Guardian* Tuesday 12 December, p. 25.

Taylor, H., 1989. *Scarlett's Women: Gone With the Wind and its female fans.* Rutgers, NJ: The University Press.

Thomson E.P. (1963; 1968) *The Making of the English Working Class.* London: Victor Gollancz. Second edition with new postscript. Harmondsworth: Penguin.

Tomlinson, S., 2013. My university life as a woman professor. *The Guardian* in the Higher Education Network series January 31, www.guardian.co.uk/higher-education-network/blog/2013/Jan/31/female-professoir-university-life-equality

Townsend, L.F., and Weiner, G., 2011. *Deconstructing and Reconstructing Lives Auto/biography in Educational Settings.* The University of Western Ontario, London, Canada: The Althouse Press.

Ungerson, C., 1990. *Policy is Personal: Sex, gender and informal care.* London: Tavistock.

Unterhalter, E., 2013. Connecting the private and the public: Pregnancy, exclusion, and the expansion of schooling in Africa. *Gender and Education* Special Issue*: Thinking Education Feminisms: Engagements with the work of Diana Leonard* 25 (1) pp. 75–91.

Unterhalter, E., and Carpentier, V., eds., 2010. *Global Inequalities and Higher Education. Whose interests are we serving?* Basingstoke: Palgrave.

UNESCO, 2012. *World Atlas on Gender Equality in Education* http://www.unesco.org/new/typo3temp/pics/d7af2fe604.jpg

Walby, S., 2011. *The Future of Feminism?* Cambridge: Polity Press.

Walker, A., 1982. *The Color Purple.* New York: Harcourt Brace Janovitch.

Walker, A., 1982. *You Can't Keep a Good Woman Down: Stories.* New York: Harcourt Brace Janovitch.

Walker, A., 1983. *In Search of Our Mothers' Gardens: Womanist prose.* New York: Harcourt Brace Janovitch.

Walkerdine, V., 1997. *Daddy's Girl: Young girls and popular culture.* London: Macmillan.

Walkerdine, V., 2011. Neoliberalism, working-class subjects and higher education. *Contemporary Social Science* Special Issue: *Challenge, Change or Crisis in Global Higher Education* 6 (2) pp. 255–73.

Walkerdine, V., Lucey, H., and Melody, J., 2002. *Growing Up Girl: Psychosocial explorations of gender & class.* London: Palgrave.

Weaver-Hightower, M.B., and Skelton, C., eds., 2013. *Leaders in Gender and Education: Intellectual self-portraits.* Rotterdam: Sense Publishers.

Weedon, C., 1996. *Feminist Practice and Poststructuralist Theory.* Second edition. Oxford: Blackwell.

Weiler, K., 1988. *Women Teaching for Change: Gender, class and power.* Greenwood, CT: Bergin and Garvey.

Weiler, K., 1998. *Country Schoolwomen: Teaching in rural California 1850–1950.* Stanford, CA: Stanford University Press.

Weiler, K., 2008. The feminist imagination and educational research. *Discourse: Studies in the Cultural Politics of Education* 29 (4) pp. 499–509.

Weiler, K., 2011. *Democracy and Schooling in California: Historical studies in education.* London: Palgrave Macmillan.

Weiler, K., and Arnot, M., eds. 1993. *Feminism and Social Justice in Education.* Brighton: Falmer Press.

Weiler, K., and David, M.E., eds., 2008. Introduction *Discourse: Studies in the Cultural Politics of Education* Special Issue: *Second Wave Feminism and educational research* 29 (4) pp.433–7.

Weiner, G., 2008. Olive Banks and the collective biography of British feminism. *British Journal of Sociology of Education:* Special Issue: Olive Banks (1923–2006) 29 (4) pp. 403–11.

Weis, L., 2004. *Class Reunion: The remaking of the American white working class.* New York: Routledge.

Weis, L., and Fine, M., 2004. *Working Method: Research and social justice.* New York: Routledge.

West, J., and Austrin, T., 2002, From work as sex to sex as work: Networks, 'others' and occupations in the analysis of work. *Gender, Work and Organization,* 9 (5) pp.

Willetts, D., 2011. *The Pinch: How the baby boomers took their children's future – and why they should give it back* Second edition. London: Atlantic Books.

Willetts, D., 2013. *Robbins Revisited: Bigger and better higher education.* London: Social Market Foundation.

Williams, F., 1989. *Social Policy: A critical introduction. Issues of race, gender and class.* Cambridge: Polity Press.

Wilson, E., 1977. *Women and the Welfare State.* London: Tavistock.

Wilson, E., 1977. Women in the community. In M. Mayo, ed., *Women in the Community.* London: Routledge.

Wilson, E., 1980. *Only Halfway to Paradise: Women in Postwar Britain, 1945–1968.* London: Tavistock.

Wilson, E., 1982. *What is to be done about Violence Towards Women?* Harmondsworth: Penguin.

Wilson, E., 1983. *Mirror Writing.* London: Virago.

Wolf, A., 2013. *The XX Factor: How working women are creating a new society.* London: Profile Books.

Wollstonecraft, M., 1792. *A Vindication of the Rights of Woman with Strictures on Moral and Political Subjects.* London: Joseph Johnson.

Women's Studies Without Walls (WSWW), 2013. Conference at the Feminist Library January 20–21.

Wright Mills, C., 1959. *The Sociological Imagination.* Oxford: Oxford University Press.

Yates, L., 2004. *What does Good Education Research Look Like? Situating a field and its practices.* Milton Keynes: Open University Press.

Yates, L., 2008. Revisiting feminism and Australian education: Who speaks? What questions? What contexts? What impact? *Discourse: Studies in the Cultural Politics of Education* Special Issue. 29 (4) pp. 471–83

Young, I.M., 1990. *Justice and the Politics of Difference.* Princeton, NJ: Princeton University Press.

Yousafzai, M., with Lamb, C., 2013. *I am Malala: The girl who stood up for education and was shot by the Taliban.* London: Weidenfeld & Nicholson.

Yuval-Davis, N., 2011. *The Politics of Belonging. Intersectional Contestations.* London: Sage.

Index

121, 124, 136, 150, 152, 164, 208;
  see also life histories
student movement 127, 193
students, *see* graduates, postgraduates,
  undergraduates
studentships 168
subjectivity 146, 206

Taylor, Helen x, 13, 62, 195, 210
teachers, *see* academics or school teachers
teaching and learning 162, 176
teaching profession 64
tertiary education 26, 29, 32
Thatcherism 58, 120
Third-wave feminism 54, 60, 66, 67, 70,
  185; *see also* post-structuralism
Times Higher Education, The 3, 164
Tinkler, Penny x, 68, 195
Tomlinson, Sally 84, 210

undergraduates 28, 36, 75, 77, 14
United Nations (UN) xv, 26, 27, 30
  UNESCO xv, 4, 6, 15, 26, 27, 28,
  29, 211
United States of America (USA) ix, xv, 3,
  7, 9, 11, 13, 15, 18, 20, 25, 28, 34,
  45, 49, 58, 74, 75, 77, 78, 82, 87,
  88, 96, 97, 98, 100, 113, 114, 124,
  125, 153, 155, 159, 168, 179, 186,
  187, 194, 195
university v, vii, x, xi, xv, 4–9, 17–24,
  28, 37–48, 52, 56–59, 61, 64,
  70, 73–94, 95–121, 123; *see
  also* academia, academy, higher
  education, tertiary education
university professors 7, 17, 85
Ungerson, Clare x, 195, 211
Unterhalter, Elaine x, 116, 195, 211,

Valentine's Day 3, 187
Vietnam War 102
violence against women 2, 3, 27, 66, 130,
  148, 184, 187, 190, 191
voices 6, 13, 19, 55, 56, 64, 65, 142, 173,
  174, 185, 200, 202
vulnerability 76

wages 121

Walby, Sylvia 15, 27, 100, 136, 208
Walkerdine, Valerie xii, 111, 127, 134, 147,
  153, 161, 210, 211
wars, *see* First World War, Second World
  War, Vietnam War
Ward, Linda x, 195
wave analogy, The 9, 21, 51, 58–60, 67–8,
  187
wave metaphor, The 59, 63, 70
Weiler, Kathleen x, 11, 70, 74, 75, 82, 96,
  195, 211
Weiner, Gaby x, 52, 53, 64, 101, 116, 138,
  140, 195, 197, 210, 211
Weis, Lois x, 94, 96, 101, 126, 195, 202,
  211, 212
welfare state 8, 174, 212
West, Jackie x, 17, 62, 81, 117, 118, 195
Willetts, David 5, 25, 35, 38, 41, 43, 73, 212
Williams, Fiona x, 64, 80, 91, 117, 195,
  212
Wilson, Elizabeth x, 79, 103, 195, 212,
Wilson, Gail x, 97, 195
wisdom x, 1, 2, 7, 9, 14, 54, 151, 152, 190
Wollstonecraft, Mary 111, 141, 212
Wolf, Alison 14, 15, 19, 212
Women's Abortion and Contraception
  Campaign (WACC) xv, 117
Women's Aid 115, 159
Women's Budget Group 115
Women's Equality Unit 28
Women in Higher Education Management
  (WHEM) network 47
Women's Liberation Movement ix, xv, 1,
  4, 6, 12
Women's Library ix, xi, 187
Women's Movement ix, xv, 1, 2, 4, 9, 10,
  12, 19, 51, 54, 55, 60, 61, 62, 69,
  70, 83, 96, 97, 101, 102, 103, 104,
  108, 112, 113, 131, 155, 157, 175,
  179, 202, 210
women's oppression 16, 127
women's rights 4, 27, 59, 108, 131, 141,
  142, 186, 188
Women's studies 2, 5, 6, 7, 10, 14, 16,
  17, 19, 52, 55, 60, 62, 64, 68, 77,
  100, 102, 103, 104, 106, 110, 116,
  117, 119, 120, 121, 125, 127, 130,
  137, 138, 140, 143, 148, 152, 153,